The Essential
BRIGHAM
YOUNG

The Essential
BRIGHAM
YOUNG

FOREWORD BY

EUGENE E. CAMPBELL

SIGNATURE BOOKS
SALT LAKE CITY
1992

Cover Design: Randall Smith Associates

∞ Printed on acid free paper.

13   12   11   10   09   2008   7   6   5   4   3   2

LIBRARY OF CONGRESS CATALOGING-IN-PUBLICATION DATA

Young, Brigham, 1801-1877.
    [Selections. 1992]
    The essential Brigham Young / foreword by Eugene E. Campbell.
       p.   cm.
    Includes bibliographical references and index.
    ISBN: 1-56085-010-8
    1. Church of Jesus Christ of Latter-day Saints—Doctrines.
    2. Mormon church—Doctrines. 3. Church of Jesus Christ of Latter
    -day Saints—Sermons. 4. Mormon Church—Sermons. 5. Sermons,
    American.   I. Title.
BX8635.Y682 1992   90-39883
289.3'32—dc20   CIP

Contents

Publisher's Preface

Brigham Young preached thousands of sermons during his thirty-three-year administration as second leader of the Church of Jesus Christ of Latter-day Saints. As church president and territorial governor, he dictated both spiritually and temporally. In his speeches he expounded doctrines from Adam-as-God to Republican Party-as-devil, interspersed with practical advice on baby-bathing and agriculture. The range of Young's sermons reflects the enormity of his chief concerns: preserving the legacy of Joseph Smith's life and teachings while forging a theocratic kingdom out of the Great Basin wilderness.

Young's expansive thought escapes easy definition, for no single wholly consistent theological system emerges from his far-reaching discourses. He adapted his sermons to fit the changing circumstances of his followers. He challenged Mormons who rigidly took counsel of ancient Hebrew prophets. "With regard to the Bible," he said, "we believe the Bible, but circumstances alter cases, for what is now required for the people may not be required of a people that may live a hundred years hence." Consequently, Young's pronouncements do not allow for satisfying prooftexts. The present compilation focuses on some of the larger themes of Young's thought as they developed.

Young's ideas arose spontaneously as he spoke. "I will present such views as shall come into my mind," he said. His style was to rely on extemporaneous inspiration, and to change his mind if he wanted. His addresses began hesitatingly—even awkwardly—and gained momentum as he found a topic and traced it through various permutations. "Our language is deficient, and I do not possess in this particular the natural endowment that some men enjoy," he admitted. "I am a man of few words, and unlearned." He referred to the "timidity" he felt "when rising to address a congregation."

When an idea came to Young's mind it was because God placed it there. This was the source of his famous self-confidence. But prefacing every seemingly dogmatic statement was an acknowledgment of his own fallibility. "You may go home," he assured the Saints, "and sleep as sweetly as a babe in its mother's arms as to any danger of your leaders leading you astray." But, he cautioned, "do not come to my office to ask me whether I am mistaken, for I want to tell you now perhaps I am." "I will acknowledge that all the time," he elaborated, "but I do not acknowledge that I designedly lead this people astray." Rather, "according to the best light and intelligence we are in possession of we will tell you what we think the Lord wishes of us and his policy concerning this people."

Young never referred to himself as prophet. "I have never particularly desired any man to testify publicly that I am a Prophet," he cautioned his followers, "nevertheless if any man feels joy in doing this, he shall be blest in it." The title of prophet was reserved exclusively for Joseph Smith. Young was administrator—president of the Quorum of Twelve Apostles. After Smith's assassination in 1844, Young asked the Saints if they wanted "a prophet and guardian" to lead them, to which they responded "No!" Young looked forward to the time when Smith's son David would claim his place as prophet and Young could resume his role as one of the traveling high council, or Twelve. When David chose to align himself with the Reorganized Church of Jesus Christ of Latter Day Saints, Young expressed disappointment that unless "he [David] repent of his sins and embrace the Gospel . . . he never can walk up to possess his right."

As for education, Young claimed he "went to school eleven days, that was the extent of my schooling." His boyhood training was in "splitting rails and fencing fields." He questioned much of science, which he referred to suspiciously as "natural philosophy." He disputed the idea that matter was composed of common elements; like his colleague Orson Pratt, he rejected Newton's theory of gravity. As Young aged, however, he became impressed by the accomplishments of science, which, he decided, came from God. Defensive about the lack of technological progress among Mormons, he said, "I know that the Latter-day Saints are looked upon by the world as dupes, as a low, degraded, imbecile race, and that we are so unwise and short-sighted, so vain and foolish, that through the great amount of enthusiasm within us we have embraced an error." But, he explained, "Joseph Smith was a poet, and poets are not like other men; their gaze is deeper, and reaches the roots of the soul; it is like that of the searching eyes of angels, they catch the swift thought of God and reveal it to us."

Young's view of deity was decidedly human. He believed Adam and Eve came to the earth from another world bringing with them plants and animals. Then, through sexual intercourse, they bore the first human children. Adam later also bore Jesus through intercourse with Mary. All this showed that sexuality was good, as was polygamy. When the Millennium came, probably before the Salt Lake Temple was completed, Mormons would be vindicated in these beliefs and practices, according to Young.

Few topics escaped Young's attention. He favored capital punishment as a blessing to those who would otherwise elude God's grace.

"This is loving our neighbor as ourselves," he argued. "If he needs help, help him; and if he wants salvation and it is necessary to spill his blood on the earth in order that he may be saved, spill it." Those who were worthy of capital punishment included apostates and adulterers. Regarding men who left their wives for younger women, Young bellowed, "I want to cut their damned throats and will if I catch any of them. Hell is full of such creatures, so full that their elbows stick out at the windows."

One of the great puzzles to antebellum Americans was the origin and meaning of race, and Young wondered why people were "different shades of color—the tawny, and copper-colored, the black and white." He decided that "if there are any who are not white and delightsome, it is because of their sins and iniquities." Blacks especially were "cursed" and were "uncouth, uncomely, disagreeable, wild, deprived of intelligence, and pre-ordained to be servants." Young's sympathies were with the South during the Civil War.

Other vestiges of Young's influence remain in contemporary Mormon culture. The work ethic, for example, which was a prerequisite to taming the Great Basin, continues to be preached from the pulpit. When the prospect of easy money lured fortune-seekers to California, Young warned that gold and silver would "ruin any nation. Give them iron and coal, good hard work, plenty to eat, good schools and good doctrine, and it will make them a healthy, wealthy, and happy people."

Young's homilies were compelling to nineteenth-century Utahns because they were filled with down-to-earth metaphors drawn from family life and farm work. Young "would not give the ashes of a rye straw" for those who abandoned an assignment. Those who did not follow counsel were likely to "fall into a ditch." He compared the church to a cotton mill. Sabbath-breakers were challenged with, "I will draw cuts with any man who would go and plough to-morrow [Sunday] [as to who] grows the most wheat, [the one who, by] staying here to-morrow gets [his] heart warmed, or [those who] go ploughing." He talked of hauling potatoes, playing cards, dancing. He cursed his enemies with a plague of mildew.

Perhaps Young's most masterful sermon was his 1858 address at a special gathering in the tabernacle. In the face of approaching federal troops, Young asked the community, which had struggled to survive in barely cultivatable valleys, to burn their houses and follow him to an unspecified desert sanctuary. This would certainly have been a shock to those assembled expecting to hear a call to arms. Like Mark Antony's monologue in *Julius Caesar*, people left the meeting prepared to do the inconceivable.

"No doubt some of the brethren will be a little surprised at this move, and think it hard," Young reasoned. "Who should be the first to volunteer, in all the settlements of the Saints? You who have never been driven, or those who have been driven twice, thrice, or four or five times? Were I to call for volunteers, generally those who have suffered the most would be soonest on hand. . . . You may ask whether I am willing to burn up my houses? Yes, and to be the first man that will put the torch to my own dwellings. . . .

"If we are obliged to remove . . . and lay waste, it is for our good. He that cannot take . . . the spoiling of his goods, whenever the Lord requires it, . . . is not worthy to be a follower of the Lamb; and when the moving is over I will have [a] better house than my present one [and much] better than the old row of log cabins we used to live in. . . . So also will your buildings be . . . better than the ones you now occupy[,] as they are better than your old shanties which you first lived in, and the earth will be more productive. . . . "

Besides, the fresh air would be good for everyone's health. "As I have told you often," asserted Young, "if people lived in their old log houses, in their tents and . . . wickiups you would not hear one cough where you now hear a hundred. . . . Send out these women and children, many of whom are not in health, and let them sleep in wagons and they will become healthy."

In one of his more confident moments, Young roared that "God is the captain of this company, the general of this church, its ruler and dictator. If I am the instrument which he chooses to use in the prosecution of his great work, it is all right. I am as willing as any other man to be used." At other times, Young let this stern façade drop and his audience caught a glimpse of the humanity underneath—the compassion, humor, commitment, authenticity. He was a complex leader and father, and he discloses more in his sermons than one might expect about his public and private life.

Brigham Young was born 1 June 1801 in Whitingham, Vermont, and his family moved to central New York in 1804. He forsook the family's farming occupation to learn the carpentry trade. Thereafter, throughout his life, he favored vocational education and distrusted liberal arts.

Like contemporaries Joseph Smith, Orson Pratt, and Parley Pratt, Young experienced the New York religious revivals of the 1820s. But unlike the others he did not remain aloof. He became a Methodist first, then, after moving to Oswego, New York, on Lake Ontario, he changed to the Congregational church.

In 1830, Phineas, Young's brother, purchased a copy of the Book of Mormon from Joseph Smith's brother Samuel. "I examined the matter studiously for two years," commented Young after borrowing Phineas's copy, "before I made up my mind." In 1832 he joined Smith's

Church of Christ.

Smith commanded his followers to gather to Kirtland, Ohio, which Young soon did. Young was then called on several short proselytizing missions, culminating in his lifetime appointment to the travelling ministry as member of the Quorum of Twelve Apostles. When opponents assailed Smith over the economically devastating collapse of the Kirtland Safety Society—a savings and loan institution—Young surfaced as Smith's staunchest defender, leading excommunication proceedings against the prophet's adversaries. When dissenters drove Smith from Kirtland in 1837, Young followed him to Missouri.

The Missouri Mormons were already embroiled in their own controversies. Older settlers distrusted Mormons, viewing them as interlopers whose growing numbers and communitarianism made them a potential political force. The Missouri militia attacked Mormon settlements in October 1838, capturing Smith and other Mormon leaders. Young, unknown to Missourians, escaped imprisonment.

With Smith under guard, Young and colleague Heber C. Kimball were left to lead the church. They oversaw the evacuation of Mormons from Missouri to Illinois. When Smith was released, he relieved the apostles of their leadership duties and asked them to resume their ministry. In September 1839, Young and the apostles left Illinois for England to recruit new Mormons.

The apostles converted several thousand British and charged the latter to emigrate to American church settlements. Young's reputation grew with the success of the British mission and influx of British converts to Mormon towns. When the apostles returned to Illinois in 1841, Smith expanded their calling to include administration of some church business at home.

During the 1840s, Smith introduced the church to new doctrines. He taught Mormons to baptize each other in behalf of dead relatives in 1841 and began introducing polygamy to a loyal few the same year. Smith's endowment, a ritual ceremony transmitting sacred knowledge required to enter heaven, was administered to apostles in 1842-43. This theological development tried the credulity of some Mormons. Reports of strange practices also incurred the suspicion and antagonism of non-Mormon neighbors. Young and other apostles travelled throughout neighboring communities to counter gossip.

Smith also became politically active in the 1840s. He wanted to redress wrongs committed by Missourians and ensure that similar persecution would not occur in the Saints' new Illinois home. He decided to run for the presidency of the United States early in 1844. In May, Young and other apostles were called to a campaigning mission in the eastern states.

With the apostles away, Smith confronted opposition at home virtually alone. Disaffected Mormons began printing a newspaper to publicize polygamy and other scandals. Smith was arrested after authorizing the destruction of the newspaper. While he was awaiting trial, a vigilante group broke into the jail and killed him and his brother Hyrum.

Receiving the news, the apostles returned quickly home. Young, as president of the quorum, competed against claims of other prominent Mormons for leadership of the church. The apostles swayed a majority of Mormons, many of whom originally converted through the apostles' missionary efforts. Young, now in control, abated further mob action by promising to lead Mormons from Illinois.

In February 1846 Mormons crossed the Mississippi River into Iowa. After a haphazard, mostly leaderless trek across Iowa to Nebraska, Young secured control and thereafter directed minute details in preparing for the exodus to the Rocky Mountains. Early the next year, Young and 143 Mormon pioneers began their vanguard expedition, travelling along the Platte River through present-day Nebraska and Wyoming to the frontier outpost of Fort Bridger. On the trail beyond the fort, Young contracted mountain fever. He entered the Salt Lake Valley two days after the first pioneers, lying sick and delirious in a wagon.

At the end of the Saints' first year in the Salt Lake Valley, Young returned to Iowa to direct emigration of the remaining Mormons. Since Smith's death, Young was de facto leader of the church, but in December 1847, at an Iowa church conference, he officially assumed Smith's role as president. He returned to the Salt Lake Valley in September 1848 and never again left the Great Basin.

From 1848 until his death in August 1877, Young directed extensive Mormon colonization and development of the Utah territory. As part of a Mormon elite, holding political and economic power, Young gained national notoriety while he tried to maintain an uneasy truce with the federal government. This eroded during the 1856-57 "Utah War." Later western gentile expansion, particularly the coming of the transcontinental railroad, undermined the control that Mormon leaders had enjoyed during Young's administration.

Of the twenty-five selections in the present compilation, Young delivered twenty-two in connection with the emigration, economic development, and colonization of the West. He gave the other three while in the eastern Utah States or in England. Approximately eight hundred of Young's sermons remain. Almost half were published in the *Journal of Discourses*. Twenty-five of Young's most frequently cited sermons are presented here as they were first published or recorded. Only obvious, unintentional typesetting mistakes such as letter transpositions have been corrected. Archaic constructions of usage and variant spellings remain. We remind readers that the earliest publication of these sermons was based on stenographers' notes.

Foreword

Eugene E. Campbell

Writing one of the first biographies of Andrew Jackson, American historian James Parton made a despairing admission. From the evidence he had gathered Parton noted that Jackson could be termed both a "patriot" and a "traitor." "He was," Parton explained, "one of the greatest of Generals and wholly ignorant of the art of war. A writer, brilliant, elegant, eloquent, without being able to compose a correct sentence or spell words of four syllables. . . . He was the most candid of men, and was capable of the profoundest dissimulation. A most law-abiding, law-defying citizen. . . . A democratic autocrat, an urbane savage, an atrocious Saint. . . . At home and among dependents, all tenderness and generosity: to opponents, violent, ungenerous, prone to believe the very worst of them."[1]

Perhaps such a description can help explain Brigham Young (1801-77). There can be no doubt that his forceful personality dominated the Church of Jesus Christ of Latter-day Saints during the years 1845 to 1877, the tenure of his presidency. Non-Mormons as well as Mormons have acknowledged his powerful influence. Historian Allen Nevins regarded him as "the most commanding single figure of the West," while Herbert E. Bolton concluded that no one "so completely molded his people and their institutions as Brigham Young molded the Mormons."[2]

A great deal has been written about Brigham Young. Limitations of space preclude touching upon every aspect of his career, but I will consider aspects of colonization; relations with the federal government; Indian policy; business practices; attitudes towards women, blacks, and co-workers; and finally I will try to come to terms with the paradoxical aspects of the life and influence of this exceptional American.

Perhaps Brigham Young's greatest claim to fame resulted from his leadership in the Mormon colonization of the Great Basin and contiguous areas. This achievement included not only the founding of over three hundred towns and cities in a desert wilderness but the organization of an immigration system that transported over 80,000 people from various parts of the world to the Great Basin, welding them into a cohesive society. Young certainly deserves to be listed among the greatest American colonizers, yet he may have been given more credit than he deserves. I believe that he did not plan or carry out a successful program of encircling the Great Basin with a chain of control colonies as has been suggested by other historians. And there are additional aspects of his colonizing policies that require a closer look. One was the calling of people to colonize areas during the winter season, resulting in unnecessary suffering and family separation without justifiable reason. Two cases in point are the Manti and Fort Supply colonies.

The Manti colonists, consisting of approximately thirty-five families (100 male and 124 female), were called to settle near Chief Walker's band of Utes for the purpose of teaching them to become farmers (hopefully Mormon, as well). Leaving Salt Lake on 28 October 1849, they moved slowly, consuming almost an entire month before settling in present-day Manti. Dissension over the choice of location was increased by the advent of a very cold and snowy winter. Although the leader, Isaac Morley, proclaimed that God had chosen the spot, his counselor, Seth Taft, insisted that "not even a jack rabbit could exist on its desert soil," and Jacob Butterfield declared "that neither God, angels [n]or Brigham Young had anything to do with locating this place."[3] (Taft was subsequently excommunicated and fined twenty-five dollars for voicing such criticism.[4]) Three nights after their arrival, it snowed heavily, and by 10 December the temperature had plummeted to twenty-one degrees below zero and more snow fell. By Christmas the snow was so deep that the cattle could not reach winter grass for grazing. Some colonists labored for weeks shoveling snow from the grass, while others left it in the hands of the Lord, saying, "If the Lord was of a mind to send deep snows and cold weather to destroy the cattle, all right."

Of course, Brigham Young was not responsible for the cold winter, but having endured the bitter winter of 1848-49, he could have realized the difficulty colonists might experience when called to settle such an area in winter. All these first settlers could do was struggle to survive.

The call to colonize the Green River Valley in November 1853 is another example. In this case only 92 men were sent into the high-country wilderness near Fort Bridger. They finally decided on a location twelve miles south of Bridger, but nearer the Uinta Mountains, and began building Forty Supply on 27 November, completing the A block house in two weeks—"not an hour too soon for the weather was very cold and threatening."[5] By 23 December eight men had risked their lives to get additional supplies from Salt Lake City, but the winter was so severe that they were unable to return until spring. The men who remained at Fort Supply spent the winter trying to survive and to keep their cattle alive. Fear of the Indians forced them to accept guard duty in below-zero weather. By February 1854 some of the cabins were buried by snow blown by high winds; by spring many of the men had deserted their mission. When, on 30 May, the thermometer registered only ten degrees above zero, others finally gave up. Such examples could be multiplied, but the point is that much unnecessary inconvenience, sacrifice, and physical suffering were endured by faithful Saints because of Brigham Young's apparent lack of foresight.

Then, too, the calls to colonize were not nearly as well planned as Mormons today might believe. The idea that Young chose people carefully based on their talents and occupations does not hold up under scrutiny, especially during the early years.

There can be no doubt as to the importance of the "call" from Brigham Young in promoting the settlement of many communities in the territory, but Davis County settlers called themselves. Young later appointed leaders and called families to strengthen the Davis settlements after they were established. The Ogden area was settled by James Brown under the direction of the Salt Lake stake presidency while Young was still in Winter Quarters. Brown's call probably came as a result of his interest in purchasing Fort Buenaventura from Miles Goodyear. The Tooele colony was organized by one of the twelve apostles who had an assignment to build mills and herd livestock. Isaac Morley was assigned to select a group to settle Sanpete County, and he enlarged his group as he passed through communities in Salt Lake and Utah valleys. During the fall general conference of 1850, Morley was given the right to choose one hundred additional men and to call them to bring their families to his settlement.

Two years later "Father" James Allred was assigned to go to Sanpete and choose a location for his "numerous posterity," resulting in the founding of Spring City. Joseph Heywood was told to "pick up volunteers" to settle Nephi, and Anson Call was assigned to "raise fifty families" to settle Fillmore. Brigham City was settled by volunteers, although President Young soon began directing Scandinavian groups to settle there. Wellsville was founded by Peter Maughn, who received permission to leave Tooele and look for a new location; any of the Tooele settlers who wished to follow Maughn were given permission to do so.

The calls to the "outer colonies" were much more specific. For example, men called on Indian missions heard their names read aloud from the pulpit at general conference. A notable exception was when apostles Amasa Lyman and Charles C. Rich had so many volunteers to go to the San Bernardino region that they had to limit the group to a quota.

Brigham Young's attitude towards the federal government may be described as ambivalent to paranoid, resulting in almost constant difficulties with federal officials. He succeeded in antagonizing every president from Zachary Taylor to Ulysses S. Grant and in alienating almost every territorial officer who came to Utah between 1850 and 1877. Of course it can be argued that federal officials were incompetent, self-seeking politicians and that Mormons had good reason to fear the federal government. But many federal appointees came expressing good will toward Mormons, only to be disillusioned by the anti-government sentiment pronounced in public gatherings. Young seemed convinced that federal officials were in a conspiracy to destroy the community.[6]

Part of the problem was Brigham Young's rhetoric. The president addressed the Saints almost every Sunday, almost daily when on tour, often giving practical advice, but on occasion he would lash out at the federal government using hyperbole, sarcasm, and rough frontier humor. The Saints loved his style, but non-Mormon officials believed he was a dangerous despot and demagogue, if not a fanatic. John M. Bernhisel, Utah's representative in Congress, begged Young to "tone down" his public utterances, but without success. When the *Baltimore Daily Sun* reported that Young had said that he would remain territorial governor "until the Lord Almighty says, 'Brigham, you need not be governor longer,'" Bernhisel asked Young to tell reporters that such statements were intended for the Saints only. "I have to meet all of these things here face-to-face and explain, palliate, contradict, deny as the case may be," wrote Bernhisel. Even when successful, Bernhisel felt that such remarks left a "deep black stain behind."[7]

Young's preaching set the tone, and he was emulated by Heber C. Kimball, George A. Smith, Jedediah M. Grant, and Daniel Wells among others. During the Civil War Governor Stephen Harding reported that Brigham Young and other preachers "are constantly asserting every Sabbath that the United States was being destroyed in fulfillment of prophecy, and that all governments of the earth are false and ought to be overthrown."[8] There can be little doubt that Brigham Young's rhetoric helped set an attitude which convinced federal officials that Mormons were disloyal and federal officers sent to govern them required the support of military units.

Young's Indian policy is usually expressed in the pragmatic statement, "It is cheaper to feed them than to fight them." But this is misleading in many ways. First, it does not actually reveal any humanitarian concern, only an economic motive—"cheaper." Second, anyone who has studied Brigham Young's attitudes on eating and working recognizes that such a policy could only be a temporary expedient. The Saints could barely feed themselves during those early years. It might be cheaper to feed the Indians than fight them, but it would be cheaper still if they were left to feed themselves. This was Brigham Young's real policy. Third, there is no evidence that Young made such a statement until after his people had first fought the Indians.

There can be no doubt that Young sympathized with the plight of native Americans and wanted to help them. He generally advocated fairness in dealing with them and tried to teach them to farm and to develop other rudiments of civilization. He also sent letters to the chiefs accompanied by gifts and advice. However, he was a realist and most consistently advocated a policy of segregation. During the first three years in the Great Basin, the plan was land occupation without recompense, extermination of non-cooperatives, and removal of all of Utah tribes to distant locations. Later Young reflected that Mormons "were prepared to meet all the Indians in these mountains and kill every soul of them if we had been obliged to."[9] He also said, "I shall live a long time before I will believe that an Indian is my friend when it is to his advantage to be my enemy."[10] Despite such attitudes and policies, Young tried to help the Indians and was successful in establishing some farms and in ending the slave trade. He encouraged the adoption of Indian children and sent sizable contingents of missionaries to work with various tribes. Unfortunately, while serving as territorial superintendent of Indian affairs, Young also antagonized both his superiors and subordinates in the Federal Indian Program, resulting in suspicion, a lack of cooperation, and withholding of government aid to the Indians of Utah territory.

By the end of the 1860s, despite Young's genuine concern, the Indian population had been greatly reduced, and the survivors were either forced to live on unattractive reservations or to remain on the outskirts of Mormon villages, dependent on charity for the necessities of life.

Young prided himself on being an astute businessman, and he had good reason for such pride. As he once said in a general conference address, "I am as good a financier as can be found—money and property do multiply in my hands."[11] By 1855, when he deeded his property to the trustee-in-trust of the church as an act of consecration, he listed his assets as almost $200,000.[12] Four years later he told the *New York Daily Tribune* that he considered himself to be "worth $250,000."[13] But in 1862, while discussing love of property with some of his friends, Young asserted "that he didn't think that there was a prophet on earth, Jesus excepted, that cared less for the things of this world than he did."[14]

Historian Leonard J. Arrington has given a broad overview of Young's business activities both in private ventures and as leader of the church and has summarized his holdings at the time of his death. Arrington indicated that "it came as a great surprise to many, including his close associates, that the obligations of Brigham Young to the Church at the time of his death totalled $999,632.90."[15] Part of this enormous debt had come as a result of Young's mixing private affairs with those of the church and drawing on church funds whenever necessary to further his private interests, which he invariably saw as benefitting the church. According to David James Croft, it is doubtful that the "other General

Authorities . . . could draw a distinction between Brigham Young as trustee-in-trust, and Brigham Young as a private enterpriser. It appears that Young was not always conscious of the distinction. Although he kept separate accounts, and knew the difference between Church funds and his own, it is likely that he viewed many Church projects as his."[16]

While both Arrington and Croft are generous in their interpretations of Young's financial dealings, some of his own brethren were not so kind. George Q. Cannon wrote in his diary, "Some of my brethren, as I have learned since the death of President Brigham Young, did have feelings concerning his course. They did not approve of it, and felt opposed, and yet they dare not exhibit their feelings to him, he ruled with so strong and stiff a hand, and they felt that it would be of no use. In a few words, the feeling seems to be that he transcended the bounds of the authority which he legitimately held. I have been greatly surprised to find so much dissatisfaction in such quarters. It is felt that the funds of the Church have been used with a freedom not warranted by the authority which he held."[17] That feeling resulted in a decision by the Quorum of the Twelve Apostles to establish a fixed salary for themselves because they did not want to allow "any man in the Church President or Apostle to draw funds from the Church without limit for their own use or any other purpose."

Brigham Young's attitude toward women is filled with paradox. Married to at least twenty-seven wives and father of fifty-seven children by sixteen different women, he once remarked that there were few men who enjoyed the company of women less. He seemed to command the respect and love of most of his wives; and his daughters, two of whom described their family life as idyllic, seemed to adore him. However, there were some marriage failures, including five separations, five divorces, and one annulment; and there must have been a great deal of heartache and jealousy, especially when at the age of sixty-two he married Amelia Folsom, thirty-seven years his junior, who demanded a special home and social position. The possibility of family dissatisfaction increased two years later when Young married Mary Van Cott, forty-three years younger than he, and finally when at the age of sixty-seven, he married Ann Eliza Webb, who was twenty-eight. Lucy Bigelow Young, his wife since 1846, had been sent to live in St. George and must have had mixed feelings when Young decided to relieve her of the burden of serving and entertaining his clerks, drivers, friends, and visitors. Young built a larger house and office in St. George "with an extra large barn, vineyard and garden" and brought "Aunt Amelia with some good help with her, to care for him in the new house when he came, and there to entertain his many guests." Lucy's daughter Susa wrote that "it would be impossible to deny that mother's heart twisted with sorrow at the thought of her dear husband coming down to spend the winters in another wife's home."[18]

Young was generous in granting divorces to women who found it difficult to live plural marriage. Many of the almost 2,000 divorces he granted were to unhappy wives. But on occasion he lashed out at wives for requesting divorce. During October conference in 1861, after scolding the people for requesting divorces, Young said, "I now inform every one of my sisters that when they come to get a divorce, paying me ten dollars for it, you may just as well tare off a piece of your shirt tail and lay it by and call it a divorce, so far as any good that piece of paper called a divorce will do . . . a bill of divorce from me does not free her. . . . How can a woman be made free from a man to whom she has been sealed for time and all eternity? There are two ways." He then explained that if a man does not magnify his priesthood callings, he will find in the hereafter that his wives will be given to those who are more worthy, but that if a man magnifies his priesthood, observing faithfully his covenants to the end of life, all the wives and children sealed to him, all the blessings, are immutably and eternally fixed.

"You may inquire," he continued, "in the case a wife becomes dissatisfied with her husband, her affections lost, she becomes alienated from him, and wishes to be the wife of another can she not leave him? I know of no law in heaven or on earth by which she can be made free while her husband remains faithful and magnifies his priesthood before God, and he is not disposed to put her away, she having done nothing worthy of being put away. If that dissatisfied wife could behold the transcendent beauty of person, the Godlike qualities of the resurrected husband she now despises, her love for him would be unbounded and unutterable. Instead of despising him she would feel like worshiping him he is so holy, so pure, so perfect, and so filled with God in his resurrected body. . . . The second way in which a wife can be separated from her husband, while he continues to be faithful to his God and his priesthood, I have not revealed, except to a few persons in this Church, and few have received it from Joseph the prophet as well as myself. If a woman can find a man holding the keys of the priesthood with higher power and authority than her husband, and he is disposed to take her, he can do so, otherwise she has got to remain where she is. In either of these ways of separation, you can discover, there is no need for a bill of divorcement." He then asserted that women were not accountable for the sins that are in the world. God requires obedience from man, he is the Lord of creation, but women will not be held responsible. "The woman is the glory of man; what is the glory of the woman? It is her virginity until she gives it into the hands of the man who will be her Lord and Master to all eternity."[19]

Certainly a case can be made to show Brigham Young's respect for women. But I doubt that he ever regarded them as equal to men—especially those who held the priesthood.

Some have admired Young's self-confidence. American traveler and writer Fritz Hugh Ludlow found that Young had "absolute certainty of himself and his own opinion"[20] and saw this quality as a key factor in his ability to motivate his people. Certainly an effective leader needs to be resolute, but Young had developed self-confidence to such a degree that few dared to challenge his statements. Apostle Orson Pratt questioned his teachings concerning the nature of God and was threatened with excommunication from the Quorum of the Twelve. Young's pronouncements of withholding priesthood ordination from blacks were so definite that the concept was accepted as doctrine by the church for over a century.[21]

Too, I wonder if Elder Orson Hyde understood that Young was probably indulging in simple hyperbole when he said that Hyde "ought to be Cut off from the Quorum of the Twelve & the Church. He is no more fit to stand at the Head of the Quorum of the Twelve than a dog! . . . He is a stink in my norstrels."[22] Or how the Saints felt during the difficult winter of 1848-49 when Young lashed out at those who were hoarding food: "If those that have do not sell to those who have not, we will just take it and distribute among the poor and those that have and will not divide willingly may be thankful that their heads are not found wallowing in the snow. There is some of the meanest spirits here among the Saints that ever graced this footstool. They are too mean to live among the gentiles. The gentiles would be ashamed of them."[23] Or later, when Young found that Mormon immigrants owed $56,000 to the Perpetual Emigrating Fund and said, "I want you to understand fully that I intend to put the screws on you, and you who have owed for years, if you do not pay up now and help us, we will levy on your property and take every farthing you have on earth."[24]

One of the more extreme examples of this occurred in November 1856 when Young learned that members were blaming him for the plight of the Willie and Martin Handcart companies. He in turn put the blame squarely on Franklin D. Richards, insisting that "if any person on this earth or even a bird had chirped in Brother Franklin's ears in Florence, and the brethren had held a council, they would have known better than to rush men, women and children onto the prairie in the autumn months." After publicly castigating Richards, Young declared, "If any man or woman complains of me or my Counselors, in regards to the lateness of some of this season's immigration, let the curse of God be on them and blast their substance with mildew and destruction, until their names are forgotten from the earth."[25]

Earlier he had lashed out at the courts and lawyers, exclaiming, "Men who love competition, contention . . . I curse you in the name of the Lord Jesus Christ. I curse you, and the fruits of your land shall be smitten with mildew, your children shall sicken and die, your cattle shall waste away, and I pray God to root you out from the Society of the Saints."[26]

My point is simply that Brigham Young's rhetoric was so positive and so powerful that no one dared to challenge his pronouncements. If he had only expressed his opinion, some things might have been different. Brigham Young became close to a law unto himself, not only in economic affairs and doctrinal pronouncements but in church appointments as well. For example, on 17 April 1864 he casually told John Taylor and George A. Smith, "I have ordained my sons, Joseph A., Brigham, and John W., apostles and my counselors, have you any objections?" Taylor and Smith replied that they had not, that it was his own affair, and that they considered it to be under his own direction.[27]

Despite such actions and scoldings, Young was "Brother Brigham" to thousands of people. They recognized his leadership, sought his judgment, and believed him to be God's representative on earth. What was the source of his power? Of course the obvious answer to faithful members is that Brigham Young was God's representative on earth. But for those seeking other explanations, the experience of Elizabeth Wood Kane might help.

Invited to come to Utah with her husband, Thomas L. Kane, in 1874, Elizabeth met Brigham Young for the first time in Lehi as the caravan prepared to travel to St. George. Later in her book, *Twelve Mormon Homes*, she gave a detailed account of that first meeting and her subsequent observations of his effective leadership. She wrote:

"I strolled out on the platform afterwards, to find President Young preparing for our journey—as he did every morning afterwards—by a personal inspection of the condition of every wheel, axle, horse and mule, and suit of harness belonging to the party. He was peering like a well-intentioned wizard into every nook and cranny, pointing out a defect here and there with his odd, six-sided staff engraved with the hieroglyphs of many measure; more useful though less romantic, than a Runic wand. He wore a great surtout, reaching almost to his feet, of dark-green cloth (Mahomet color?) lined with fur, a fur collar, cap, and pair of sealskin boots with the undyed fur outward. I was amused at his odd appearance; but as he turned to address me, he removed a hideous pair of green goggles, and his keen, blue-gray eyes met mine with their characteristic look of shrewd and cunning insight. I felt no further inclination to laugh. His photographs, accurate enough in other respects, altogether fail to give the expression of his eyes."[28]

At Parowan she continued: "When we reached the end of a day's journey, after taking off our outer garments and washing off the dust, it was the custom of our party to assemble before the fire in the sitting room, and the leading 'brothers and sisters' of the settlement would come in to pay their respects. The front door generally opened directly from the piazza into the parlor, and was always on the latch, and the circle 'round the fire varied constantly as the neighbors dropped in or went away. At these informal audiences, reports, complaints, and petitions were made; and I think I gathered more of the actual working of Mormonism by listening to them than from any other source. They talked away to Brigham Young about every conceivable mater, from the fluxing of an ore to the advantages of a Navajo bit, and expected him to remember every child in every cotter's family. And he really seemed to do so, and to be at home, and be rightfully deemed infallible on every subject. I think he must make fewer mistakes than most popes, from his being in such constant intercourse with his people. I noticed that he never seemed uninterested, but gave an unforced attention to the person addressing him, which suggested a mind free from care. I used to fancy that he wasted a great deal of power in this way; but I soon saw that he was accumulating it. Power, I mean, at least as the driving-wheel of his people's industry."[29]

Surely this partially explains the paradox of Brigham Young, for although Young criticized, scolded, and threatened his people, he also stayed close to them, remembered their names, listened to their problems, and from his own experience, his powers of observation, and his reservoir of common sense, gave them counsel and advice. And because he was so sure of himself and so sincere in his devotion to the building up of the Mormon kingdom, his followers took the scoldings and threats as part of the package, following him as their divinely inspired leader even if it meant taking another wife, moving to an uninhabited wilderness, or simply staying home and trying to live with a difficult situation.

As I reflect on the life of Brigham Young and his influence on the Mormon church and Utah's history, I find that I have mixed feelings. Perhaps Allen Nevins was right when he asserted that "no man of less strength could have succeeded; he had taken a heterogenous people, foreign and native, skilled and unskilled, and molded them into an industrious, orderly, devoted, and homogenous community."[30] Certainly Young was a great leader and was especially effective as a colonizer and in dealing with practical things. So, in a very real sense, he saved the church by leading his followers into the Great Basin where they could be the first settlers and become strong enough to establish their concept of God's kingdom without serious opposition during the first decade.

But Young also left his people with another heritage. He was responsible for expanding the practice of plural marriage in the face of federal law declaring it illegal. He fostered an attitude of antagonism toward the federal government which led to hardship and almost resulted in the destruction of the church. His strong statements concerning blacks and the priesthood fastened an unfortunate concept on the church. His antagonism toward precious-metal mining resulted in the great mineral wealth of the Mormon country being exploited by non-Mormons— many of whom became wealthy and powerful opponents of the church. His criticism of Orson Pratt caused other quorum members to assert that a living prophet is to be followed, even though he should be out of harmony with both scripture and the teachings of Joseph Smith.

But just as James Parton wrote of Andrew Jackson, after criticizing some of his actions, "I think most citizens of the United States will concur in the wish, that when next a European Army lands upon American soil, may there be a Jackson to meet them at the landing place," so many Mormons today would no doubt hope that when the next major threat to their survival arises, may there be a strong man like Brigham Young to lead them to a place of refuge and safety. If such an emergency arises and Mormons survive because of a strong leader, they will no doubt be willing to live with his weaknesses because they value his strengths.

NOTES

1. James Parton, *Life of Andrew Jackson*, quoted in James L. Bugg, Jr., and Peter C. Stewart, eds., *Jacksonian Democracy*, 2d ed. (Hinsdale, IL: Dryden Press, 1976).

2. Leonard J. Arrington and Ronald K. Esplin, "Building a Commonwealth: The Secular Leadership of Brigham Young," *Utah Historical Quarterly* 45 (Summer 1977): 218.

3. Adelia Belva Cox Sidwell, *Reminiscences of Early Days in Manti* (N.p.: n.p. [1950?]), 1.

4. Isaac Morley to Brigham Young, 20 Feb. 1850, Brigham Young Papers, archives, Historical Department, Church of Jesus Christ of Latter-day Saints, Salt Lake City; hereafter LDS archives.

5. Fred R. Gowans and Eugene E. Campbell, *Fort Supply* (Provo, UT: Brigham Young University Press, 1976), 25.

6. John Pulsipher, who attended a council meeting in December 1848, claimed that Young said he planned to "petition for a territorial government each year until the honest in heart had been gathered out of the nations and the armies of Israel had become very great, and then we will say 'We don't care whether you grant it [the territorial recognition] or not. Damn you, we are here and we ask no odds of you'" (John Pulsipher Journal, Dec. 1848, LDS archives).

7. Gwynn Barrett, "Mormon Elder in Congress," Ph.D. diss., Brigham Young University, 1968, 122-23.

8. Gustive O. Larson, "Utah and the Civil War," *Utah Historical Quarterly* 33 (Winter 1965): 68.

9. Floyd O'Neil and Stanford J. Layton, "Of Pride and Politics: Brigham Young as Indian Superintendent, *Utah Historical Quarterly* 46 (Summer 1978): 237.

10. Brigham Young, "Manuscript History," 18 May 1853, LDS archives.

11. Leroy and Ann Hafen, *Handcarts to Zion: The Story of a Unique Western Migration, 1856-1860* (Glendale, CA: Arthur H. Clark Co., 1960), 243.

12. Leonard J. Arrington, Feramorz Y. Fox, and Dean L. May, *Building the City of Zion: Community and Cooperation Among the Mormons* (Salt Lake City: Deseret Book, 1976), 374-75. Also David James Croft, "The Private Business Activities of Brigham Young, 1847-1877," *Journal of the West* (Oct. 1977): 49.

13. Croft, 48.

14. Brigham Young, Office Journal, 29 Jan. 1862, Brigham Young Papers.

15. Leonard J. Arrington, "The Settlement of the Brigham Young Estate, 1877-1879," *The Pacific Historical Review* 21 (Feb. 1952): 13.

16. Croft, 39.

17. George Q. Cannon Journal, 17 Jan. 1878, in D. Michael Quinn, "The Mormon Hierarchy, 1832-1932: An American Elite," Ph.D. diss., Yale University, 1976, 127.

18. Susa Young Gates, "From Impulsive Girl to Patient Wife: Lucy Bigelow Young," *Utah Historical Quarterly* 45 (Summer 1977): 285.

19. Brigham Young, unpublished address, 8 Oct. 1861, Brigham Young Papers.

20. Arrington and Esplin, 219.

21. Ronald Esplin has defended Brigham Young's role in establishing and promoting this doctrine. But even if we accept Esplin's assertion that "his audience" understood Young's use of hyperbole, Esplin does not deny that it was Young who said that the curse was from God, could only be removed by God, and that only when all of Abel's descendants "were assured their birthright" would blacks be given the priesthood. Such a concept suggested a time in the far-distant future—perhaps the Millennium. See Ronald K. Esplin, "Brigham Young and the Priesthood Denial to the Blacks: An Alternate View," *Brigham Young University Studies* 19 (Spring 1979): 401.

22. Wilford Woodruff, *Wilford Woodruff's Journal, Typescript,* 9 vols., ed. Scott G. Kenney (Midvale, UT: Signature Books, 1983-85), 4:477.

23. Juanita Brooks, ed., *A Mormon Chronicle,* 88.

24. *Journal of Discourses,* 26 vols. (Liverpool: Latter-day Saints' Book Depot, 1855-86), 3:6.

25. Hafen and Hafen, 245-46.

26. Andrew Love Neff, *History of Utah, 1847 to 1869* (Salt Lake City: Deseret News Press, 1940), 96.

27. "Acts of the Twelve," 17 Apr. 1864, microfilm, LDS archives.

28. Elizabeth Wood Kane, *Twelve Mormon Homes Visited in Succession on a Journey through Utah to Arizona* (Salt Lake City: Tanner Trust Fund, 1974), 5-6.

29. Ibid., 101.

30. Arrington and Esplin, 232.

"Election and Reprobation"
(with Willard Richards)

(from *Latter-day Saints' Millennial Star*
I [January 1841]: 217-25)

"Do you believe in Election and Reprobation?" To prevent the necessity of repeating a thousand times what may be said at once, we purpose to answer this oft asked question in writing; so that the Saints may learn doctrine, and all who will, may understand that such election and reprobation as is taught in the Old and New Testaments, and other revelations from God, we fully believe, in connexion with every other principle of righteousness; and we ask this favour of all, into whose hands our answer may come, that they will not condemn till they have read it through, in the spirit of meekness and prayer.

The Lord (Jehovah) hath spoken through Isa. (42, 1) saying, behold my servant, whom I uphold, mine elect in whom my soul delighteth; evidently referring to the Lord Jesus Christ, the Son of God chosen or elected by the Father, (1 Peter i. 20, who verily was fore-ordained before the foundation of the world, but was manifest in these last times for you, who by him do believe in God,) to serve him in the redemption of the world, to be a covenant of the people, (Isa. xlii, 6) for a light of the Gentiles, and the glory of his people Israel; having ordained him to be the judge of quick and dead, (Acts x, 42) that through him forgiveness of sins might be preached (Acts xiii, 38) unto all who would be obedient unto his gospel (Mark xvi, 16, 17).

Every high priest must be ordained (Heb. v, 1,) and if Christ had not received ordination, he would not have had power to ordain others, as he did when he ordained the twelve (Mark iii, 14) to take a part in the ministry which he had received of his father: also, (John xv, 16) ye have not chosen me, but I have chosen you, and ordained you, that ye should go and bring forth fruit, (Heb. v, 4) for no man taketh this honour unto himself but he that is called of God as was Aaron (v. 5.) So also Christ *glorified not himself* to be *made* an *high priest*, but he that said unto him thou art my Son, this day have I begotten thee.

No being can give that which he does not possess; consequently no man can confer the priesthood on another, if he has not himself first received it; and the priesthood is of such a nature that it is impossible to investigate the principles of election, reprobation, &c., without touching upon the priesthood also; and, although some may say that Christ as God needed no ordination, having possessed it eternally, yet Christ says (Matt. xxviii, 18) all *power* is *given* unto me in heaven and on earth; which could not have been if he was in eternal possession; and in the previously quoted verse we discover that he that said unto him, (i.e.) his father glorified him *to be made* an high priest, or ordained him to the work of creating the world and all things upon it; (Col. i, 16) for by him were all things created that are in heaven and that are in the earth, &c., and of redeeming the same from the fall; and to the judging of the quick and dead; for the right of judging rests in the priesthood; and it is through this medium that the father hath *committed* all judgment unto the Son (John v, 22) referring to his administration on earth.

If it was necessary that Christ should receive the priesthood to qualify him to minister before his father unto the children of men so as to redeem and save them, does it seem reasonable that any man should take it upon him to do a part of the same work, or to assist in the same priesthood, who has not been called by the spirit of prophecy or revelation as was Aaron, and ordained accordingly? And can it be expected that a man will be called by revelation who does not believe in revelation? Or will any man submit to ordination, for the fulfilment of a revelation or call in which he has no faith? We think not.

That we may learn still further that God calls or elects particular men to perform particular works, or on whom to confer special blessings, we read (Isa. xlv, 4) for Jacob my servant's sake, and Israel mine elect, I have called thee (Cyrus) by thy name; to be a deliverer to my people Israel, and to help to plant them on my holy mountain, (Isa. lxv, 9, see connexion) for mine elect shall inherit it, and my servants shall dwell there; even on the mountains of Palestine, the Land of Canaan, which God had before promised to Abraham and his seed; (Gen. xvii, 8) and the particular reason why Abraham was chosen or elected to be the father of this blessed nation, is clearly told by the Lord, (Gen. xviii, 19) for I know him, that he will command his children and his household after him; and they shall keep the way of the Lord, to do justice and judgment; that the Lord may bring upon Abraham that which he hath spoken of him; and this includes the general principle of election (i.e.) that God chose, elected, or ordained, Jesus Christ, his son, to be the Creator, governor, Saviour, and judge of the world; and Abraham to be the father of the faithful, on account of his foreknowledge of their obedience to his will and commandments; which agrees with the saying in the 2d Timothy ii, 21, if a man purge himself from these, he shall be a vessel unto honour, sanctified and meet for the masters use, and prepared unto every good work.

Thus it appears that God has chosen or elected certain individuals, to certain blessings, or to the performance of certain works; and that we may more fully understand the movements of the Supreme Governor of the universe in the order of election, we proceed to quote the sacred writers.

Rom. viii, 29, 30, For whom he did foreknow, he also did predestinate to be conformed to the image of his son, that he might be the first born among many brethren: moreover, whom he did predestinate, them he also called, and whom he called, them he also justified, and whom he justified, them he also glorified. And whom did he foreknow? Those that loved him, as we find in the 28th verse of the same chapter, for we know that all things shall work together for good to them that *love God*, to them who are the *called* according to his purpose. And who are the called according to his purpose? Those whom he foreknew, for he foreknew that those, who loved him, would do his will and work righteousness, and it is vain for men to say they love God, if they do not keep his commandments. Cain found it so when he presented an unrighteous offering, for God said unto him (Gen. iv, 7) if thou doest well shalt thou not be accepted; and yet he was not accepted; but whoso keepeth his word, in him verily is the love of God perfected; and hereby we know that we are in him, (1 John ii, 5) or, that we are the called according to his purpose.

But did not God foreknow all things, and all men? Surely, known unto God are all his works, from the beginning of the world; (Acts xv, 18;) but does that prove that all men would love him and keep his commandments, so that he would predestinate them unto eternal life? Certainly not, for that would make God to foreknow things which were not to be, and to predestinate men to that, unto which they could never attain; (Mat. vii, 13) for wide is the gate and broad is the way that leadeth to destruction, and many there be which go in thereat.

The principles of God's kingdom are perfect and harmonious, and the scriptures of truth must also agree in all their parts, so that one sentiment thereof shall not destroy another, and when we read that whom he did foreknow, he also did predestinate; and that known unto God are all his works; so that it might appear from an abstract view thereof, that God foreknew all, and consequently predestinated all to be conformed to the image of his son; we ought also to read (Mark xvi, 16) he that believeth not shall be damned; and (John viii, 24) if ye believe not that I am he, ye shall die in your sins; also, (Mat. xxv, 41) depart from me ye cursed, for I was an hungered and ye gave me no meat, &c.

Paul referring to the Saints, (Rom. i, 7) calls them beloved of God, *called* to be Saints; and says (Rom. viii, 1) there is no condemnation to them which are in Christ Jesus, who walk not after the flesh, but after the spirit; and goes on to shew in his Epistle to the Romans, that the law,

3

(the law of carnal commandments given to the children of Israel, the covenant people,) could not make the comers thereunto perfect, (see also Heb. x, 1) but was given for a school master, to bring us unto Christ; (Gal. iii, 24,) so that when he had come, and offered himself without spot to God, (Heb. ix, 14) the sacrifice of the law should be done away in him that the honest in heart all might come unto the perfect law of liberty, (James i, 25) or the gospel of Christ, walking no longer after the flesh, but after the spirit, and be of that number who love God and keep his commandments, that they might be the called according to his purpose; (Rom. viii, 28) and these were the individuals referred to, whom God foreknew; such as Abel, Seth, Enoch, Noah, Melchizedec, Abraham, Lot, Isaac, Jacob, Joseph, Moses, Caleb, Joshua, the harlot Rahab who wrought righteousness by hiding the servants of God when their lives were sought by their enemies, Gideon, Barak, Sampson, Jeptha, David, Samuel, and the Prophets, (Heb. xi,) who, through faith, subdued kingdoms, wrought righteousness, obtained promises, stopped the mouths of lions, quenched the violence of fire, escaped the edge of the sword, out of weakness were made strong, waxed valiant in fight, and turned to flight the armies of the aliens; these all died in faith having kept the commandments of the Most High, having obtained the promise of a glorious inheritance, and are waiting the fulfilment of the promise which they obtained, (Heb. xi, 40) God having provided some better thing for us, that they, without us, should not be made perfect.

The prophet Alma bears a similar testimony to the other prophets concerning election in his 9th chapter (Book of Mormon) saying, this is the manner after which they were ordained: being called and prepared from the foundation of the world, according to the foreknowledge of God, on account of their exceeding faith and good works; in the first place being left to choose good or evil; therefore they having chosen good, and exercising exceeding great faith, are called with a holy calling, yea, with that holy calling which was prepared with, and according to, a preparatory redemption for such; and thus they have been called to this holy calling on account of their faith, while others would reject the spirit of God on account of the hardness of their hearts and blindness of their minds, while if it had not been for this, they might have had as great privilege as their brethren. Or in fine; in the first place they were on the same standing with their brethren; thus this holy calling being prepared from the foundation of the world for such as would not harden their hearts, being in and through the atonement of the only begotten son; who was prepared; and thus being called by this holy calling, and ordained unto the high priesthood of the holy order of God, to teach his commandments unto the children of men, that they might also enter into his rest, this high priesthood being after the order of his son, which order

4

was from the foundation of the world; or in other words being without beginning of days or end of years, being prepared from eternity to all eternity, according to his foreknowledge of all things.

Rom. ix. 11, 12. For the children being not yet born, neither having done any good or evil, that the purpose of God, according to election, might stand, not of works, but of him that calleth; it was said unto her, the elder shall serve the younger. As we have before shewn why God chose Abraham to be the father of the faithful, (viz.) because he knew he would command his children and his household after him, so now we see by this why the purposes of God according to election should stand, and that for his oath's sake. Gen. xxii, 16, 17, 18. By myself have I sworn saith the Lord; for because thou hast done this thing, and hast not withheld thy son, thine only son; that in blessing I will bless thee, and in multiplying I will multiply thy seed as the stars of heaven, and as the sand which is upon the sea shore; and thy seed shall possess the gate of his enemies; and in thy seed shall all the nations of the earth be blessed, because thou hast obeyed my voice. Here the Lord Jesus, coming through the seed of Abraham, is again referred to, through whose sufferings and death, or in whom all the nations of the earth were to be blessed, or made alive as they had died in Adam, (1 Cor. xv, 22). In this election is made manifest, for God elected or chose the children of Israel to be his peculiar people, and to them belong the covenants and promises, and all the blessings received by the Gentiles come through the covenants to Abraham and his seed; for through the unbelief of the Jews (Rom. xi, 17) they were broken off, and the Gentiles were grafted in; but they stand by *faith*, (Rom. xi, 20) and not by the *oath* of *election*; therefore it becometh them to fear lest they cease quickly to bear fruit, and be broken off (verse 21) that the Jews may be grafted in again, for they shall be grafted in again (verse 23) if they abide not in unbelief.

The Gentiles became partakers of the blessings of election and promises through faith and obedience, as Peter says, writing to the strangers scattered abroad, (1 Peter 1st chap.) who were the Gentiles, the elect according to the foreknowledge of God the Father, through sanctification of the spirit *unto obedience*: (1 Peter ii, 9) for ye are a chosen *generation*, a royal priesthood, an holy nation, a peculiar people; that ye should shew forth the praises of him, who hath called you out of darkness into his marvellous light, (verse 10) which in *time past were not a people* but now are the people of God; which *had not obtained mercy*, but now have obtained mercy.

Why were they a peculiar people? Because God had chosen that generation of Gentiles, and conferred on them the blessings, which descended through the priesthood, and the covenants unto the house of Israel, or grafted them into the good olive tree; (Rom. xi, 17) and thus

5

the house of Israel became ministers of salvation to the Gentiles; and this is what the house of Israel was elected unto, not only their own salvation, but through them salvation unto all others, (John iv, 22) for salvation is of the Jews; (Rom. xi, 11) and through their fall salvation is come unto the Gentiles. Among the promised seed, we find Jesus Christ neither last nor least, but the great high priest and head of all, who was chosen to lay down his life for the redemption of the world, for without the shedding of blood there could be no remission of sins, (Heb. ix, 22).

(Deut. vii, 6, 7, 8, 9.) Moses bears a similar testimony with Peter and Paul to the principles of election; for thou art an holy people unto the Lord thy God; the Lord thy God hath chosen thee to be a special people unto himself, above all people that are upon the face of the earth. The Lord did not set his love upon you, nor choose you, because ye were more in number than any people; for ye were the fewest of all people; but because the Lord loved you, and because he would keep the oath which he had sworn unto your fathers, hath the Lord brought you out with a mighty hand, and redeemed you out of the house of bondmen, from the hand of Pharoah king of Egypt.—Know therefore that the Lord thy God, he is God, the faithful God, which keepeth covenant and mercy with them that love him and keep his commandments to a thousand generations, which proves the long continuance of the blessings of this highly favoured people.

And the Lord said unto her, (Rebecca, Gen. xxv, 23) the elder shall serve the younger. And why? Because that Isaac, the father of Esau and Jacob, the husband of Rebecca, and the son of promise to Abraham, was the heir; and as Esau was the elder son of his father Isaac, he had a legal claim to the heirship; but through unbelief, hardness of heart, and hunger, he sold his birthright to his younger brother, Jacob, (Gen. xxv, 33) and God knowing before hand that he would do this of his own free will and choice, or acting upon that agency which God has delegated to all men, said to his mother, the elder shall serve the younger; for as the elder son, Esau, has sold his birthright and by that means lost all claim to the blessings promised to Abraham, those blessings and promises must have failed, if they had not descended with the purchased birthright unto the younger son, Jacob, for their [sic] was no other heir in Israel's family; and if those blessings had failed, the purposes of God according to election must have failed, in relation to the posterity of Israel, and the oath of Jehovah would have been broken, which could not be, though heaven and earth were to pass away.

Rom. ix, 13,—As it is written Jacob have I loved, but Esau have I hated. Where is it written? Malachi, i, 1, 2, verses. When was it written? About 397 years before Christ, and Esau and Jacob were born about 1773 years before Christ, (according to the common computation of time in

6

scripture margin,) so that Esau and Jacob lived about 1376 years before the Lord spoke by Malachi, saying, Jacob have I loved but Esau have I hated, as quoted by Paul. This text is often brought forward to prove that God loved Jacob and hated Esau, before they were born; or, before they had done good or evil; but if God did love one and hate the other, before they had done good or evil, he has not seen fit to tell us of it, either in the Old or New Testament, or any other revelation; but this only we learn that 1376 years after Esau and Jacob were born, God said, by Malachi, Jacob have I loved and Esau have I hated; and surely that was time sufficient to prove their works, and ascertain whether they were worthy to be loved or hated.

And why did he love the one and hate the other? For the same reason that he accepted the offering of Abel, and rejected Cain's offering; because Jacob's works had been righteous, and Esau's wicked; and where is there a righteous father who would not do the same thing? Who would not love an affectionate and obedient son, more than one who was disobedient, and sought to injure him and overthrow the order of his house? (objection) "But God seeth not as men seeth, and he is no respecter of persons," (Acts, x. 34.) True, but what saith the next verse, "He that *feareth God* and *worketh righteousness* is *accepted* of him; but it does not say that he that worketh wickedness is accepted, and this is a proof that God has respect to the *actions* of persons; and if he did not, why should he commend obedience to his law? for if he had no respect to the actions of men, he would be just as well pleased with a wicked man for breaking his law, as a righteous man for keeping it; and if Cain had done well he would have been accepted as well as Abel, (Gen. iv. 7) and Esau as well as Jacob, which proves that God does not respect persons, only in *relation to their acts*, (see Mat. xxv. 34, to the end,) Come ye blessed of my Father, inherit the kingdom prepared for you from the foundation of the world, for I was an hungred and ye gave me meat, &c.; and because that God blessed Abel and Jacob, this would not have hindered his blessing Cain and Esau, if their works had been righteous like unto their brethren; so God's choosing one nation to blessing, does not doom another to cursing, or make them reprobate, according to the reprobation of God, as some suppose; but by resisting the truth, they become reprobate concerning the faith, (2 Tim. iii. 8) and are abominable, and disobedient, and unto every *good work* reprobate, (Titus, i. 16) consequently, are not fit subjects for the blessings of election.

Rom. ix. 15, for he saith to Moses I will have mercy on whom I will have mercy, and I will have compassion on whom I will have compassion, (see Ex. xxxiii. 13, to the 19.) My presence shall go with thee, and I will give thee rest, for thou hast found grace in my sight, and I know thee by name, and I will make all my goodness to pass before thee, and I will proclaim the name of the Lord before thee: and I will be gracious to whom I will be gracious, and will shew mercy on whom I will shew mercy, (Rom. ix. 16.) So then it is not of him that willeth, nor of him that runneth, but of God that sheweth mercy; having his eye at the same time directed towards his covenant people in Egyptian bondage.

For the scripture saith unto Pharoah, (Ex. ix. 16, 17.) and in very deed for this cause have I raised thee up, for to shew in thee my power; and that my name may be declared throughout all the earth. As yet exaltest thou thyself against my people, that thou wilt not let them go? God had promised to bring the house of Israel up out of the land of Egypt, at his own appointed time; and with a mighty hand and an out-stretched arm, and great terribleness, (Deut. xxvi. 8.) he chose to do this thing, that his power might be known and his name declared throughout all the earth, so that all nations might have the God of heaven in remembrance, and reverence his holy name; and to accomplish this it was needful that he should meet with opposition to give him an opportunity to manifest his power; therefore he raised up a man, even Pharoah, who, he fore-knew, would harden his heart against God, of his own free-will and choice, and would withstand the Almighty in his attempt to deliver his chosen people, and that to the utmost of his ability; and he proved himself worthy of the choice, for he left no means unimproved, which his wicked heart could devise to vex the sons of Abraham, and defeat the purposes of the Most High, which gave the God of Abraham an opportunity to magnify his name in the ears of the nations, and in sight of this wicked king, by many mighty signs and wonders, sometimes even to the convincing the wicked king of his wickedness, and of the power of God, (Ex. viii. 28, &c.) and yet he would continue to rebel, and hold the Israelites in bondage; and this is what is meant by God's hardening Pharaoh's heart; he manifested himself in so many glorious and mighty ways, that Pharaoh could not resist the truth without becoming harder, so that at the last, in his madness to stay the people of God, he rushed into the Red sea, with all his host, and was covered with the floods.

Had not the power of God been exerted in a remarkable manner, it would seem as though the house of Israel must have become extinct, for Pharaoh commanded the midwifes to destroy the sons of the Israelitish women as soon as they were born, (Ex. i, 15, 16) and called them to account for saving the men children alive, (verse 18) and charged all his people saying every son that is born ye shall cast into the river, (verse 22) and yet God would have mercy on whom he would have mercy, (Rom. ix, 18) for he would have mercy on the goodly child, Moses, (when he was hid and laid in the flags (Ex. ii, 3) by his mother, to save him from Pharaoh's cruel order) and caused that he should be preserved as a prophet and deliverer to lead his people up to their own country; and whom he would be [sic] hardened, for he hardened Pharaoh by passing before him in mighty power, and withdrawing his spirit and leaving him to his own wicked inclination, for he had set taskmasters over the Israelites, to afflict them with their burdens; and caused them to build treasure-cities for Pharaoh, and made them to serve with rigour; and made their lives bitter with hard bondage, in mortar and brick and all manner of service in the field (Ex. 1st ch.); beside destroying the men children: thus proving to the God of heaven and all men that he had hardened his own hard heart, until he become a vessel of wrath fitted for destruction, (Rom. ix, 22) all this, long before God said unto Moses, I will harden his (Pharoah's) heart (Ex. iv, 21).

Are men then to be saved by works? Nay, verily, by grace are ye saved through faith, and that not of yourselves, it is the gift of God, (Eph. ii, 8.) Not of works, lest any man should boast. (v. 9.) Not by works of righteousness which we have done, but according to his mercy he saved us, (Titus iii, 5) and yet faith without works is dead being alone, (James ii, 17.) Was not Abraham our father justified by works? (v. 21.) Shall we then be saved by faith? Nay, neither by faith nor works; but by works is faith made perfect, (v. 22) but by grace are ye saved, (Eph. ii, 8,) and if by grace, then it is no more of works, otherwise grace is no grace and if it be of works then it is no more work. (Rom. xi. 6.) Ye see then how that a man is justified by works, and not by faith only, (James ii, 24).

Rom. x, 3, 4. For they, (Israel) being ignorant of God's righteousness, and going about to establish their own righteousness, have not submitted themselves unto the righteousness of God; for Christ is the end of the law for righteousness to every one that believeth. Thus the righteousness of God is made manifest in the plan of salvation by his crucified son; for there is none other name under heaven, given among men whereby we must be saved, but the name of Jesus Christ of Nazareth; (Acts iv, 10, 12) but of this the Jews were ignorant, although they themselves crucified him; and they have been going about wandering among all the nations of the earth ever since, for the space of eighteen hundred years, trying to establish their own righteousness, which is of the law of Moses; which law can never make the comers thereunto perfect, (Heb. x, 1;) yet notwithstanding their darkness and long dispersion, there is a remnant according to the election of grace, (Rom. xi, 5) whom God will gather from among all people whither they are scattered, and will be sanctified in them in the sight of the heathen; then shall they dwell in their land which God gave to his servant Jacob, and they shall dwell safely therein, and shall build houses and plant vineyards, yea they shall dwell with confidence, when I have executed judgments upon all those that despise them round about; and they shall know that I am the Lord their God; (Eze. xxviii, 25, 26. Isa. xi, 11 to 16,) and when this gathering shall be completed, it shall no more be said the Lord liveth that brought up the children of Israel out of the land of Egypt; but the Lord liveth that brought up the children of Israel from the land of the north, and from all the lands whither he had driven them; and I will bring them again unto this land which I gave unto their fathers, (Jer. xvi, 14, 15, &c. to the end).

Rom. xi, 7. What then? Israel hath not obtained that which he seeketh for, but the election hath obtained it. And why have they not obtained it? Because they sought it not by faith, but it were by the works of the law, for they stumbled at that stumbling-stone; as it is written, behold I lay in Zion a stumbling stone and rock of offence, (Rom. ix, 32, 33) to both the houses of Israel; and for a gin and for a snare to the inhabitants of Jerusalem; and many of them shall stumble, (Isa. viii, 14, 15) but have they stumbled that they should fall? God forbid; but rather through their fall salvation is come unto the Gentiles, (Rom. xi, 11) and Jerusalem shall be trodden down by the Gentiles until the times of the Gentiles be fulfilled, (Luke xxi, 24,) and when the house of Israel shall be restored to their possession in Canaan, it may truly be said the election hath obtained it; for the fulfilment of God's oath of election to Abraham, as the father of the faithful, and the promises to his children, will obtain that for Israel, which he has sought for in vain by the law of Moses.

This is the election that we believe in, viz.:—such as we find in prophets and apostles, and the word of the Lord himself, and as we have not room to give all the quotations in full, relating to election in this epistle, we would invite the Saints, to examine the Scriptures in connection with these quoted: and whenever they find election or any other principle or blessing given or applied to the house of Israel, let those principles continue with the house of Israel; and not apply that to Esau, which belongs to Jacob; or to the churches of modern times, which belong to the ancient covenant people; and always *ascertain* how the *Lord*, the *apostles*, and *prophets*, *have applied* their words, and *ever continue* the *same application*, and wisdom and knowledge will be added unto you: and in the words of the beloved Peter and Paul, we would exhort you to work out your own salvation with fear and trembling: for it is God which worketh in you, both to will and to do, of his good pleasure; (Phil. ii. 12, 13,) giving all diligence to make your calling and election sure, (2 Peter, i. 10.) for this is that sealing power spoken of in Eph. i. 13, 14. In whom ye also trusted, after that ye heard the word of truth; the gospel of your salvation, in whom also, *after that ye believed ye were sealed with that Holy Spirit of promise*, which is the earnest [?] of our inheritance, until the *redemption* of the *purchased possession*, until the praise of his glory, (2 Peter, i. 11,) for so an entrance shall be ministered unto you abundantly into the everlasting kingdom of our Lord and Saviour Jesus Christ. *Amen.*

{2}

"The Remarks of President Young in Behalf of the Claim of the Twelve to Lead the Church in the Absence of the First Presidency," A Sermon in Two Parts Delivered on 8 August 1844

(from Joseph Smith et al., *History of the Church of Jesus Christ of Latter-day Saints*, ed. B. H. Roberts, 7 vols. [Salt Lake City: Deseret Press, 1932], 7:231-36, 239-42)

The meeting being opened, President Brigham Young arose and said:—

"*Attention all!* This congregation makes me think of the days of King Benjamin, the multitude being so great that all could not hear. I request the brethren not to have any feelings for being convened this afternoon, for it is necessary; we want you all to be still and give attention, that all may hear. Let none complain because of the situation of the congregation, we will do the best we can.

For the first time in my life, for the first time in your lives, for the first time in the kingdom of God in the 19th century, without a Prophet at our head, do I step forth to act in my calling in connection with the Quorum of the Twelve, as Apostles of Jesus Christ unto this generation—Apostles whom God has called by revelation through the Prophet Joseph, who are ordained and anointed to bear off the keys of the kingdom of God in all the world.

This people have hitherto walked by sight and not by faith. You have had the Prophet in your midst. Do you all understand? You have walked by sight and without much pleading to the Lord to know whether things were right or not.

Heretofore you have had a Prophet as the mouth of the Lord to speak to you, but he has sealed his testimony with his blood, and now, for the first time, are you called to walk by faith, not by sight.

The first position I take in behalf of the Twelve and the people is, to ask a few questions. I ask the Latter-day Saints: do you, as individuals, at this time, want to choose a Prophet or a guardian? Inasmuch as our Prophet and Patriarch are taken from our midst, do you want some one to guard, to guide and lead you through this world into the kingdom of God, or not? All that want some person to be a guardian or a Prophet, a spokesman or something else, signify it by raising the right hand. (No votes).

When I came to this stand I had peculiar feelings and impressions.

The faces of this people seem to say, we want a shepherd to guide and lead us through this world. *All that want to draw away a party from the church after them, let them do it if they can, but they will not prosper.*

If any man thinks he has influence among this people to lead away a party, let him try it, and he will find out that there is power with the Apostles which will carry them off victorious through all the world, and build up and defend the church and kingdom of God.

What do the people want? I feel as though I wanted the privilege to weep and mourn for thirty days at least, then rise up, shake myself, and tell the people what the Lord wants of them; although my heart is too full of mourning to launch forth into business transactions and the organization of the church, I feel compelled this day to step forth in the discharge of those duties God has placed upon me.

I now wish to speak of the organization of the Church of Jesus Christ of Latter-day Saints. If the church is organized, and you want to know how it is organized, I will tell you. I know your feelings—do you want me to tell your feelings?

Here is President Rigdon, who was counselor to Joseph. I ask, where are Joseph and Hyrum? They are gone beyond the veil; and if Elder Rigdon wants to act as his counselor, he must go beyond the veil where he is.

There has been much said about President Rigdon being President of the Church, and leading the people, being the head, etc. Brother Rigdon has come 1,600 miles to tell you what he wants to do for you. If the people want President Rigdon to lead them they may have him; but I say unto you that the Quorum of the Twelve have the keys of the kingdom of God in all the world.

The Twelve are appointed by the finger of God. Here is Brigham, have his knees ever faltered? Have his lips ever quivered? Here is Heber and the rest of the Twelve, an independent body who have the keys of the priesthood—the keys of the kingdom of God to deliver to all the world: this is true, so help me God. They stand next to Joseph, and are as the First Presidency of the Church.

I do not know whether my enemies will take my life or not, and I do not care, for I want to be with the man I love.

You cannot fill the office of a prophet, seer and revelator: God must do this. You are like children without a father and sheep without a shepherd. You must not appoint any man at our head; if you should, the Twelve must ordain him. You cannot appoint a man at our head; but if you do want any other man or men to lead you, take them and we will go our way to build up the kingdom in all the world.

I know who are Joseph's friends, and who are his enemies. I know where the keys of the kingdom are, and where they will eternally be.

You cannot call a man to be a prophet; you cannot take Elder Rigdon and place him above the Twelve; if so, he must be ordained by them.

I tell you there is an overanxiety to hurry matters here. You cannot take any man and put him at the head; you would scatter the saints to the four winds, you would sever the priesthood. So long as we remain as we are, the heavenly Head is in constant cooperation with us; and if you go out of that course, God will have nothing to do with you.

Again, perhaps some think that our beloved Brother Rigdon would not be honored, would not be looked to as a friend; but if he does right and remains faithful he will not act against our counsel nor we against his, but act together, and we shall be as one.

I again repeat, no man can stand at our head, except God reveals it from the heavens.

I have spared no pains to learn my lesson of the kingdom in this world and in the eternal worlds; and if it were not so, I could go and live in peace; but for the gospel and your sakes I shall stand in my place. We are liable to be killed all the day long. You have never lived by faith.

Brother Joseph, the Prophet, has laid the foundation for a great work, and we will build upon it; you have never seen the quorums built one upon another. There is an almighty foundation laid, and we can build a kingdom such as there never was in the world: we can build a kingdom faster than satan can kill the saints off.

What do you want? Do you want a patriarch for the whole church? To this we are perfectly willing. If Brother Samuel H. Smith had been living, it would have been his right and privilege; but he is dead, he is gone to Joseph and Hyrum, he is out of the reach of bullets and spears, and he can waft himself with his brothers, his friends and the saints.

Do you want a patriarch? Here is brother William [Smith] left; here is Uncle John Smith, uncle to the Prophet Joseph left; it is their right. The right of patriarchal blessings belongs to Joseph's family.

Do you want a Trustee-in-Trust? Has there been a bishop who has stood in his lot yet? What is his business? To take charge of the temporal affairs, so that the Twelve and the elders may go on their business. Joseph condescended to do their business for them. Joseph condescended to offer himself for president of the United States, and it was a great condescension.

Do you want a spokesman? Here are Elder Rigdon, Brother Amasa Lyman [whom Joseph expected to take as a counselor] and myself. Do you want the church properly organized, or do you want a spokesman to be chief cook and bottle-washer? Elder Rigdon claims to be spokesman to the Prophet. Very well, he was; but can he now act in that office? If he wants now to be a spokesman to the Prophet, he must go to the other side of the veil, for the Prophet is there, but Elder Rigdon is here.

13

Why will Elder Rigdon be a fool? Who knows anything of the priesthood, or of the organization of the kingdom of God. I am plain.

Does this church want it as God organized it? Or do you want to clip the power of the priesthood, and let those who have the keys of the priesthood go and build up the kingdom in all the world, wherever the people will hear them?

If there is a spokesman, if he is a king and priest, let him go and build up a kingdom unto himself; that is his right and it is the right of many here, but the Twelve are at the head of it.

I want to live on the earth and spread truth through all the world. You saints of latter-day want things right. If 10,000 men rise up and say they have the Prophet Joseph Smith's shoes, I know they are imposters. In the priesthood you have a right to build up a kingdom, if you know how the church is organized.

Now, if you want Sidney Rigdon or William Law to lead you, or anybody else, you are welcome to them; but I tell you, in the name of the Lord that no man can put another between the Twelve and the Prophet Joseph. Why? Because Joseph was their file leader, and he has committed into their hands the keys of the kingdom in this last dispensation, for all the world; don't put a thread between the priesthood and God.

I will ask, who has stood next to Joseph and Hyrum? I have, and I will stand next to him. We have a head, and that head is the Apostleship, the spirit and power of Joseph, and we can now begin to see the necessity of that Apostleship.

Brother Rigdon was at his side—not above. No man has a right to counsel the Twelve but Joseph Smith. Think of these things. You cannot appoint a prophet; but if you let the Twelve remain and act in their place, the keys of the kingdom are with them and they can manage the affairs of the church and direct all things aright.

Now, all this does not lessen the character of President Rigdon; let him magnify his calling, and Joseph will want him beyond the veil—let him be careful what he does, lest that thread which binds us together is cut asunder. May God bless you all." . . .

President Brigham Young again arose and said:—

"There is more business than can be done this afternoon, but we can accomplish all we want to have done without calling this convention of the whole church. I am going to present to you the leading items.

I do not ask you to take my counsel or advice alone, but every one of you act for yourselves; but if Brother Rigdon is the person you want to lead you, vote for him, but not unless you intend to follow him and support him as you did Joseph. Do not say so without you mean to take his counsel hereafter.

And I would say the same for the Twelve, don't make a covenant to support them unless you intend to abide by their counsel; and if they do not counsel you as you please, don't turn round and oppose them.

I want every man, before he enters into a covenant, to know what he is going to do; but we want to know if this people will support the priesthood in the name of Israel's God. If you say you will, do so.

We want men appointed to take charge of the business that did lay on the shoulders of Joseph. Let me say to you that this kingdom will spread more than ever.

The Twelve have the power now—the seventies, the elders and all of you can have power to go and build up the kingdom in the name of Israel's God. Nauvoo will not hold all the people that will come into the kingdom.

We want to build the Temple, so as to get our endowment; and if we do our best, and satan will not let us build it, we will go into the wilderness and we will receive the endowment, for we will receive an endowment anyhow.

Will you abide our counsel? I again say, my soul for any man's, if they will abide our counsel, that they will go right into heaven. We have all the signs and tokens to give to the porter at the door, and he will let us in.

I will ask you as quorums, Do you want Brother Rigdon to stand forward as your leader, your guide, your spokesman. President Rigdon wants me to bring up the other question first, and that is, Does the church want, and is it their only desire to sustain the Twelve as the First Presidency of this people?

Here are the Apostles, the *Bible*, the *Book of Mormon*, the *Doctrine and Covenants*—they are written on the tablet of my heart. If the church want the Twelve to stand as the head, the First Presidency of the Church, and at the head of this kingdom in all the world, stand next to Joseph, walk up into their calling, and hold the keys of this kingdom, every man, every woman, every quorum is now put in order, and you are now the sole controllers of it.

All that are in favor of this, in all the congregation of the saints, manifest it by holding up the right hand. (There was a universal vote). If there are any of the contrary mind, every man and every woman who does not want the Twelve to preside, lift up your hands in like manner. (No hands up). This supersedes the other question, and trying it by quorums.

We feel as though we could take Brother Rigdon in our bosom along with us; we want such men as Brother Rigdon. He has been sent away by Brother Joseph to build up a kingdom; let him keep the instructions and calling; let him raise up a mighty kingdom in Pittsburgh, and we will lift up his hands to Almighty God. I think we may have a printing office and a gathering there. If the devil still tries to kill us he will have enough to do.

The next is President Marks. Our feelings are to let him stand as president of the stake, as heretofore. We can build the Temple, etc.

You did not know who you had amongst you. Joseph so loved this people that he gave his life for them; Hyrum loved his brother and this people unto death. Joseph and Hyrum have given their lives for the church. But very few knew Joseph's character; he loved you unto death—you did not know it until after his death: he has now sealed his testimony with his blood.

If the Twelve had been here we would not have seen him given up—he should not have been given up. He was in your midst, but you did not know him; he has been taken away, for the people are not worthy of him.

The world is wide. I can preach in England, Ireland, Scotland, France, Germany, etc. I can preach in all the world, and the devils cannot find us. I'll swear to you I will not be given up.

There is much to be done. You have men among you who sleep with one eye open. The foundation is laid by our Prophet, and we will build thereon; no other foundation can be laid but that which is laid, and we will have our endowment, if the Lord will.

As the authorities do not want us to do military duty, don't do it. If it is necessary, my neck is ready for the knife; as for myself, I am determined to build up the kingdom of God: and by and by there will be a gleaning of grapes, and it may be said, 'To your tents, O Israel'.

We can build on the foundation that was laid by the Prophet. Joseph has finished his work, and all the devils in hell and all the mobbers on earth could not take his life until he had accomplished his work. God said, I will put a veil over his eyes and lead him up to the slaughter like a sheep to be killed, for the people are not worthy of him, though God loves this people.

Let no man suppose that the kingdom is rent from you; that it is not organized. If all the quorums of the church were slain, except the high priests, they would rise up with the keys of the kingdom, and have the powers of the priesthood upon them, and build up the kingdom, and the devil cannot help himself.

You can go to a healthy country, buy the land, and don't let a cursed scoundrel get in your midst. Let there be good men, good women, and whenever a man comes with a wheelbarrow-full of goods don't sell him land, don't let him a house, nor buy of him.

Suppose we had ten thousand such places, and increasing in greatness, perfectly free from these poor devils, we should feel better than we do now. Let us all be humble and get our endowments—all be humble, industrious and prudent, what sort of a kingdom would it be? The foundation is laid for more than we can think or talk about today.

Is it the will of this congregation that they will be tithed until the Temple is finished, as they have hitherto been? If so, signify it by the uplifted hand. (The vote was unanimous).

The men will act that have never acted before, and they will have the power and authority to do it. Is it the mind of this congregation to loose the hands of the Twelve, and enable us to go and preach to all the world? We want to know the feelings of the people. Is it your will to support the Twelve in all the world in their missions? (The congregation sustained this question by a unanimous vote). Will you leave it to the Twelve to dictate about the finances of the church? and will it be the mind of this people that the Twelve teach what will be the duties of the bishops in handling the affairs of the church? I want this, because twelve men can do it just as well as calling this immense congregation together at any other time. (A unanimous vote).

We shall have a patriarch, and the right is in the family of Joseph Smith, his brothers, his sons, or some one of his relations. Here is Uncle John, he has been ordained a patriarch. Brother Samuel would have taken the office if he had been alive; it would have been his right; the right is in Uncle John, or one of his brothers (read sec. iii, par. 17, *Doctrine and Covenants*). I know that it would have belonged to Samuel. But as it is, if you leave it to the Twelve, they will wait until they know who is the man. Will you leave it to the Twelve, and they dictate the matter. (A unanimous vote). I know it will be let alone for the present.

I feel to bring up Brother Rigdon; we are of one mind with him and he with us. Will this congregation uphold him in the place he occupies by the prayer of faith and let him be one with us and we with him. (Unanimous). The Twelve will dictate and see to other matters. There will be a committee for the Temple; and now let men stand to their posts and be faithful."

{3}

"Speech Delivered by President B. Young, in the City of Joseph, April 6th 1845"

(from *Times and Seasons* 6 [1 July 1845]: 953-57)

I hope there may be faith enough in this congregation of Saints to still the wind, and strengthen me so that I may be heard by all of this vast assemblage of people; and in order that my voice may extend, and be heard by all it will be necessary for the brethren and sisters to be as quiet as possible, and I will do my best to speak that you may all hear and understand.

We shall devote this day to preaching—exhortation—singing—praying and blessing children, (such as have not been blessed,) and all those who have not been able to come to meeting: such women may be, who have not had their children blessed, and have the privilege this afternoon.

Last Sunday I proposed to the Saints, to speak to day on the subject of the baptism for the dead in connexion with other items, that the Saints may be satisfied—that all doubt and darkness may be removed with regard to certain principles of the doctrine of redemption.

But before I undertake to explain or give correct views upon this important subject, I would say to all those who are satisfied with all the knowledge they have, and want no more: to you I do not expect to be an apostle this day; but for those who are hungering and thirsting after righteousness, I pray, that they may be filled and satisfied with the intelligence of God, even his glory.

What I have stated in the winter past relative to the baptism for the dead, has been a matter of discussion among the elders, and among the brethren and sisters in general, but I will endeavor to show to this congregation of Saints the propriety of it; and that the people could not run at hap-hazard, and without order to attend to this ordinance and at the same time it be valid, and recognized in heaven.

We are building a house at present unto the Lord in the which we expect to attend to the fulfilment of this doctrine; you all believe that this is a doctrine revealed by God to his servant Joseph. Admitting this to be the fact, that he has revealed through him a plan by which we may bring to life the dead, and bless them with a great and glorious exaltation in the presence of the Almighty with ourselves; still we want to know how to do these things right; to do them in a manner that shall be acceptable to the Almighty, if otherwise he will say unto us at the last day, "ye have not known me right, because of your slothfulness and your wickedness depart from me for I know you not." O ye Latter-day Saints! I don't want one of you to be caught in that snare, but that you may do things right, and thus be enabled to make your calling and election sure. I might say the plan of salvation is perfect of itself—it is a system that can save, redeem, honor and glorify all who are willing to apply themselves to it according to the pattern—it is a plan of salvation to all men both male and female; it has been handed down, and known from the days of Adam, and those who will open their eyes to see, their ears to hear, and their hearts to understand, they will acknowledge at once that it is a perfect system; but those whose eyes, ears and hearts are shut up by incorrect tradition and prejudice, they acknowledge by their lives, by their practices, by their walk and conversation, and by their actions in general, that they do not understand it, yet they plead the atonement, and say we believe the atonement is sufficient for all—only believe and he will save you; yet at the same time the bible, reason, common sense and every other righteous principle positively testifies that there must be means made use of to put you in possession of the blessings of the atonement, as well as any other blessing.

I believe the plan of salvation is comeatable, and may be understood—and the inhabitants of the world who will come to God can be made acquainted with all the ordinances and blessings by which they may know how to save themselves and their friends, as we know how to build a house, or as the mechanic knows how to make any piece of mechanism; but mechanism is not to be compared with the perfection of the machine of salvation, or with the beauty of the plan of redemption: it is the most perfect system of any other creature under heaven.

The gospel is adapted to the capacity of all the human family, whether they be high or low, rich or poor, bond or free, black or white, young or old, it is adapted to their capacities, all can understand and be saved: no comparison of its purity can be made; you may investigate the laws of nations, and gather together all the laws of the kingdoms of this world, and make a selection of the best part of the purest principles of the laws of justice and equity, and they would not compare, nor would there be any resemblance to the purity of the laws of heaven. He who gives that law is perfect, and reduces it to the capacity of finite beings in order that they may understand it and then receive more: thus the infinite being gives line upon line, reveals principle after principle, as the mind of the finite being expands, and when he has learned all his life he will then begin to see, that he has not yet entered upon the threshold of the eternal things that are to be gained by the children of men. I have now about got through with my preliminaries, and shall occupy your attention with some items in relation to the doctrine of the baptism for the dead.

I do not say that you have not been taught and learned the principle; you have heard it taught from this stand from time to time, by many of the elders, and from the mouth of our beloved and martyred prophet Joseph; therefore my course will not be to prove the doctrine, but refer to those things against which your minds are revolting. Consequently I would say to this vast congregation of Saints, when we enter into the Temple of God to receive our washings, our anointings, our endowments and baptisms for the saving of ourselves, and for the saving of our dead: that you never will see a man go forth to be baptized for a woman, nor a woman for a man. If your minds should be in any dubiety with regard to this, call to mind a principle already advanced, that when an infinite being gives a law to his finite creatures, he has to descend to the capacity of those who receive his law, when the doctrine of baptism for the dead was first given, this church was in its infancy, and was not capable of receiving all the knowledge of God in its highest degree; this you all believe. I would keep this one thing in your minds, and that is, that there is none, no not one of the sons and daughters of Adam and Eve, that ever received the fullness of the celestial law at the first of the Lord's commencing to reveal it unto them.

The doctrine of baptism for the dead you have been taught for some time, and the first account that I heard of it was while I was in England; it was there I got the glad tidings that the living could go forth and be baptised for those who had fallen asleep. This doctrine I believed before anything was said or done about it in this church; it made me glad when I heard it was revealed through his servant Joseph, and that I could go forth, and officiate for my fathers, for my mothers, and for my ancestors, to the latest generation who have not had the privilege of helping themselves; that they can yet arise to the state of glory and exaltation as we that live, have a privilege of rising to ourselves. The next year I came home and requested Brother Joseph to preach upon the subject, which he did, I also heard many of the elders preach upon the same subject.

There has been many things said, and notions imbibed concerning this doctrine. Allow me to advance an idea, and it is this; except we attend to this ordinance according to the law of heaven in all things it will not be valid or be of any benefit either to the living or the dead; when it was first revealed all the order of it was not made known, afterwards it was made known, that records, clerks, and one or two witnesses were necessary or else it will be of no value to the saints.

The Lord has led this people all the while in this way, by giving them here a little and there a little, thus he increases their wisdom, and he that receives a little and is thankful for that shall receive more and more, and more even to the fullness of the eternal Godhead: there is no stopping place, but the weak capacity of man cannot understand it unless the spirit of the eternal God is in their hearts, and then they can comprehend but a little of it. In this is the glory, power, and excellency of the gospel of the Son of God to poor weak finite man.—Look, O ye Latter-day Saints, at the nations of the earth, Christendom, look at them; but look at ourselves (although we have received a great deal) yet who is there here that has seen Jesus Christ, that have beheld angels, that have conversed with the spirits of just men made perfect, and the assembly of the church of Enoch, and with God the judge of all? who is there here that has been caught up to the third heavens and gazed upon the order and glory of the celestial world? don't you see brethren we have yet a great deal to learn, but is it not our privilege to be filled with all the fullness of Godliness? (cries of yes.) When you receive all that is for you, you will say O the blindness of Christendom! O the ignorance of the world!! even the Latter-day Saints that have assembled themselves together at the April conference in the year eighteen hundred and forty-five, will say, what am I?

Joseph in his life time did not receive every thing connected with the doctrine of redemption, but he has left the key with those who understand how to obtain and teach to this great people all that is necessary for their salvation and exaltation in the celestial kingdom of our God. We have got to learn how to be faithful with the few things, you know the promise is, if we are faithful in a few things we shall be made rulers over many things. If we improve upon the small things, greater will be given unto us.

I have said that a man cannot be baptized for a woman, nor a woman for a man, and it be valid. I have not used any argument as yet; I want now to use an argument upon this subject, it is a very short one; and I will do it by asking this congregation, if God would call a person to commence a thing that would not have power and ability to carry it out? Would he do it? (no.) Well then, what has been our course on former occasions? Why, here goes our beloved sisters, and they are baptised in the river or in the fount for their uncles, for their fathers, for their grand-fathers and great grandfathers.

Well, now I will take you and confirm you for your uncles, for your fathers, for your grandfathers, and for your great grandfathers, and let you go; after a while here comes our beloved sisters, saying, I want to be ordained for my uncle, and for my father, and for my grandfather, and great grandfather; I want my father ordained to the high priesthood, and my grandfather, I want to be patriarch, and you may ordain me a prophet for my uncle! What would you think about all that, sisters, come now you have been baptised and confirmed for your father, wont you be ordained for him? You could cast on a stocking and finish it.—You could take wool and card and spin it and make it into cloth, and then make it into garments. A person that commences a work and has not ability and power to finish it, only leaves the unfinished remains as a monument of folly. We will not commence a work we cannot finish; but let us hearken to the voice of the spirit and give heed to his teachings and we will make ourselves perfect in all things.

I would now call your attention to some of the sayings of the apostle Paul. I hope you will not stumble at them. Paul says, "nevertheless, neither is the man without the woman, neither the woman without the man, in the Lord, for as the woman is of the man, even so is the man also by the women, but all things of God." The same Apostle also says, "The woman is the glory of the man." Now brethren, these are Paul's sayings, not Joseph Smith's spiritual wife system sayings.

And I would say, as no man can be perfect without the woman, so no woman can be perfect without a man to lead her, I tell you the truth as it is in the bosom of eternity; and I say so to every man upon the face of the earth: if he wishes to be saved he cannot be saved without a woman by his side. This is spiritual wife *ism*, that is, the doctrine of spiritual wives.

Lest these my sisters should think I give power into the hands of their husbands to abuse them, I would say there is no man has a right to govern his wife and family unless he does it after the order of the church of Christ, unless he does it upon this principle he need not expect to receive a celestial glory. He that does not govern as Jesus governs his church, breaks his bonds and solemn obligations to his family.

Now ye elders of Israel will you go and beat your wives? will you neglect and abuse them? You may ask, is that anything about being baptised for the dead, or the laws of the celestial kingdom?

With regard to the laws of the celestial kingdom, I say it always was, and is, and always will be, a system of beauty and order. When the angel visited Cornelius, and commanded him to send men to Joppa for Peter, who should tell him words whereby he and his house should be saved. Would it not have saved a good deal of trouble if the angel had told these words to Cornelius? It certainly would, but it was not the angel's privilege, it remained for Peter to do, because it was Peter's calling; it was Peter's duty. In this case we see the principle of order. Again, in the case of the Savior, did he offer to baptise Paul? No, he had to go to Damascus, to a certain street, in order to find Ananias, who administered to him. Thus you see the angel honored Peter, the Savior honored Ananias by permitting them to attend to the calling they had received power to act in. So let fathers honor their families, husbands honor your wives, honor your children that they may learn to honor you; and if you come and are baptised for the father of your wife, and you want your mother baptised for, let your wife do it; give honor to her.—Ananias had the glory and honor of ordaining Paul and sending him to preach. Christ had done his work, and then gave honor and glory to his servants; when the elders have done their work, let them give their wives honor, and let them say to them, come be baptised for my mother, and for my sister, and save them, and I will preside over the whole of you.

Thus let every person stand in their own order, and do that which belongs to them to do, that there may be no confusion, but let order and beauty be the characteristics of this people. I used to think that the sectarian world would certainly get to heaven for they tried hard enough. And we boys would frequently wish ourselves in heaven with our backs broke that we could not get out again. The sectarian world is just like that, they are scrambling up in the greatest confusion, saying to each other, I hope you will get to heaven, and may your back be broke that you cannot get out again, and that is all they know about it.

The religion of heaven teaches us to give every man and every woman their due, that rightly belongs to them. And he that walks up to his privilege and duty, he has honor and glory, and shall never be removed out of his place.

I have shown to the brethren and sisters that Brother Joseph did not tell them all things at once, consequently you may expect to hear and see many things you never thought of before. One thing is that we have taken down the wooden fount that was built up by the instructions of Brother Joseph. This has been a great wonder to some, and says one of the stone-cutters the other day, "I wonder why Joseph did not tell us the fount should be built of stone." The man that made that speech is walking in darkness. He is a stranger to the spirit of this work, and knows nothing. In fact he does not know enough to cut a stone for the house of God. There is not a man under the face of the heavens that has one particle of the spirit about him, but knows that God talks to men according to their circumstances. God knew that old Abraham could not build a temple, therefore he said unto him, go to the mountain I shall tell thee of, and there offer up your sacrifice. He tells us to build an house here in this place, according to our means. And when we get a little more strength, he will say, go now and execute your means upon the next house we have got to build, and it is just to stretch our faith until it shall become exceeding great, that we can command the elements and they will obey. And when we get into Jackson county to walk in the courts of that house, we can say we built this temple: for as the Lord lives we will build up Jackson county in this generation, (cries of amen,) and we will be far better off with regard to temporal things, when we have done, than ever we were before. If we had the means to build a fount in that house, say one of marble, the Lord would just as like as not tell us to cover it with gold just to stretch our faith. Brother Joseph said to me with regard to the fount, "I will not go into the river to be baptised for my friends, we will build a wooden fount to serve the present necessity; brethren does that satisfy you? This fount has caused the Gentile world to wonder, but a sight of the next one will make a Gentile faint away. This brings to my memory a circumstance that transpired in the temple at Kirtland. A very pious lady came to see the temple, she walked up and down in the house, with her hands locked together, and after the escape of one or two of the sectarians most sanctified groans, she explained, "The Lord does not like such extravagance." Poor thing, I wonder how she will walk upon the streets when they are paved with gold; she could not bear to see the temple of God adorned and beautified, and the reason was because she was *full of the devil.*

I would put you on your guard against those who wear a long face, and pretend to be so holy, and so much better than every body else—They cannot look pleasant because they are full of the devil. Those who have got the forgiveness of their sins have countenances that look bright, and they will shine with the intelligence of heaven. If you dont believe it, try yourselves and then look up into the glass.

We will have a fount that will not stink and keep us all the while cleansing it out: and we will have a pool wherein to baptise the sick, that they may recover. And when we get into the fount we will show you the priesthood and the power of it: therefore, let us be diligent in observing all the commandments of God. Put away all fears of mobs, let not these things trouble you, for I say to the people I believe myself we shall have a healthy season, and that we shall have a summer of peace—The devils will growl without, and if they could get in here they would growl, but if they do they must look out. And I dare venture to say, that there could not be found as healthy a looking congregation in all the United States as I see here this day.

Brethren and sisters, for the sake of your dead and for the sake of yourselves, be faithful and have no feelings in your hearts against one another, but learn to suffer wrong rather than do wrong, and by so doing we will outstrip all our enemies and conquer the evil one, for know ye not that here is Zion? know ye not that the millennium has commenced? We have had Zion upon the earth this fourteen years. Peace reigns among this people which is Zion. Union and true charity dwells with this people: this is the most orderly and peaceable people upon the face of the whole earth. Well, this is Zion, and it is increasing and spreading wider and wider, and this principle of Zion, which is peace, will stretch all over the earth; that is the millennium.

The saints will increase, and continue to increase, and virtue, love, holiness and all good principles, will continue to spread and spread, and will rule the nations of the earth, and who is there that can stop its progress? None, but it will roll until there is no room for the devil; then he will be bound and shut up. The principles of the kingdom of God will prevail, from city to city, from nation to nation, until the devil shall be bound and there is no place for him. They killed the prophet Joseph for fear he would spread this principle, but it will go and fill the whole earth; this is true and will come to pass as the Lord lives. Amen.

{4}

"I Remarked Last Sunday that I had not Felt Much Like Preaching to the Brethren," A Sermon Delivered on 29 May 1847

(from George D. Smith, ed., *An Intimate Chronicle: The Journals of William Clayton* [Salt Lake City: Signature Books in association with Smith Research Associates, 1991], 325-30)

I remarked last Sunday that I had not felt much like preaching to the brethren on this mission. This morning I feel like preaching a little, and shall take for my text, "That as to pursuing our journey with this company, with the spirit they possess, I am about to revolt against it." This is the text I feel like preaching on this morning, consequently I am in no hurry. In the first place, before we left Winter Quarters, it was told to the brethren, and many knew it by experience, that we had to leave our homes, our houses our lands and our all because we believed in the gospel as revealed to the Saints in these last days. The rise of the persecutions against the Church, was in consequence of the doctrines of eternal truth taught by Joseph. Many knew this by experience. Some lost their husbands, some lost their wives, and some their children through persecution, and yet we have not been disposed to forsake the truth, and turn and mingle with the gentiles, except a few who have turned aside, and gone away from us, and we have learned in a measure, the difference between a professor of religion, and a possessor of religion. Before we left Winter Quarters, it was told to the brethren that we were going to look out a home for the saints where they would be free from persecution by the gentiles, where we could dwell in peace and serve God according to the Holy priesthood, where we could build up the kingdom, so that the nations would begin to flock to our standard. I have said many things to the brethren, about the strictness of their walk and conduct, when we left the gentiles, and told them that we would have to walk uprightly or the law would be put in force &c. Many have left and turned aside through fear, but no good, upright, honest man will fear. The gospel does not bind a good man down, and deprive him of his rights and privileges. It does not prevent him from enjoying the fruits of his labors. It does not rob him of blessings. It does not stop his increase. It does not diminish his kingdom, but it is calculated to enlarge his kingdom as well as to enlarge his heart. It is calculated to give him privileges, and power, and honor, and exaltation, and everything which his heart can desire in righteousness all the days of his life, and then, when he gets exalted into the eternal world, he can still turn round and say it hath not entered into the heart of man to conceive the glory and honor and blessings which God hath in store for those that love and serve Him. I want the brethren to understand, and comprehend the principles of eternal life, and to watch the spirits, be wide awake and not be overcome by the adversary. You can see the fruits of the spirit, but you cannot see the spirit itself with the natural eye, you behold it not. You can see the result of yielding to the evil spirit and what it will lead you to, but you do not see the spirit itself, nor its operations only by the spirit thats in you. Nobody has told me what has been going on in the Camp, but I have known it all the while. I have been watching its movement, its influence, its effects, and I know the result if it is not put a stop to. I want you to understand that inasmuch as we are beyond the power of the gentiles, where the devil has tabernacles in the priests and the people, but we are beyond their reach, we are beyond their power, we are beyond their grasp, and what has the devil now to work upon? Upon the spirits of men in this camp, and if you do not open your hearts so that the spirit of God can enter your hearts, and teach you the right way, I know that you are a ruined people. I know that you will be destroyed, and that without remedy; and unless there is a change and a different course of conduct, a different spirit to what is now in this Camp I go no further. I am in no hurry. Give me the man of prayer, give me the man of faith, give me the man of meditation, a sober-minded man, and I would far rather go amongst the savages, with six or eight such men, than to trust myself with the whole of this camp with the spirit they now possess. Here is an opportunity for every man to prove himself, to know whether he will pray and remember his God, without being asked to do it every day; to know whether he will have confidence enough to ask of God that he may receive, without my telling him to do it. If this camp was composed of men who had newly received the gospel, men who had not received the priesthood, men who had not been through the ordinances in the Temple and who had not had years of experience, enough to have learned the influence of the spirits and the difference between a good and an evil spirit, I should feel, like preaching to them and watching over them, and teaching them all the time, day by day. But here are the Elders of Israel, men who have had years of experience, men who have had the priesthood for years, and have they got faith enough to rise up and stop a mean, low, grovelling, covetous, quarrelsome spirit? No they have not, nor would they try to stop it unless I rise up in the power of God and put it down. I don't mean to bow down to the spirit thats in this camp, and which is rankling in the bosoms of the brethren, and which will lead to knock downs, and perhaps to the use of the knife to cut each other's throats if it is not put a stop to. I don't mean to bow down to the spirit which causes the brethren to quarrel and when I wake up in the morning the first thing I hear is some of the brethren jawing each other and quarrelling because a horse has got loose in the night. I have let the brethren dance, and fiddle, and act the nigger night after night to see what they will do, and what extremes they would go to, if suffered to go as they would but I don't love to see it. The brethren say they want a little exercise to pass away time, but if you can't tire yourselves bad enough with a days journey without dancing every night, carry your guns on your shoulders, and walk, carry your wood to Camp instead of lounging and laying sleeping in your wagons, increasing the load untill your teams are tired to death and ready to drop into the earth. Help your teams over mud holes and bad places instead of lounging in your wagons and that will give you exercise enough without dancing. Well, they will play cards, they will play checkers, they will play dominoes, and if they had the privilege and were where they could get whiskey, they would be drunk half their time, and in one week they would quarrel, get to high words and draw their knives to kill each other. This is what such a course of things would lead to. Don't you know it? Yes. Well then why don't you try to put it down? I have played cards once in my life since I became a Mormon to see what kind of a spirit would attend it, and I was so well satisfied that I would rather see the dirtiest thing you could find on the earth, than a pack of cards in your hands. You never read of gambling, playing cards, checkers, Dominoes &c. in the scriptures, but you do read of men praising the Lord in the dance, but who ever read of praising the Lord in a game at cards? If any man had sense enough to play a game at Cards, or dance a little without wanting to keep it up all the time, but exercise a little, and then quit it and think no more of it, it would do well enough. But you want to keep it up till midnight and every night, and all the time. You don't know how to control your selves. Last winter when we had our seasons of recreation in the council house, I went forth in the dance frequently, but did my mind run on it? No! To be sure when I was dancing, my mind was on the dance, but the moment I stoppt in the middle or the end of a tune, my mind was engaged in prayer and praise to my heavenly father, and whatever I engage in my mind is on it while engaged in it, but the moment I am done with it, my mind is drawn up to my God.

The devils which inhabit the gentiles priests are here. The tabernacles are not here, we are out of their power, we are beyond their grasp, we are beyond the reach of their persecutions, but the devils are here, and the first thing you'll know if you don't open your eyes, and your hearts, they will cause divisions in our Camp, and perhaps war, as they did the

Lamanites, as you read in the book of Mormon.

Do we suppose that we are going to look out a home for the saints, a resting place, a place of peace, where they can build up the Kingdom and bid the nations welcome, with a low, mean, dirty, trifling Covetous, wicked spirit dwelling in our bosoms? It is vain! vain! Some of you are very fond of passing jokes, and will carry your jokes very far. But will you take a joke? If you don't want to take a joke, don't give a joke to your brethren. Joking, nonsense, profane language, trifling conversation and loud laughter do not belong to us. Suppose the Angels were witnessing the hoe down the other evening, and listening to the haw, haw's, the other evening would they not be ashamed of it. I am ashamed of it. I have not given a joke to any man on this journey nor felt like it; neither have I insulted any mans feelings, but I have hollowed pretty loud and spoke sharp to the brethren when I have seen their awkwardness at coming into Camp. The revelations in the bible, in the book of Mormon, and doctrine and covenants teaches us to be sober; and let me ask you Elders that have been through the ordinances in the Temple, what were your covenants there? I want you should remember them. When I laugh I see my folly, and nothingness, and weakness, and am ashamed of myself. I think meaner and worse of myself than any man can think of me; but I delight in God, and in his commandments, and delight to meditate on him and to serve him and I mean that every thing in me shall be subject to him, and I delight in serving him. Now let every man repent of his weaknesses, of his follies, of his meanness, and every kind of wickedness, and stop your swearing and your profane language for it is in this camp, and, I know it, and have known it. I have said nothing about it, but I now tell you, if you don't stop it, you shall be cursed by the Almighty, and shall dwindle away and be damned. Such things shall not be suffered in this Camp. You shall honor God, and confess his name or else you shall suffer the penalty. Most of this Camp belongs to the church, nearly all; and I would say to you brethren and to the Elders of Israel, if you are faithful, you will yet be sent to preach this gospel to the nations of the earth and bid all welcome whether they believe the Gospel or not, and this kingdom will reign over many who do not belong to the Church, over thousands who do not believe in the gospel. Bye and bye, every knee shall bow, and every tongue confess and acknowledge and reverence, and honor the name of God and His priesthood and observe the laws of the Kingdom whether they belong to the Church and obey the gospel or not, and I mean that every man in this camp shall do it. That is what the scripture means, by every Knee shall bow &c. and you cannot make anything else out of it.

I understand there are several in this Camp who do not belong to the church. I am the man who will stand up for them and protect them in all their rights. And they shall not trample on our rights nor on the priesthood. They shall reverance [sic] and acknowledge the name of God and His priesthood, and if they set up their heads and seek to introduce iniquity into this Camp, and to trample on the priesthood, I swear to them, they shall never go back to tell the tale. I will leave them where they will be safe. If they want to retreat they can now have the privilege, and any man who chooses to go back rather than abide the law of God can now have the privilege of doing so before we go any further.

Here are the Elders of Israel who have the priesthood, who have got to preach the gospel, who have to gather the nations of the earth, who have to build up the Kingdom, so that the nations can come to it, they will stoop to dance as niggers. I don't mean this as debasing the negroes, by any means; they will hoe down all, turn summersets, dance on their knees, and haw, haw, out loud, they will play cards, they will play checkers, and Dominoes, they will use profane language, they will swear. Suppose when you go to preach the people should ask you what you did when you went on this mission to seek out a home for the whole church, what was your course of conduct. Did you dance? Yes. Did you hoe down all? Yes. Did you play cards? Yes. Did you play checkers? Yes. Did you use profane language? Yes. Did you swear? Yes. Did you quarrel with each other and threaten each other? Why Yes. How would you feel? What would you say for yourselves? Would you not want to go and hide up? Your mouths would be stopt and you would want to creep away in disgrace. I am one of the last to ask my brethren to enter into solemn covenants, but if they will not enter into a covenant to put away their iniquity and turn to the Lord and serve him, and acknowledge and honor his name I want them to take their wagons and retreat back, for I shall go no further under such a state of things. If we don't repent and quit our wickedness we will have more hinderances than we have had, and worse storms to encounter. I want the brethren to be ready for meeting tomorrow at the time appointed, instead of rambling off, and hiding in their wagons to play cards &c. I think it will be good for us to have a fast meeting tomorrow and a prayer meeting to humble ourselves and turn to the Lord and he will forgive us.

{5}

"With Joy and Gratitude to My Heavenly Father, I Look Upon this Congregation with Admiration," A Sermon Delivered on 6 April 1850 following the dedication of the Bowery

(from *Latter-day Saints' Millennial Star* 12 [15 September 1850]: 273-76)

With joy and gratitude to my Heavenly Father, I look upon this congregation with admiration. I rejoice to see my brethren and my sisters congregate together to worship the Lord. It is a feast to me to look upon the Saints. It is a joy and gladness to mingle in their society. I feel thankful for the goodly number that are safely landed in the mountains. I look forward to the day when scores of thousands will join us in our secluded retreat. It is a matter of consolation to me to have the privilege of looking at the Saints. I can truly say, it is sweeter to me than the honey comb. The greatest luxury I can enjoy, is to associate with those who delight to serve the Lord with all their hearts. And in the midst of all afflictions and privations we have the privilege that we never before had, of assembling unmolested from our oppressors. I esteem the providences of God as a fresh manifestation of his kindness in removing the Saints to this place, to suffer the wickedness of the wicked to remove us to this place. I hope we will improve on the same. I would be thankful if I could have my feelings satisfied at this conference; to a certain degree they are, and will be. When I realize what a struggle and labor we have undergone, I would rejoice at the privilege to look at my brethren for days and days. It is a place of happiness to me—the day I have long looked for, to enjoy the privileges now around me. I can truly say, ten or fifteen years ago, I looked upon this people with an expectation that every man and woman would be worn into the grave, their lives spent in preaching, in watching their houses and protecting their families, before we could enjoy the present privilege. I expected it would be enjoyed by my children, but not by me. I am disappointed—it is all I could have anticipated—my life, my labor, all that I could anticipate eight or ten years ago, is now realized by me. The providences of the Almighty speak volumes to me, and say to Israel, be on the look out. Latter-day Saints be on the watch-tower. The providences of God as they are dealt out to the earth speak to us, and should be realized as peals of thunder, that the Lord will cut short his work in righteousness, for a short work will he do on the earth.

I can say to all Israel, it is time we should awake from our lethargy, from our drowsy and sleepy feelings; awake to righteousness, and hasten the work that is upon us, for in a day and hour that we are not aware of, behold, the Son of Man cometh, as fast as the wheels of time roll round, to bring calamities, famine, fire, pestilence, sword, and the destroyer that walks abroad at noon-day, or at midnight, and lays wastes its thousands; nations are revolutionised; kingdoms are tottering and falling: a whole world is in commotion, what can we say? I can say, watch! watch!! watch!!! brethren, and be faithful! When I came yesterday morning, my feelings were peculiar; I realised that for years we have been deprived of such a privilege to meet together to worship the Lord. This is the most comfortable place I have ever seen for the Saints to hold their meetings in at our gathering place. When I have been abroad in the world, we have had splendid halls; but, at the gathering place, this is the best. What next, brethren? Some think I will go to the conference; but if I do, I cannot stay there. I must go to the kanyons, or hunt my cattle. I would like to go to conference, but I want to plough my lot, or fence my field, or to go to mill, or to my farm. This I feel—I felt it yesterday. I have the same cares that other men have—the care of my family, the daily labour that is upon me; my business is before me; but I said to my flocks and herds, and teams, now rest: workmen stop your business, all hands; my family prepare to entertain those who call upon us; do the best you can; prepare the best to feed them with; and to all around me, I said rest while I go and worship the Lord; it has been a great struggle, like two immense armies contending; the enemy of all righteousness contending by storms and thunder, that we should not prepare a place to meet; we have been fighting and struggling for years. I recollect four years last February, we left Nauvoo; from that time to this we have been struggling to build a place to assemble in, we were thwarted in getting a Council House, we have not got it yet; we have been two winters idle, and some of the Elders have forgotten there is a God; they have forgotten their covenants, their vows, and their prayers; they have forgotten what they once remembered, as the first and foremost in their hearts. I will draw cuts with any man who would go and plough foremost in their hearts. I will draw cuts with any man who would go and plough to-morrow, which grows the most wheat, by staying here to-morrow and getting our hearts warmed, or go ploughing; I have seen it tried, and proved that when the Lord requires anything of his Saints, and they do it, he can give the increase better, than if they served themselves; there is not the first man who has gained the first picayune by going to a kanyon on Sunday, or by labouring on the Sabbath day; necessity does not drive a man to do it, no such thing, but it is their own dispositions, and the spirit that is in them. There is no necessity to go to the kanyons, or hunt your cattle on the Sabbath

32

day, you might as well plough; but some feel that they cannot spare time on a week day. We have tried it in travelling since we left Nauvoo, and not one time having travelled on the Sabbath day, have we gained by it, but we have lost a day or two the next week to pay for it. What is the harm? It proves that you treat lightly the rules of the God of nature,—the God we serve. The laws that organised the elements knows what they can endure; he said to man, when you have laboured six days, rest one, to refresh your bodies; let your horses and cattle that labour rest; your men and women, let them rest; I don't mean to rest like Christians, ride ten miles to a meeting, and then ride twenty-five miles for pleasure; but I mean a Saint's Sabbath: there is not a nation nor a people that keep the Sabbath, not a christian, from the Pope to the latest reformer; there is not one who keeps it, no not one, unless sick, if there is one it is by mistake or by accident. Now you gain nothing by transforming the ordinances of natures to your own desires; let them all rest, and when the earth has brought forth six years let it rest the seventh; you will not make anything by transgressing any rule of the God of nature, and if our eastern neighbours had done so, their land would have been as good as when they first saw it. I would as soon rest a whole week and let every thing rest a week; for have we not worked more than six Sabbaths? If we tarry a whole week, it would not pay the debt, and the God of nature will bring it all back again. If I hurry this Conference, I have got to hurry every business transaction, and every speech, and then the spirit would not abide with us. I want you to feel as I feel; stay right here, and spend a week in Conference, if necessary. A great many persons feel that they are so poor they have to go to the gold mines, they will be in such a hurry they will forget to pray; another cannot spend a week day to go after wood or hunt his cattle; you can see the example, poor they are and poor they will be, and by and by they will wake up in hell. It is not a polite expression, but it is true doctrine, they will go down to hell, poverty stricken and naked; are those who go to meeting every Sabbath going to get rich? Not just yet. They will have more wheat; you may take economy and rest on the seventh day, and he will be the best off. I am not going to desire anything but the will of my Father in Heaven; if my Father makes me rich I will be contented, and if I am poor I will be contented still, and I will be content with all good men and good people. It is disgusting to me to see a person love this world in its present organization; look at kings on their thrones, their crowns fall at their feet, their almighty dollars do them no good, their wealth and opulence are gone, nation after nation are dethroned and crumble to ashes. Take the very youth of beauty; it is laid low in the grave! Riches take the wings of the morning and fly away; it is beneath the heart of a man who loves God and His spirit.

33

I wish the brethren to listen to the principles this morning set forth on speculation, and their daily walk; we are here, and it is our duty to sustain ourselves in this place, and also those who will come to us; we have a duty to perform to our brethren; we are under holy christian covenants to assist our brethren who are left in the states, until they are gathered here; remember the poor who are yet in bondage, and say what we can do for our poor brethren this season; it is one of the most important things that we can do, to raise grain to sustain ourselves, and those who come here.

I have a few words to say on Mormonism as it is called, but to us, the doctrine of salvation; I can say I know it is true. I have known for years and years that Joseph was a prophet. I did not embrace Mormonism, because I hoped it was true, but because it was that principle that would save all the human family that would obey it, and it would make them righteous. Joseph Smith lived and died a prophet, and sealed his testimony with his blood; he lived a good man, and died a good man, and he was as good a man as ever lived; and the voice of the Lord is still heard for this people. For myself I am here just as I was in the days of Joseph. I never pretended to be Joseph Smith. I am not the man who brought forth the Book of Mormon, but I do testify to the truth of it. I am an apostle to bear testimony to the Gentiles of this last dispensation, and also the Jews. I can say the heart of man is always eager for something, just like little children; we often see children when they have been feasted on pumpkin pie and sweet cake, and other good things, eat until they are filled with pain, and cry for more. The Elders have had so much revelation, that it has put them in pain, because they did not know how to digest it, and yet they cry for more. You live and see the time that kings and prophets have desire to see, but have died without the sight. It is your privilege, and it is mine, to receive revelation, and my privilege to dictate to the church. Here are a cloud of witnesses from the death of Joseph or the return of the Twelve to Nauvoo, that all things have been dictated by the Twelve, with your humble servant at their head; could it have been bettered? Was this people or any other people ever led, fed, or administered to more kindly and faithfully than this people have been by the Twelve and those that helped them? No, not even in the days of Joseph. From the day that I was baptized until this present time, I have felt as if I was in another world, in another existence. I never look back upon the old world, but it is like looking into hell. I have only one desire, and that is to do the will of my God, and that is all the will I ever had. I do chastise my brethren, find fault with them, and give them counsel, but the counsel I give let any one say it is not right; I am at the defiance of any one to say that I have not told them just right.

Next thing. Just as soon as any of the Twelve become dissatisfied, they lop off, they have not the boldness to go to the Council and say "good bye, I am going to hell my own road;" no, not even John E. Page. I remember once at the commencement of this church, a necromancer embraced it, but he could not be satisfied; he came and said he had fingered and handled the perverted priesthood so much, the course I have taken is downwards, the devil has too fast hold of me, I cannot go with you; but the rest slide off.

Let me tell you it is the truth of the Lord God Almighty, and if a man will not do right, God will remove him out of his place forthwith.

I never was afraid of Joseph, although many would falter and feared Joseph would go astray. I did not serve Joseph, but I patterned after the doctrine the Lord has revealed through him. There was no possibility of Joseph leading the people astray. If I thought that God would suffer a man to lead a righteous people astray I would not serve him, I would leave him and seek another; I serve the God of Abraham, of Isaac, and Jacob, the God of our fathers; he has called Joseph and will never let him lead this people astray, but when he has done his work he will take him to himself. I never was afraid of my friends, and you need not be; the Lord Almighty will never suffer his people to go astray, unless they as a people want to follow iniquity; never, no never, no never.

Do you know the word of the Lord when you hear it? It is the will of the Lord that he wants his people to do. As for revelation, some say it has ceased; it has no such thing. I could give you revelation as fast as a man could run, I am in the midst of revelation. Do you want more revelation written? Wait till you obey what is already written.

The last two years of Joseph's life, Joseph laid out as much work as we can do for twenty years. I have no disposition to seek for more, until I see these we have obeyed. I tell you one thing, if we obey the word of the Lord, this people have got to quit drinking whisky, and leave off using so much tobacco, tea, and coffee. It is not religion to spend our time in light visits, or squandering your time as many have. When I look at the world and hear the blasts of the devil, I say blow away. I trust that I shall live to accomplish my designs of fighting the devil, and if I do not live, there are other men who will step into my place who are just as good for a hang on, as I am, or Joseph was.

My feelings are the same as they were when I was baptized, to do the will of my God. When we have the spirit of the Lord, we work together in oneness, and we shall accomplish the design sooner or later. Joseph used to say, "do not be scared, I have not apostatized yet;" and he did not. I say, brethren I have not apostatized, and there are a good many who have not. We have got to gather Israel, and see the redemption of Israel, and if I do not live to accomplish it, I shall come back to enjoy it. I say come on ye Elders of Israel and preach the mysteries of the kingdom. When a principle comes to your understanding, it is no more a mystery; but, behold, the mystery has flown, and all things are easy to be comprehended; all is simple; all is childlike; and all is Godlike.

"The Gospel of Salvation—A Vision— Redemption of the Earth and All that Pertains to It," A Sermon Delivered on 8 August 1852

(from *Journal of Discourses*, 26 vols. [Liverpool: Latter-day Saints' Book Depot, 1855-86], 3:89-96)

I will read a revelation given to Joseph Smith, junior, and Sidney Rigdon. But previous to my doing so, and commencing upon the subject that I expect to lay before the people this morning, I will say to them, my understanding with regard to preaching the Gospel of Salvation is this: there is but one discourse to be preached to all the children of Adam; and that discourse should be believed by them, and lived up to. To commence, continue, and finish this Gospel sermon, will require all the time that is allotted to man, to the earth, and all things upon it, in their mortal state; that is my idea with regard to preaching. No man is able to set before a congregation all the items of the Gospel, in this life, and continue these items to their termination, for this mortal life is too short. It is inseparably connected, one part with the other, in all the doctrines that have been revealed to man, which are now called the various doctrines of Christianity, of which all the professors of religion believe a portion; but severally reject, or desire to reject, other portions of the truth; each sect or individual, taking to themselves portions of the Bible, portions of the doctrine of salvation, that are the most pleasing to them, rejecting all the rest, and mingling these doctrines with the tenets of men.

But let a Gospel sermon be preached, wherein all the principles of salvation are embodied, and we will acknowledge, at the end of the mortality of this earth, and all things created upon it—at the closing up scene, at the final consummation of all things that have been from the commencement of the creation of the world, and the peopling of it unto the latest generation of Adam and Eve, and the final finishing up of the work of Christ—I say, we shall acknowledge that there is the Gospel sermon, and that it could not be preached to finite beings, in one short life.

I make these remarks for the purpose of extricating myself from the arduous task of undertaking to set before this congregation, every item of the doctrine of salvation, in all of their various significations, as they are presented in this life, and according to our understanding. I make these introductory remarks to free myself from the great task of finishing the discourse I shall commence. I did not expect to finish it; I do not expect to see the end of it, until the winding up scene. I do not even commence at the beginning of it; I only catch at it, where it comes to me, in the 19th century, for it has been before me; it is from eternity to eternity.

Christ is the author of this Gospel, of this earth, of men and women, of all the posterity of Adam and Eve, and of every living creature that lives upon the face of the earth, that flies in the heavens, that swims in the waters, or dwells in the field. Christ is the author of salvation to all this creation; to all things pertaining to this terrestrial globe we occupy.

This, however, would be contrary to our prejudices, to admit for a moment, that Christ, in his redeeming properties, has power to redeem any of the works of his hands—any other living creature, but the children of Adam and Eve—this would not be in accordance with our pre-possessed feelings, and long-imbibed prejudices, perhaps; but he has redeemed the earth; he has redeemed mankind and every living thing that moves upon it; and he will finish his Gospel discourse when he overcomes his enemies, and puts his last enemy under his feet—when he destroys death, and him that hath the power of it—when he has raised up this kingdom, and finished his work which the Father gave him to do, and presents it to his Father, saying, "I have done the work, I have finished it; I have not only created the world, but I have redeemed it; I have watched over it, and I have given to those intelligent beings, that you have created by me, their agency, and it has been held with perfection to every creature of intelligence, to every grade of mankind; I have preserved inviolate their agency; I have watched over them, and over-ruled all their actions, and held in my hand the destinies of men; and I have finished up my Gospel sermon," as he presents the finished work to his Father.

It takes just such a character as the Savior, to preach one Gospel discourse; and this was commenced with the commencement of all men upon this earth or any other; and it will never close until the winding up scene, and all is finished, and the kingdom is presented to the Father.

I expect only to look into some portions of it, as it comes to me in the 19th century of the Christian era.

I will now read a revelation that was given to Joseph Smith, junior, and Sidney Rigdon, called

A VISION.

"1. Hear O ye heavens, and give ear O earth, and rejoice, ye inhabitants thereof, for the Lord is God, and beside him there is no Savior: great is his wisdom, marvellous are his ways, and the extent of his doings none can find out; his purposes fail not, neither are there any who can stay his hand; from eternity to eternity he is the same, and his years never fail.

38

"2. For thus saith the Lord, I, the Lord, am merciful and gracious unto those who fear me, and delight to honour those who serve me in righteousness and in truth unto the end, great shall be their reward and eternal shall be their glory; and to them will I reveal all mysteries; yea, all the hidden mysteries of my kingdom from days of old, and for ages to come will I make known unto them the good pleasure of my will concerning all things pertaining to my kingdom; yea, even the wonders of eternity shall they know, and things to come will I show them, even the things of many generations; and their wisdom shall be great, and their understanding reach to heaven: and before them the wisdom of the wise shall perish, and the understanding of the prudent shall come to naught; for by my Spirit will I enlighten them, and by my power will I make known unto them the secrets of my will; yea, even those things which eye has not seen, nor ear heard, nor yet entered into the heart of man.

"3. We, Joseph Smith, junior, and Sidney Rigdon, being in the Spirit on the sixteenth of February, in the year of our Lord, one thousand eight hundred and thirty-two, by the power of the Spirit our eyes were opened and our understandings were enlightened, so as to see and understand the things of God—even those things which were from the beginning before the world was, which were ordained of the Father, through his only begotten Son, who was in the bosom of the Father, even from the beginning, of whom we bear record, and the record which we bear is the fulness of the gospel of Jesus Christ, who is the Son, whom we saw and with whom we conversed in the heavenly vision; for while we were doing the work of translation, which the Lord had appointed unto us, we came to the twenty-ninth verse of the fifth chapter of John, which was given unto us as follows: speaking of the resurrection of the dead, concerning those who shall hear the voice of the Son of man, and shall come forth; they who have done good in the resurrection of the just, and they who have done evil in the resurrection of the unjust. Now this caused us to marvel, for it was given unto us of the Spirit; and while we meditated upon these things, the Lord touched the eyes of our understandings and they were opened, and the glory of the Lord shone round about; and we beheld the glory of the Son, on the right hand of the Father, and received of his fulness; and saw the holy angels, and they who are sanctified before his throne, worshipping God, and the Lamb, who worship him forever and ever. And now, after the many testimonies which have been given of him, this is the testimony last of all, which we give of him, that he lives; for we saw him, even on the right hand of God, and we heard the voice bearing record that he is the only begotten of the Father—that by him, and through him, and of him the worlds are and were created, and the inhabitants thereof are begotten sons and daughters unto God. And this we saw also, and bear record, that an angel of God who was in authority in the presence of God, who rebelled against the only begotten Son, whom the Father loved, and who was in the bosom of the Father—was thrust down from the presence of God and the Son, and was called Perdition, for the heavens wept over him—he was Lucifer, a son of the morning. And while we were yet in the Spirit, the Lord commanded us that we should write the vision, for we beheld Satan, that old serpent—even the devil—who rebelled against God, and sought to take the kingdom of our God, and his Christ, wherefore he maketh war with the saints of God, and encompasses them round about. And we saw a vision of the sufferings of those with whom he made war and overcame, for thus came the voice of the Lord unto us.

"4. Thus saith the Lord, concerning all those who know my power, and have been made partakers thereof, and suffered themselves, through the power of the devil, to be overcome, and to deny the truth and defy my power—they are they who are the sons of perdition, of whom I say that it had been better for them never to have been born, for they are vessels of wrath, doomed to suffer the wrath of God, with the devil and his angels in eternity; concerning whom I have said there is no forgiveness in this world nor in the world to come, having denied the Holy Spirit after having received it, and having denied the only begotten Son of the Father—having crucified him unto themselves, and put him to an open shame. These are they who shall go away into the lake of fire and brimstone, with the devil and his angels, and the only ones on whom the second death shall have any power; yea, verily, the only ones who shall not be redeemed in the due time of the Lord, after the sufferings of his wrath; for all the rest shall be brought forth by the resurrection of the dead, through the triumph and the glory of the Lamb, who was slain, who was in the bosom of the Father before the worlds were made. And this is the gospel, the glad tidings which the voice out of the heavens bore record unto us, that he came into the world, even Jesus, to be crucified for the world, and to bear the sins of the world, and to sanctify the world, and to cleanse it from all unrighteousness; that through him all might be saved whom the Father had put into his power and made by him, who glorifies the Father, and saves all the works of his hands, except those sons of perdition, who deny the Son after the Father has revealed him; wherefore he saves all except them: they shall go away into everlasting punishment, which is endless punishment, which is eternal punishment, to reign with the devil and his angels in eternity, where their worm dieth not, and the fire is not quenched, which is their torment; and the end thereof, neither the place thereof, nor their torment, no man knows, neither was it revealed, neither is, neither will be revealed unto man, except to them who are made partakers thereof: nevertheless I the Lord show it by vision unto many, but straightway shut it up again;

wherefore the end, the width, the height, the depth, and the misery thereof, they understand not, neither any man except them who are ordained unto this condemnation. And we heard the voice, saying, write the vision, for lo! this is the end of the vision of the sufferings of the ungodly!

"5. And again, we bear record, for we saw and heard, and this is the testimony of the gospel of Christ, concerning them who come forth in the resurrection of the just; they are they who received the testimony of Jesus, and believed on his name and were baptized after the manner of his burial, being buried in the water in his name, and this according to the commandment which he has given, that by keeping the commandments they might be washed and cleansed from all their sins, and receive the Holy Spirit by the laying on of the hands of him who is ordained and sealed unto this power, and who overcome by faith, and are sealed by the Holy Spirit of promise, which the Father sheds forth upon all those who are just and true. They are they who are the church of the first-born. They are they into whose hands the Father has given all things—they are they who are priests and kings, who have received of his fulness, and of his glory, and are priests of the Most High, after the order of Melchisedek, which was after the order of Enoch, which was after the order of the only begotten Son; wherefore, as it is written, they are Gods, even the sons of God—wherefore all things are theirs, whether life or death, or things present, or things to come, all are theirs and they are Christ's and Christ is God's; and they shall overcome all things; wherefore let no man glory in man, but rather let him glory in God, who shall subdue all enemies under his feet—these shall dwell in the presence of God and his Christ forever and ever. These are they whom he shall bring with him, when he shall come in the clouds of heaven, to reign on the earth over his people. These are they who shall have part in the first resurrection. These are they who shall come forth in the resurrection of the just. These are they who are come unto mount Zion, and unto the city of the living God, the heavenly place, the holiest of all. These are they who have come to an innumerable company of angels, to the general assembly and church of Enoch, and of the first-born. These are they whose names are written in heaven, where God and Christ are the judge of all. These are they who are just men made perfect through Jesus the mediator of the new covenant, who wrought out this perfect atonement through the shedding of his own blood. These are they whose bodies are celestial, whose glory is that of the sun, even the glory of God, the highest of all, whose glory the sun of the firmament is written of as being typical.

"6. And again, we saw the terrestrial world, and behold and lo, these are they who are of the terrestrial, whose glory differs from that of the church of the first-born, who have received the fulness of the Father, even as that of the moon differs from the sun of the firmament. Behold, these are they who died without law, and also they who are the spirits of men kept in prison, whom the Son visited, and preached the gospel unto them, that they might be judged according to men in the flesh, who received not the testimony of Jesus in the flesh, but afterwards received it. These are they who are honorable men of the earth, who are blinded by the craftiness of men. These are they who receive of his glory, but not of his fulness. These are they who receive of the presence of the Son, but not of the fulness of the Father; wherefore they are bodies terrestrial, and not bodies celestial, and differ in glory as the moon differs from the sun. These are they who are not valiant in the testimony of Jesus; wherefore they obtained not the crown over the kingdom of our God. And now this is the end of the vision which we saw of the terrestrial, that the Lord commanded us to write while we were yet in the Spirit.

"7. And again, we saw the glory of the telestial, which glory is that of the lesser, even as the glory of the stars differs from that of the glory of the moon in the firmament. These are they who received not the testimony of Jesus. These are they who deny not the Holy Spirit. These are they who are thrust down to hell. These are they who shall not be redeemed from the devil, until the last resurrection, until the Lord, even Christ the Lamb shall have finished his work. These are they who receive not of his fulness in the eternal world, but of the Holy Spirit through the ministration of the terrestrial; and the terrestrial through the ministration of the celestial; and also the telestial receive it of the administering of angels who are appointed to minister for them, or who are appointed to be ministering spirits for them, for they shall be heirs of salvation. And thus we saw in the heavenly vision, the glory of the telestial, which surpasses all understanding, and no man knows it except him to whom God has revealed it. And thus we saw the glory of the terrestrial, which excels in all things the glory of the telestial, even in glory, and in power, and in might, and in dominion. And thus we saw the glory of the celestial, which excels in all things—where God, even the Father, reigns upon his throne forever and ever; before whose throne all things bow in humble reverence and give him glory forever and ever. They who dwell in his presence are the church of the first-born, and they see as they are seen, and know as they are known, having received of his fulness and of his grace; and he makes them equal in power, and in might, and in dominion. And the glory of the celestial is one, even as the glory of the sun is one. And the glory of the terrestrial is one, even as the glory of the moon is one. And the glory of the telestial is one, even as the glory of the stars is one, for as one star differs from another star in glory, even so differs one from another in glory in the telestial world; for these are they who are of Paul, and of Apollos, and of Cephas. These are they who say they are some of one and some of another—some of Christ, and some of John, and some of Moses, and some of Elias, and some of Esaias, and some of Isaiah, and some of Enoch; but received not the gospel, neither the testimony of Jesus, neither the prophets, neither the everlasting covenant. Last of all, these all are they who will not be gathered with the saints, to be caught up into the church of the first born, and received into the cloud. These are they who are liars, and sorcerers, and adulterers, and whoremongers, and whosoever loves and makes a lie. These are they who suffer the wrath of God on the earth. These are they who suffer the vengeance of eternal fire. These are they who are cast down to hell and suffer the wrath of Almighty God, until the fulness of times when Christ shall have subdued all enemies under his feet, and shall have perfected his work, when he shall deliver up the kingdom, and present it unto the Father spotless, saying—I have overcome and have trodden the winepress alone, even the winepress of the fierceness of the wrath of Almighty God. Then shall he be crowned with the crown of his glory, to sit on the throne of his power to reign for ever and ever. But behold, and lo, we saw the glory and the inhabitants of the telestial world, that they were as innumerable as the stars in the firmament of heaven, or as the sand upon the sea shore, and heard the voice of the Lord, saying—these all shall bow the knee, and every tongue shall confess to him who sits upon the throne forever and ever; for they shall be judged according to their works, and every man shall receive according to his own works, his own dominion, in the mansions which are prepared, and they shall be servants of the Most High, but where God and Christ dwell they cannot come, worlds without end. This is the end of the vision which we saw, which we were commanded to write while we were yet in the Spirit.

"8. But great and marvellous are the works of the Lord, and the mysteries of his kingdom which he showed unto us, which surpasses all understanding in glory, and in might, and in dominion, which he commanded us we should not write while we were yet in the Spirit, and are not lawful for man to utter; neither is man capable to make them known, for they are only to be seen and understood by the power of the Holy Spirit, which God bestows on those who love him, and purify themselves before him; to whom he grants this privilege of seeing and knowing for themselves; that through the power and manifestation of the Spirit, while in the flesh, they may be able to bear his presence in the world of glory. And to God and the Lamb be glory, and honor, and dominion forever and ever. Amen."

These are the words of the vision that were given to Joseph and Sidney. My mind rests upon this subject, upon this portion of the Gospel of salvation; and has done so, more or less, for a great many years. The circumstances that surround me, almost daily; things that I see and hear,

43

cause my mind to reflect upon the situation of mankind; create in me an anxiety to find out—to learn why things are as they are; why it is that the Lord should build a globe like this earthly ball, and set it in motion—then people it with intelligent beings, and afterwards cast a vail over the whole, and hide Himself from His creation—conceal from them the wisdom, the glory, the truth, the excellency, the true principles of His character, and His design in forming the earth.

Why cast this vail over them, and leave them in total darkness—leave them to be carried away with erroneous doctrines, and exposed to every species of wickedness that would render them obnoxious to the presence of God, who placed them upon the face of this earth. My daily experience and observation cause me to enquire into these things. Can I attribute all to the wisdom of Him that has organized this earth, and peopled it with intelligent beings, and see the people honestly desiring to do right all the day long, and would not lift hand or heel against the Almighty, but would rather have their heads taken from their bodies than dishonor him? And yet, we hear one crying on the right hand, this is the law of God, this is the right way; another upon the left, saying the same; another in the front; and another in the rear; and to every point of the compass, hundreds and thousands of them, and all differing one from another.

They do the best they can, I admit. See the inhabitants of the earth, how they differ in their prejudices, and in their religion. What is the religion of the day? What are all the civil laws and governments of the day? They are merely traditions, without a single exception. Do the people realize this—that it is the force of their education that makes right and wrong, with them? It is not the line which the Lord has drawn out; it is not the law which the Lord has given them; it is not the righteousness which is according to the character of Him who has created all things, and by His own law governs and controls all things; but by the prejudice of education—the prepossessed feeling that is begotten in the hearts of the children of men, by surrounding objects; they being creatures of circumstances, who are governed and controlled by them more or less. When they, thus, are led to differ one from another, it begets in them different feelings; it causes them to differ in principle, object, and pursuit; in their customs, religion, laws, and domestic affairs, in all human life; and yet every one, of every nation there is under heaven, considers that they are the best people; that they are the most righteous; have the most intelligent and best of men for their priests and rulers, and are the nearest to the very thing the Lord Almighty requires of them. There is no nation upon this earth that does not entertain these sentiments.

Suppose a query arising in the minds of the different sects of the human family—"Do not the Latter-day Saints think they are the best people under the whole heavens, like ourselves?" Yes, exactly; I take that

44

to myself. The Latter-day Saints have the same feelings as the rest of the people; they think also, that they have more wisdom and knowledge, and are the nearest right of any people upon the face of the earth.

Suppose you visit China, and mingle among the "celestial" beings there; you will find a people who hold in scorn and ridicule every other people, and especially those of Christendom. They consider themselves more holy, more righteous, more upright, more honest; filled with more intelligence; they consider themselves better educated; better in every respect, in all their civil and religious rites than any other nation under heaven.

Suppose you next visit Spain; there you will find the mother, and grandmother, and great-grandmother of all the Christian denominations upon the face of the earth—though these are but a scanty proportion of mankind, compared with all the inhabitants upon the face of the globe. I suppose not one twelfth, or one sixteenth part of the inhabitants of the earth, believe in Jesus Christ—and probably not one thirtieth part of them.

Take the mother of modern Christianity; go into Italy—to Rome, the seat of her government, and we find that they also consider themselves to be the best people in the world—the nearest the Lord and the path of right—more so than any other people upon the face of the earth.

Then visit the first Protestant church that was organized, and they consider themselves nearer right than their mother, or any of their sisters. You may thus follow it down to the last reformer upon the earth; and then step back to those we call heathen; to all that ever lived, from the place where Noah landed his ark, to the building of the tower of Babel; and in their dispersion, trace their footsteps to the islands and continents, under the whole heavens, and you cannot find a people that do not believe they are nearest right in their religion—more so than their neighbors—and have the best form of civil government.

Suppose you call upon the aborigines of our country, here, these wild Indians; we call them savages; we call them heathens. Let yourselves be divested of prejudice; let it be entirely forgotten and out of the question, together with all your education, and former notions of things, your religious tenets, &c., and let your minds be in open vision before the Almighty, seeing things as they are, you will find that that very people know just as much about the Lord as anybody else; like the rest of mankind, they step into a train of ideas and ordinances, peculiar to the prejudices of their education.

All this I admit; and I admit it upon the resources of my own knowledge that I have pertaining to the inhabitants of the earth; this, also, every person knows, who is acquainted with the different customs and religions of different countries.

Let me step over into England, and carry with me my Yankee notions and manners, and I should be a burlesque to them. Let an Englishman pass over into Scotland, and speak and act according to English customs, it would differ so far from them, that they would laugh at him. Let a Scotchman or an Englishman go to Ireland, and it would be just the same. This difference of feeling, sentiment, and custom, exists in those countries that are so near each other. If you go to France, you find that they walk over the customs and manners of England, as unworthy of their notice. Should you thus go, from one people to another, throughout all nations, you would find that they differ in their religions and national customs, according to the teachings of their mother, and the priest. In this manner the *consciences* of mankind are formed—*by the education they receive.* You know this to be true, by your own experience.

That which you once considered, perhaps, to be a non-essential in religion, you now consider to be very essential. That which you once esteemed to be unbecoming in society, has become so interwoven in your feelings, by being accustomed to it, that it ultimately appears quite rational to you.

When you survey the inhabitants of the world, you will find that the religious tenets of all nations have sprung from their education; consequently, if we should summon the whole earth before us, and strictly examine them, we should find that the nations of the earth, as far as they know and understand, are doing about the best they know how; they are just about as near right as they know how to be.

These tribes of Indians differ from one another in their sentiments and feelings; they war with each other, and try to destroy each other; and why do they do it? Why, "you are not as righteous as I am, and I want to bring you over to my holy faith." You see these bands of Indians doing these things, and you spurn the idea. Suppose you extend the principle, and carry it among the greatest nations of the earth; and you would see Queen Victoria, one of the most powerful sovereigns, sitting at the head of one of the most powerful nations upon the earth, sending her forces among these "celestial" ones, battering down the walls of China, bombarding their cities, throwing confusion into their States, and destroying thousands of their people—extending their sway of empire over India, And why all this? "To subdue you heathens, and bring you over to our more enlightened customs and religion."

Does one nation rise up to war with another without having motives, and those which they will substantiate as being good and sufficient? Will one people rise up to war with another people, except the motive that moves them is of a nature to justify them in their own minds and judgment for doing so? No. There is not a people upon the face of this earth that would do so; they all calculate to do that which seemeth good to them.

There are the Jews—and recollect that they are a very religious people to this day; a more religious people never lived than they, that is, the tribe of Judah, and the half tribe of Benjamin that were left in Jerusalem—they are as tenacious as any people can be, to this day, for the religion of their fathers; and where can you see them among the nations of the earth, without seeing a hunted, driven, and persecuted people? The laws of nations have been framed for the express purpose of killing and destroying them from the earth. Yes, in the midst of nations that profess to adhere to the doctrines of Christianity—that legislate, and make laws, and put them in force—laws have been made to exterminate them; then cry out against them, and raise mobs to persecute and destroy, and clear the earth of the Jews. Notwithstanding all this, will they forsake their religion? No. They have suffered themselves to be stoned in the streets of the cities, their houses to be burned over their heads; but will they forsake their religion? No; they will perish rather.

The Christians say they are wrong; and the "Holy Roman Catholic Church" would have killed every one of them, hundreds of years ago, had not God promised by His holy Prophets, that they should remain and multiply. They have been distributed, dispersed, scattered abroad among the nations of the earth, to fulfil that, and many more of the sayings of their Prophets: and they are as tenacious, this day, with regard to their religion, as in the days of Moses, and are as anxiously expecting, and looking for the Messiah.

Conscience is nothing else but the result of the education and traditions of the inhabitants of the earth. These are interwoven with their feelings, and are like a cloak that perfectly envelops them, in the capacity of societies, neighborhoods, people, or individuals; they frame that kind of government and religion, and pursue that course collectively or individually, that seemeth good to themselves.

When we look at the whole creation, and that, too, from the days of Adam, down to this time, what do we see? According to the reading of the Bible, the sayings of Jesus Christ, of all the ancient Prophets, and of the Apostles, every soul, every son and daughter of Adam and Eve, that have lived from the day of transgression to this time; and that will live from this time henceforth, so long as any of the posterity of Adam and Eve shall continue upon the earth, unless they know Jesus Christ, and his Father, and receive the Holy Ghost, and be prepared to dwell with the Father and the Son; become acquainted with them, and converse with them, they will all be damned; every soul of them will be sent to hell.

And what do we see on the back of this, I ask? We see that all Christendom are ready to pounce upon them that believe in Jesus Christ,

47

and are trying to attain to this knowledge, and grind them down, and send them down, and continue to bear upon them, and crowd them down, down to the bottom of the *"bottomless pit,"* and throw upon them pig metal, and lead, to keep them down. This is what we see; and all creation may see it also, if they will open their eyes.

I shall not undertake to prove from the Bible every thing I say, yet it is all there.

With regard to the peculiar and varied formations of the religions of the day, I will say, we can see in them the first strong lines of the religion of Christ drawn out, which have existed among them from the days of the apostacy from the true order, to the present day.

If you could just humble yourselves until your eyes should be enlightened by the Spirit of God, by the spirit of intelligence, you may understand things the world cannot see; and understand that it is the privilege of every person to know the exact situation of the inhabitants of the earth, for themselves. The ancient Apostles saw it; Jesus Christ knew all about it; and the Prophets before them prophesied, and wrote, and preached about what was then upon the earth, what had been, and what would be.

The inquiry might be made, "Can any person in the world prophesy, unless he possess the spirit of it?" No, they cannot. They may prophesy lies by the spirit of lies, by the inspiration of a lying spirit, but can they see and understand things in the future, so as to prophesy truly of things to come, unless they are endowed with the spirit of prophecy? No. Is this the privilege of every person? It is. Permit me to remark here—this very people called Latter-day Saints have got to be brought to the spot where they will be trained (if they have not been there already,) where they will humble themselves, work righteousness, glorify God, and keep His commandments. If they have not got undivided feelings, they will be chastised until they have them; not only until every one of them shall see for themselves, and prophesy for themselves, have visions to themselves, but be made acquainted with all the principles and laws necessary for them to know, so as to supersede the necessity of anybody teaching them.

Is not the time to come when I shall not say to my neighbor, know the Lord, for he will know Him as well as I do? This is the very people that have to come to it, sooner or later. Can we come to it? We can. If you are industrious and faithful scholars in the school you have entered into, you shall get lessons one after another, and continue on until you can see and understand the spirit of prophecy and revelation, which can be understood according to a systematic principle, and can be demonstrated to a person's understanding as scientifically as Professor Pratt, who sits directly behind me, can an astronomical problem.

48

I do not purpose to go into that, or to say anything to the brethren or to this people with regard to their daily walk and actions. I proposed to view the inhabitants of the earth and their situation, that you and I might understand that the Lord Almighty has a hand in all these matters; that the Lord is on the earth, and fills immensity; He is everywhere; He dictates governors and kings, and manages the whole affairs of the nations of the earth, and has from the days of Adam, and will until the winding up scene, and the work shall be finished.

There is only one Gospel sermon, recollect, brethren and sisters, and the time that is required to preach it is from the day of the fall, or from the day when Adam and his wife Eve came here upon this planet, and from that time until Jesus Christ has subdued the last enemy, which is death, and put all things under his feet, and wound up all things pertaining to this earth. Then the Gospel will have been preached, and brought up and presented, and the effects thereof, to the Father.

Now what shall we do with the inhabitants of the earth? Their true situation can be presented to your minds, if you will calmly reflect. Every person, whether they have travelled or not, if they are acquainted with the history of nations, can discover at once the variety there is of religions, customs, laws, and governments; and if you will apply your hearts, you can understand the cause of this variety of effects.

Again, there are the nations that have lived before us; what shall we do with them? And what is their situation in the other world? What have we now to say of them? I can tell it in short. We are preaching to them the Gospel of salvation—to the dead—through those who have lived in this dispensation; and it is a part and parcel of the great Gospel discourse, a little here and a little there, that is necessary for the nation unto whom given. With regard to doctrine, rules, customs, and many sacraments, they are meted out to the inhabitants of the earth severally as they stand in need, according to their situations and what is required of them.

You may ask, "What is meted out to us?" I answer, the ordinances, the sacraments that the Lord Jesus Christ instituted for the salvation of the Jews, for all the house of Israel, and then for the Gentiles. This is the Gospel—the plan of salvation the Lord has given to us. This is the kingdom the Lord has presented to us; the same he presented to the Apostles in the days of Jesus. Now it is for the people to become acquainted with these laws and ordinances of salvation, then apply them to their lives, and that will save as many in the celestial kingdom, in the presence of the Father and Son, as will strictly adhere to them. This we read in the sacred book; we have it before us all the time, that just as many as will believe the Gospel of Jesus Christ, live up to its requirements in their lives, and die in the faith, shall receive a crown of life with the Apostles, and all the faithful in Christ Jesus.

What next? I will tell you a practice of the Latter-day Saint Elders generally. For instance, I get up here, and preach the fulness of the Gospel, perhaps to individuals who never heard it before in their lives, and I close by saying, you that believe this which I have told you, shall be saved; and if you do not, you shall be damned. I leave the subject there. But, says one, "don't the Bible say so?" You ought to explain yourself. "I only said what the Savior taught—he says, go into all the world, and preach the Gospel to every creature; he that believeth and is baptized, shall be saved; and he that believeth not, shall be damned. Don't I say the same?" You leave it there, don't you? "Yes; the Apostle left it there, and so do I."

I wish to explain it a little more, according to the plain, simple, English language. The sum of this practice in this; when I preach a gospel sermon, and they don't believe what I say, I straightway seal their damnation. Brethren, do you believe in such a thing as that? I do not; yet there are many of the Elders just so absurd.

I recollect, in England, sending an Elder to Bristol, to open a door there, and see if anybody would believe. He had a little more than thirty miles to walk; he starts off one morning, and arrives at Bristol; he preached the Gospel to them, and sealed them all up to damnation, and was back next morning. He was just as good a man, too, as we had. It was want of knowledge caused him to do so. I go and preach to the people, and tell them at the end of every sermon, he that believeth and is baptized, shall be saved; and he that believeth not, shall be damned. I continue preaching there day after day, week after week, and month after month, and yet nobody believes my testimony, that I know of, and I don't see any signs of it. "What shall I do in this case, if I am sent to preach there?" you may inquire. You must continue to preach there, until those who sent you shall tell you to leave that field of labour; and if the people don't manifest by their works, that they believe, as long as they come to hear me, I will continue to plead with them, until they bend their dispositions to the Gospel. Why? Because I must be patient with them, as the Lord is patient with me; as the Lord is merciful to me, I will be merciful to others; as He continues to be merciful to me, consequently I must continue in long-suffering to be merciful to others—patiently waiting, with all diligence, until the people will believe, and until they are prepared to become heirs to a celestial kingdom, or angels to the devil.

When the book of Mormon was first printed, it came to my hands in two or three weeks afterwards. Did I believe, on the first intimation of it? The man that brought it to me, told me the same things; says he, "This is the Gospel of salvation; a revelation the Lord has brought forth for the redemption of Israel; it is the Gospel; and according to Jesus Christ, and his Apostles, you must be baptized for the remission of sins, or you will be damned." "Hold on," says I. The mantle of my traditions was over me, to that degree, and my prepossessed feelings so interwoven with my nature, it was almost impossible for me to see at all; though I had beheld, all my life, that the traditions of the people was all the religion they had, I had got a mantle for myself. Says I, "Wait a little while; what is the doctrine of the book, and of the revelations the Lord has given? Let me apply my heart to them;" and after I had done this, I considered it to be my right to know for myself, as much as any man on earth.

I examined the matter studiously for two years before I made up my mind to receive that book. I knew it was true, as well as I knew that I could see with my eyes, or feel by the touch of my fingers, or be sensible of the demonstration of any sense. Had not this been the case, I never would have embraced it to this day; it would have all been without form or comeliness to me. I wished time sufficient to prove all things for myself.

The Gospel of Jesus Christ, must be preached to all nations for a witness and a testimony; for a sign that the day has come, the set time for the Lord to redeem Zion, and gather Israel, preparatory to the coming of the Son of Man. When this Gospel is preached to the people, some will believe, and some will not know whether to believe it, or not. This is the situation of the world; go forth among the people; go among your own neighbors, and you may see it; because the Lord has touched your understanding with the spirit of truth, it looks to you as though all the world will believe it, if they can only hear your testimony; you go and preach to them, but, to your astonishment, they seem perfectly uninterested; some go to sleep, and others are dreaming of their farms and possessions.

The Methodist will tell you, he has had the Gospel from his youth, and been brought up in the Methodist society; and so will the Quaker; and so will the Presbyterian; and so will the Shakers; for they say they are the only people, who are preparing for the Millennium. What is law here, is not there; and what is not there, is here. I have been used to this method of worship, or that; and have heard the good old tone, all the days of my life.

The Methodists come along and say, you may be baptized by pouring, or by sprinkling, or not at all, for there is nothing essential in it. Another man says, you can partake of the Lord's Supper if you like, or let it alone, for it is non-essential; if you have only the good old tone, you are all right.

Now I ask a question: Who is there that can know the things of God; who can discern the truth from the error? Where is the man; where are the people now in the world that can do it? They do not exist. Let the best wisdom of the world be summoned to their aid, and they cannot know the things of God. Let a man be endowed with the revelations of Jesus Christ, and he will say at once, they cannot tell—it is impossible.

Let the just Judge sound his trump, what would he say? I can read it to you in this book. (Laying his hand on the Bible.)

He is compassionate to all the works of His hands, the plan of His redemption, and salvation, and mercy, is stretched out over all; and His plans are to gather up, and bring together, and save all the inhabitants of the earth, with the exception of those who have received the Holy Ghost, and sinned against it. With this exception, all the world besides shall be saved. Is not this Universalism? It borders very close upon it.

I have preached portions of the doctrine of salvation to the people, when I travelled abroad. When I would take up this subject, the Universalists would run after me hundreds of miles, saying, "We are Universalists, where I live; we are troubled with the Methodists, and the various sects; won't you come and use them up for us; we want them whipped out."

It is only parts and portions of the Gospel that you hear; a little here, and a little there, scattered all over the world. Now let the hearts of the children of men be enlightened; let them be awakened to understand the designs of the Lord, in the salvation of man, and what will their voices echo one to another? I will tell you what would be the feeling of every heart; salvation, glory, hallelujah to God and the Lamb, forever and ever. Why? Because of His abundant mercy and compassion; because His wisdom has devised for us, that which we could not have devised for ourselves. This is what all creation would do.

I will take up another thread of my discourse, by observing, that a few men upon the earth, have found an item of truth, here and there, and incorporated it with their own wisdom, and taught the world that the Lord designs to save all mankind, no matter what they do. Another portion will catch at the Calvinistic principles; they hold that the Lord has fore-ordained this, that, and the other, and vigorously contend that the Lord *did* decree, and *did* fore-ordain whatsoever comes to pass, and away they run. Another comes along with free salvation to all; he has caught that principle, and away they all go, deprecating everything else, only the little particle each one has incorporated to himself.

It is this that makes the variance in the religious world. We see a party here, and a party there, crying, "Lo here, and lo there;" and the people are contending bitterly with each other, nation against nation, society against society, and man against man, each seeking to destroy the other, or bring them to this little particle of doctrine, that each one thinks is just right. It is right, as far as it goes.

Man is made an agent to himself before his God; he is organized for the express purpose, that he may become like his master. You recollect one of the Apostle's sayings, that when we see Him, we shall be like Him; and again, we shall become Gods, even the sons of God. Do you read anywhere, that we shall possess all things? Jesus is the elder brother, and all the brethren shall come in for a share with him; for an equal share, according to their works and calling, and they shall be crowned with him. Do you read of any such thing as the Savior praying, that the Saints might be one with him, as he and the Father are one? The Bible is full of such doctrine, and there is no harm in it, as long as it agrees with the New Testament.

I will continue the point I am now at. The Lord created you and me for the purpose of becoming Gods like Himself; when we have been proved in our present capacity, and been faithful with all things He puts into our possession. We are created, we are born for the express purpose of growing up from the low estate of manhood, to become Gods like unto our Father in heaven. That is the truth about it, just as it is. The Lord has organized mankind for the express purpose of increasing in that intelligence and truth, which is with God, until he is capable of creating worlds on worlds, and becoming Gods, even the sons of God.

How many will become thus privileged? Those who honor the Father and the Son; those who receive the Holy Ghost, and magnify their calling, and are found pure and holy; they shall be crowned in the presence of the Father and the Son. Who else? Not anybody. What becomes of all the rest. Are you going to cast them down, and sink them to the bottom of the bottomless pit, to be angels to the devil? Who are his angels? No man nor woman, unless they receive the Gospel of salvation, and then deny it, and altogether turn away from it, sacrificing to themselves the Son of God afresh. They are the only ones who will suffer the wrath of God to all eternity.

How much does it take to prepare a man, or woman, or any being, to become angels to the devil, to suffer with him to all eternity? Just as much as it does to prepare a man to go into the celestial kingdom, into the presence of the Father and the Son, and to be made an heir to His kingdom, and all His glory, and be crowned with crowns of glory, immortality, and eternal lives. Now who will be damned to all eternity? Will any of the rest of mankind? No; not one of them.

The very heathen we were talking about; if they have a law, no matter who made it, and do the best they know how, they will have a glory which is beyond your imagination, by any description I might give; you cannot conceive of the least portion of the glory of God prepared for His beings, the workmanship of His hands; for these people who are seated before me, who are the sons and daughters, legitimately so, of our Father in heaven, they all sprung from Him; it hath not entered into the heart of man to conceive what He has prepared for them.

The Lord sent forth His Gospel to the people; He said, I will give it to my son Adam, from whom Methuselah received it; and Noah received

53

it from Methuselah; and Melchisedek administered to Abraham. In the days of Noah, the people generally rejected it. All those who became acquainted with its principles, and thereby were made acquainted with, and tasted the power of salvation, and turned away therefrom, became angels to the devil.

Let us apply it directly to ourselves, who have received the truth, and tasted of the good word of God. Let me turn around with you and reject it, and teach our children that it is an untruth, teach the same to our neighbors, and that it is a burlesque to our senses; let us deny the Lord that bought us, what would be the result? Our children would grow up in unbelief, and the sin would rest upon our heads. Suppose we are faithful, and the people will not believe our testimony, we shall receive our reward, the same as though they did believe it.

Suppose the inhabitants of the earth were before me, those who have died, what shall we say of them? Have they gone to heaven, or to hell? There is a saying of a wise man in the Bible, like this: "Who knoweth the spirit of a man that goeth upward or the spirit of the beast that goeth downward?" All have spirits, I should suppose, by this. Again, there is another saying, "The Lord giveth, and the Lord taketh away, and blessed be the name of the Lord." Man dies, and his spirit goes to God who gave it. All these things are within the scope of the Gospel sermon; all these principles are embraced in this great Gospel discourse.

What shall we say without going to the Scriptures at all? Where do the spirits of this people go to, when they lay down their tabernacles? They go into the presence of God, and are at the pleasure of the Almighty. Do they go to the Father and the Son, and there be glorified? No; they do not. If a spirit goes to God who gave it, it does not stay there. We are all the time in the presence of the Lord, but our being in the presence of the Lord, does not make it follow that He is in our presence; the spirits of men are understood to go into the presence of the Lord, when they go into the spiritual world.

The Prophet lays down his body, he lays down his life, and his spirit goes to the world of spirits; the persecutor of the Prophet dies, and he goes to Hades; they both go to one place, and they are not to be separated yet. Now, understand, that this is part of the great sermon the Lord is preaching in his providence, the righteous and the wicked are together in Hades. If we go back to our mother country, we there find the righteous and the wicked.

If we go back to our mother country, the States, we there find the righteous, and we there find the wicked; if we go to California, we there find the righteous and the wicked, all dwelling together; and when we go beyond this vail, and leave our bodies which were taken from mother earth, and which must return; our spirits will pass beyond the vail; we go where both Saints and sinners go; they all go to one place. Does the devil have power over the spirits of just men? No. When he gets through with this earth, he is at the length of his chain. He only has permission to have power and dominion on this earth, pertaining to this mortal tabernacle; and when we step through the vail, all are in the presence of God. What did one of the ancients say? "Whither shall I go from thy spirit, and whither shall I flee from thy presence; if I ascend up into heaven, thou art there; if I make my bed in hell, behold, thou art there; if I take the wings of the morning, and dwell in the uttermost parts of the earth, even there shall thy hand lead me, and thy right hand shall hold me." Where is the end of His power? He is omnipotent, and fills immensity by His agents, by His influence, by His Spirit, and by His ministers. We are in the presence of God there, as we are here. Does the enemy have power over the righteous? No. Where are the spirits of the ungodly? They are in prison. Where are the spirits of the righteous, the Prophets, and the Apostles? They are in prison, brethren; that is where they are.

Now let us notice a little experience, lest some of you should be startled at this idea. How do you feel, Saints, when you are filled with the power and love of God? You are just as happy as your bodies can bear. What would be your feelings, suppose you should be in prison, and filled with the power and love of God; would you be unhappy? No. I think prisons would palaces prove, if Jesus dwelt there. This is experience. I know it is a startling idea to say that the Prophet and the persecutor of the Prophet, all go to prison together. What is the condition of the righteous? They are in possession of the spirit of Jesus—the power of God, which is their heaven; Jesus will administer to them; angels will administer to them; and they have a privilege of seeing and understanding more than you or I have, in the flesh; but they have not got their bodies yet, consequently they are in prison. When will they be crowned, and brought into the presence of the Father and the Son? Not until they have got their bodies; this is their glory. What did the holy martyrs die for? Because of the promise of receiving bodies, glorified bodies, in the morning of the resurrection. For this they lived, and patiently suffered, and for this they died. In the presence of the Father, and the Son, they cannot dwell, and be crowned, until the work of the redemption of both body and spirit is completed. What is the condition of the wicked? They are in prison. Are they happy? No; They have stepped through the vail, to the place where the vail of the covering is taken from their understanding. They fully understand that they have persecuted the just and Holy One, and they feel the wrath of the Almighty resting upon them, having a terrible foreboding of the final consummation of their just sentence, to become angels to the devil; just as it is in this world, precisely.

Has the devil power to afflict, and cast the spirit into torment? No! We have gained the ascendency over him. It is in this world only he has power to cause affliction and sickness, pain and distress, sorrow, anguish, and disappointment; but when we go there, behold! the enemy of Jesus has come to the end of his chain; he has finished his work of torment; he cannot come any further; we are beyond his reach, and the righteous sleep in peace, while the spirit is anxiously looking forward to the day when the Lord will say, "Awake my Saints, you have slept long enough;" for the trump of God shall sound, and the sleeping dust shall arise, and the absent spirits return, to be united with their bodies; and they will become personages of tabernacle, like the Father, and His Son, Jesus Christ; yea Gods in eternity.

They look forward with great anxiety to that day, and their happiness will not be complete—their glory will not attain to the final consummation of its fulness, until they have entered into the immediate presence of the Father and the Son, to be crowned, as Jesus will be, when the work is finished. When it is wound up, the text is preached, in all its divisions, pertaining to the redemption of the world, and the final consummation of all things; then the Savior will present the work to the Father, saying, "Father, I have finished the work thou gavest me to do;" and the Son will give it up to the Father, and then be subject to Him, and then he will be crowned, and that is the time you and I will be crowned also.

We will notice, by this, that all the nations of the earth, with the exception of those who have apostatized from the Gospel salvation; every son and daughter of Adam, except those who have denied the Holy Ghost, after having received it, are placed in prison with the rest of them, with Prophets, Priests, and Saints. Suppose we quote a little Scripture on this point. Jesus died to redeem the world. Did his body lay in the tomb? Did his spirit leave his body? Yes. Where did his spirit go, you may inquire? I do not know that I can tell you any better than what the ancient Apostle has told it; he says he went to preach to the spirits in prison. Who are they to whom he went to preach? The people who lived in the antediluvian world. He preached the Gospel to them in the spirit, that they might be judged according to men in the flesh.

What shall we say of the people who live in the 19th century? When any of the Latter-day Elders or Apostles die, and leave this world, suffice it to say, that their spirits go to that prison, and preach the Gospel to those who have died without hearing it; and every spirit shall be judged precisely as though he lived in the flesh, when the fulness of the Gospel was upon the earth. This leads to the subject of the saving and redeeming powers possessed by the righteous; but we shall not have time this morning to treat upon it, suffice it to say, that saviors are coming up, in

56

the last days, upon mount Zion.

This I say of every son and daughter of Adam, Prophets, Priests, and those that slew the Prophets, all go to prison; the Elders of this Church go there, and there continue their labors; and by and bye you will see Zion redeemed, and saviors will come up upon mount Zion. The faithful Elders will come, and go forward in the ordinances of God, that our ancestors, and all who have died previous to the restoration of the Gospel in these last days, may be redeemed.

Now, ye Elders of Israel, when you say that John Wesley went to hell, say that Joseph Smith went there too. When you tell about Judas Iscariot going to hell, say that Jesus went there too. The world cannot see the whole of the Gospel sermon at one glance; they can only pick up a little here, and a little there. They that do understand it from the beginning to the end, know that is as straight as a line can be drawn. You cannot find a compass on the earth, that points, so directly, as the Gospel plan of salvation. It has a place for everything, and puts everything in its place. It divides, and sub-divides, and gives to every portion of the human family, as circumstances require.

It is for us to get rid of that tradition in which we are incased, and bring up our children in the way they should go, that when they get old, they will not depart from it. It is your privilege and mine, to enjoy the visions of the Spirit of the Lord, every one in his own order, just as the Lord has ordained it, that every man and woman may know for themselves, if they are doing right, according to the great plan of salvation. I have only touched a little of the great Gospel sermon, and the time has come, that we must close our meeting; so may the Lord God of Israel bless you, in the name of Jesus. Amen.

7

"True and False Riches,"
A Sermon Delivered on 14 August 1853

(from *Journal of Discourses*, 26 vols.
[Liverpool: Latter-day Saints' Book Depot, 1855-86], 1:264-76)

I am disposed this morning to give my testimony to this congregation upon the subject of true riches. Wealth and poverty are much talked of by all people. The subject was tolerably well discussed yesterday, and according to my understanding, the most that I have heard said upon that point has been on the negative of the question.

If you wish me to take a text, I will take the Scriptures of the Old and New Testaments, referring, if you please, to both text and context, and let the people distribute, or apply them according to their own pleasure. I will, however, use one passage of Scripture as a text, that was used yesterday. Jesus said to his disciples, to them it was given to know the mysteries of the kingdom of heaven, but to them that were without, it was not given. If we were to examine the subject closely, we should learn that a very scanty portion of the things of the kingdom were ever revealed, even to the disciples. If we were prepared to gaze upon the mysteries of the kingdom, as they are with God, we should then know that only a very small portion of them has been handed out here and there. God, by His Spirit, has revealed many things to His people, but, in almost all cases, He has straightway shut up the vision of the mind. He will let His servants gaze upon eternal things for a moment, but straightway the vision is closed, and they are left as they were, that they may learn to act by faith, or as the Apostle has it, not walking by sight, but by faith.

In viewing this subject, permit me to preach what I have to preach, without framing or systematising my address. When I have endeavored to address a congregation, I have almost always felt a repugnance in my heart to the practice of premeditation, or of pre-constructing a discourse to deliver to the people, but let me ask God my heavenly Father, in the name of Jesus Christ, to give me His Spirit, and put into my heart the things He wishes me to speak whether they be for better or worse. These have been my private feelings, as a general thing. I would ask our Father in heaven, in the name of Jesus Christ, to pour His Spirit upon each one of us this morning, that we might speak and hear with an understanding heart, that a hint, a key word, or a short sentence pertaining to the things of God, might open the vision of our minds, so that we might comprehend the things of eternity, and rejoice exceedingly therein.

In the first place, suppose we commence by examining the principles that have been laid before us this Conference, taking up the negative of the question; suppose, in our social capacity here, we have a system that feeds the hungry, clothes the naked, administers to the widow and the fatherless, so that we can say of a truth, as they did in the days of the Apostles, *we have no poor among us.* Would it establish the principle that we are rich? To me it would establish no more than a good wholesome principle upon which the wicked may act, as well as the righteous—a principle upon which the world ought to act, by the moral obligations they are under to stretch out the arm of charity to every person, to fill up their days with industry, prudence, and faithfulness, procuring means to sustain themselves, and to administer to the wants of those who are unable to administer to themselves. To me, I say, this principle manifests no more than a moral obligation under which all are placed. Though some may think it a decided mark of Christianity, that it is a proof of deep piety, and bespeaks the character of Saints, and all this, if we scan the subject closely, it amounts to nothing more than a moral obligation all are under to each other.

Again, we call up the question of riches, wealth. We may behold one upon the right, that commands his thousands of gold and silver, which he has treasured up; he has houses and lands to occupy, goods and chattels to fill his store-houses, cattle to cover his fields, and servants to obey his commands; we call such an individual *rich, wealthy,* but when we take into consideration the *"true riches"* spoken of in this book [the Bible], they are not riches. We may behold another upon the left, reigning as a monarch; the gold, and the silver, yea all the treasures of the kingdom over which he reigns are at his command; and all his subjects are fully disposed to do the will of their sovereign. He reigns, he rules, he governs, and controls, and there are none to gainsay, none to offer a single word of opposition, his word is the law, his commands are supreme, he rides in his richly-adorned chariots, and wears his crown of gold set with the most precious stones. He sets up one, and drags down another. Those who have in the least incurred his displeasure, he condemns to the block, and he exalts others to sudden wealth and power. This monarch reigns for a day, a month, a year, or for half a century, according to the will of Him by whom kings sway the sceptre of power; and the world say he is a rich man, a powerful and wealthy man. But this is not riches according to the saying of the Saviour in the New Testament.

Suppose we could heap to ourselves the treasures of the earth, as was mentioned yesterday; suppose we could load our wagons with the purest of gold; with it we could open our commercial business on an extensive scale, we could build our temples and mansions, macadamise our streets, beautify our gardens, and make these valleys as it were like the Garden of Eden, but would it prove we were actually rich? It would not. As it was said yesterday, and justly, too, we might be brought into circumstances, in the midst of this supposed wealth, to be glad to give a barrel of gold for as much flour. In such a circumstance, of what benefit to us would be this wealth, so called? Would not the idea which the wicked, and, I may say, with some propriety, the Saints, have of wealth vanish like smoke, and should we not find ourselves poor indeed? If we possessed mountains of gold, *should we not perish without bread, without something to feed the body?* Most assuredly. Though an individual, or a nation of people, could command their millions of millions of gold and silver, houses, lands, goods, and chattels, horses and chariots, crowns, and thrones, or even the products of the soil—the wheat, the fine flour, the oil, and the wine, and all the precious metals of the earth in abundance—though they were flooded with all these good things, yet if the Almighty should withdraw His hand, they would be smitten with the mildew, and disappear; their wealth would become the most abject poverty. The possession of these things is not wealth to me. Not that I would cast them away as a thing of naught, or look upon the good things of this earth, and the riches of the world, as things of naught, but they are not the true riches, the pearl of great price spoken of in the Scriptures, when a man found which, he sold all he had to purchase; they do not belong to those principles couched in the saying of our Lord, touching the mysteries of the kingdom. The riches of this world are nothing more than a stepping stone, or necessary means whereby people may obtain the true riches—by which they can sustain themselves until they can procure the true riches of the kingdom of God. As such they ought to be looked upon and handled. "Seek first the kingdom of God." "*Seek* FIRST" that durable object. "*Seek* FIRST" the righteousness that will never betray you. *Obtain* "FIRST" the prize that will not forsake you. Procure to yourselves "FIRST" *of all*, that which will endure through time, and through all the eternities that will be. "Seek FIRST *the kingdom of God, and its righteousness*," and let the gold and silver, the houses, the lands, the horses, the chariots, the crowns, the thrones, and the dominions of this world be dead to you, as it is necessary you should secure for yourselves eternal riches that will never forsake you in time nor in all eternity.

The negative of the question is present with the people. If they begin to seek the kingdom of heaven, if they set out to glorify God in their souls and bodies, which are His, how quick their feelings and desires, how soon their natural propensities cling with greater pertinacity to the things that are perishable. On the right hand and on the left we see persons whose trust is wholly in the riches of this world; they say, "I have gathered to myself substance, if you rob me of it you rob me of my all. I have my flocks and herds around me, if you take these from me all is gone." Those men or women to whom this will apply have not eternal riches abiding in them. Their minds are set upon the things of this world, upon a shadow, upon the substance that passes away, like the shadow of morn, or like the morning dew upon the flowers. They are like a thing of naught to those who understand the things of the kingdom of God. They are to be used, but not abused. They are to be handled with discretion, and looked upon in their true light, without any lustful desires, as the means to feed, clothe, and make us comfortable, that we may be prepared to secure to ourselves eternal riches.

Suppose we should remain here to discuss the subject, for days, months, and years, and scan it with a scrutinizing examination, in the end of all our labor we should find that the things of this world called riches, are in reality *not riches*. We should find they are like miracles to the ignorant, mere phenomena to the inhabitants of the earth; to-day they are, to-morrow they are not; they were, but now they are gone, it is not known where. The earthly king upon his throne, who reigns triumphantly over his subjects, is blasted, with all his kingdom, and brought to naught at one breath of Him who possesses true riches. Let Him who possesses the true riches say to the elements around that kingdom, "produce no wheat, nor oil, nor wine, but let there be a famine upon that people," in such a circumstance where is the wealth of that king, his power, his grandeur, and his crown? There is no bread, no oil, there are no flocks, no herds, for they have perished upon the plains, his wheat is blasted, and all his crops are mildewed. What good does his wealth do him? His subjects are lying all around him lifeless for want of bread; he may cry to them, but in vain; his wealth, power, and influence have vanished, they are swept away like the flimsy fabric of a cobweb.

Again, the rich merchant, or private individuals, may have millions of gold and silver deposited, hid in the ground, or elsewhere, perhaps, and this is their god. Should the Lord Almighty say, as he did in the days of the Nephites, Let their substance become slippery, let it disappear that they cannot find it again; it is gone, and they may hunt for it in vain. Or let it be deposited in a bank, the first they know, the bank is broken, their substance is gone, and they are left in perfect beggary. To possess gold and silver, or earthly power and wealth, is not riches to me, but it is the negative of the question.

There are hundreds of people in these valleys, who never owned a cow in the world, until they came here, but now they have got a few cows and sheep around them, a yoke of oxen, and a horse to ride upon, they feel to be personages of far greater importance than Jesus Christ was, when he rode into Jerusalem upon an ass's colt. They become puffed up in pride, and selfishness, and their minds become attached to the things of this world. They become covetous, which makes them idolators. Their substance engrosses so much of their attention, they forget their prayers, and forget to attend the assemblies of the Saints, for they must see to their land, or to their crops that are suffering, until by and bye the grasshoppers come like a cloud, and cut away the bread from their mouth, introducing famine and distress, to stir them up in remembrance of the Lord their God. Or the Indians will come, and drive off their cattle; where then is their wealth in their grain, and in their cattle? *Are these things riches?* No. They are the things of this world, made to decay, to perish, or to be decomposed, and thus pass away.

Were we to spend the period of our lives and try to trace the history of mankind upon this world, from the beginning to the present time, by referring to the lives of kings, rulers, governors, and potentates; to the wealth, magnificence, and power of nations; also to the poverty, wretchedness, war, bloodshed, and distress there have been among the inhabitants of the earth, it could not all be told, but I have noticed some few of the items which I call the negative of the question. To possess this world's goods is not in reality wealth, it is not riches, it is nothing more nor less than that which is common to all men, to the just and the unjust, to the Saint and to the sinner. The sun rises upon the evil and the good; the Lord sends His rain upon the just and upon the unjust; this is manifest before our eyes, and in our daily experience. Old King Solomon, the wise man, says, the race is not to the swift, nor the battle to the strong, neither riches to men of wisdom. The truth of this saying comes within our daily observation. Those whom we consider swift are not always the ones that gain the mastery in the race, but those who are considered not so fleet, or not fleet at all, often gain the prize. It is, I may say, the unseen hand of Providence, that over-ruling power that controls the destinies of men and nations, that so ordains these things. The weak, trembling, and feeble, are the ones frequently who gain the battle; and the ignorant, foolish, and unwise will blunder into wealth. This is all before us, it is the common lot of man, in short, I may say, it is the philosophical providence of a philosophical world.

Suppose we look for a short time after the true riches—after the pearl of great price. In doing this were I to systematize, I would say, let us leave this subject, which is the negative of the question, and take up another, entirely different. We would have to take up the subject of salvation to the human family, calling up the characters who have officiated in this great work, and have brought forth redemption, and placed it before the world, putting it within the reach of every individual of the sons and daughters of Adam and Eve. Yet it is all the same subject.

Where shall we direct our course to find true riches? Who is there that possesses them? Were we to admit scriptural testimony, I could refer you to the Bible, where we read of people exhibiting a power that gave their beholders satisfactory proof of their possessing the true riches. The riches of the world are natural, and common to the human family, but who governs and controls them? Who holds the destiny of the wealth of the nations in his hand? Do the kings, rulers, governors, or the inhabitants of the earth generally? No, not one of them, by any means. Have there ever been persons upon the earth who have exhibited the principles of true riches? Yes. The Bible tells us who they are, and delineates the principles of true riches.

Again, here is the philosophical world, the *terra firma* on which we tread. Here is the atmosphere which the wise men of the world tell us it is surrounded with, which is congenial to the constitution of the vegetable and animal world, it is the air we breathe. Philosophers tell us that the *terra firma* on which we walk is surrounded with it 40 miles high from the surface of the earth. It revolves in this subtle element, which is a combination of other elements. This is a philosophical world. What then are the results of the philosophical world? Why, if you were to put wheat in the ground that has been well tilled, it would grow, and bring an increase to repay the husbandman for his labor. If you plant potatoes in the ground the philosophy of the earth is, it will bring forth potatoes. If you plant corn, corn will be produced in abundance, and this will apply to all the grain, and vegetables, and products of this earth.

What is there here, in the valleys of these mountains? Why, the same that was centuries ago. As I told my brethren six years ago, I said, there are here wheat, corn, potatoes, buckwheat, beets, parsnips, carrots, cabbage, onions, apples, peaches, plums, pears, and fruits of every description and kind. They are all in the philosophical world—in the air we breathe, and in the water we drink; it needs nothing more than philosophical applications to bring them forth. The most delicate silks, the finest linen, and fine cloth of every description, that were ever produced upon the earth, are right here in this valley, and it requires nothing more than a philosophical application to bring them forth to administer to our wants. What more is there here! When we first came into this valley we had no knowledge that our brethren could find gold in California, or perhaps we might have been digging gold over there at this time; but our thoughts were occupied with how we should get our wives and children here; we were thinking about wheat, potatoes, water melons, peaches, apples, plums, &c. But allow me to tell you, that gold and silver, platina, zinc, copper, lead, and every element that there is in any part of the earth, can be found here; and all that is required, when we need them, is a philosophical application to make them subservient to our wants.

Here we pause and think—"What! is there gold here, silver here? Are the finest and most beautiful silks that were ever made, to be found here? Yes. Is there fine linen here?" Yes, and the finest broad-cloths, and shawls and dresses of every description. We are walking over them, drinking them, and breathing them every day we live. They are here with us, and we can make ourselves rich, for all these things are within our reach. What hinders us from being truly rich? This is the point. I will tell you when you and I may consider ourselves truly rich—When we can speak to the earth—to the native elements in boundless space, and say to them—"Be ye organized, and planted here, or there, and stay until I command you hence;" when at our command the gold is hid so that no man can find it, any more than they could in California until within a few years back.

Again, we have a little absolute truth still nearer, and which comes under our own knowledge. There is the Sweet Water that runs into the Platte river, that this people have passed by for years. There have been no pains spared to find gold on that stream and its tributaries, but it could not be seen, and yet of late an abundance of it has been discovered, ranging over a district of country from the South Platte to the South Pass. There are men present here to-day, I have no doubt, who have it in their pockets, or in their wagons. There are as good prospects for gold *there*, as there ever were in California. How is this? Why He that hath all power and all true riches in His possession, has said, "Let that sleep, let it be out of sight to this people, until I say the word; I organized the elements, and control them, and place them where I please." When He says, "Let it be found;" it is right there on the top of the earth. Where was it before? I do not know; it was out of sight. In the very place where men have gone from this valley, to my knowledge, and hunted weeks and weeks for gold, and could not find it, there is plenty of it now. When you and I can say, "Let there be gold in this valley," and turn round again, and command it to disappear, that it is not to be found; when we can call gold and silver together from the eternity of matter in the immensity of space, and all the other precious metals, and command them to remain or to move at our pleasure; when we can say to the native element, "Be thou combined, and produce those commodities necessary for the use and sustenance of man, and to make this earth beautiful and glorious, and prepare it for the habitation of the sanctified;" then we shall be in possession of true riches. This is true riches to me, and nothing short of it constitutes them. When I have gold and silver in my possession, which a thief may steal, or friends borrow, and never pay me back again, or which may take the wings of the morning, and I behold it no more, I only possess the negative of the true riches. When the riches of this world leave me, I cannot say—"Gold, return thou to my chest." I cannot say to the gold I pick up out of the earth, "Be thou separated from every particle of dross, and let me see the pure virgin gold." I cannot do that without submitting to a tedious process of chemical action.

All those who wish to possess true riches, desire the riches that will endure. Then look at the subject of salvation, where you will find true riches. They are to be found in the principles of the Gospel of salvation, and are not to be found anywhere else. With whom abide eternally the true riches? With that God whom we serve, who holds all things in His hands, that we know anything of; He is the first and the last, the Alpha and the Omega, the beginning and the end who at one survey looks upon all the workmanship of His hands; who has the words of eternal life, and holds the hearts of the children of men in His hand, and turns them whithersoever He will, even as the rivers of waters are turned; who commands the earth to perform its revolutions, or stand still, at His pleasure; who has given the sun, the planets, the earths, and far distant systems their orbits, their times, and their seasons; whose commands they all obey. With Him abide the true riches.

I will now notice the character who exhibited the power of true riches on the earth, though he himself was in a state of abject poverty, to all human appearance, for he was made poor that we might be made rich, and he descended below all things that he might ascend above all things. When the only begotten Son of God was upon the earth, he understood the nature of these elements, how they were brought together to make this world and all things that are thereon, for he helped to make them. He had the power of organizing, what we would call, in a miraculous manner. That which to him was no miracle, is called miraculous by the inhabitants of the earth. On one occasion he commanded a sufficient amount of bread to be formed to feed his disciples and the multitude. It was in the air, in the water, and in the earth they walked upon. *He*, unperceived by his disciples and the multitude, spoke to the native elements, and brought forth bread. He had the power. We have not that power, but are under the necessity of producing bread according to a systematic plan. We are obliged to till the ground, and sow wheat, in order to obtain wheat. But when we possess the true riches, we shall be able to call forth the bread from the native element, like as Jesus Christ did. Everything that is good for man, is there. Jesus said to his disciples, Make the multitude sit down, and divide them into companies, and take this bread and break it, and distribute it among them. They did not know but that it was the few loaves and fishes that fed the whole of them as they ate. The truth is, he called forth bread from the native elements. Is that mystery to you? Did you never think of it before? How do you suppose he fed them, he did not feed them upon nothing at all, but they ate bread and fish, *substantial bread and fish!* until they were satisfied. This the Saviour called from the surrounding elements; he was quite capable of doing it, because he had the keys and power of true riches, if any man possess which, he is rich in time, and in eternity both.

Again, the Saviour changed water into wine, in the same manner, by commanding the elements. Can that be done by a chemical process. I admit it can by the persons who understand the process; and that men can make bread also. As quick as I admit that the history Moses gives of himself is true, I cannot have any question in the world but what in ancient days they understood in a measure how to command the elements. The magicians of Egypt were instructed in things pertaining to true riches, and had obtained keys and powers enough to produce a bogus in opposition to the true coin, as it were, and thus they deceived the king and the people. They could cause frogs to come upon the land, as well as Moses could. They could turn the waters of Egypt into blood, and in many more things compete with Moses. There was one thing, however, they could not do, though they produced a very good bogus, but it was not *quite* the true coin. When they threw their staffs on the floor before the king, they could not swallow the staff of Moses, but the staff of Moses swallowed the staffs of the magicians. I have no doubt that men can perform many such wonders by the principles of natural philosophy.

Again, they can deceive the inhabitants of the earth, and make them believe that things were done, which in reality were not. If there were not a true coin in existence, how could there be a bogus produced? The true coin is what we are after, the true riches. We are seeking to be made rich in the power of God, so as to be able to control the elements, and say—"Let there be light," and there is light; "Let there be water," and there is water; "Let this or that come," and it cometh; by the power that is within us to command the elements; and they obey, just as they did the Saviour when he changed the water into wine, or made bread to feed the multitudes.

What shall we say? Do the things of this world, in their present state, offer unto us true riches? *I say they are not riches*, in the true sense of the word; there is no such thing as a man being truly rich until he has power over death, hell, the grave, and him that hath the power of death, which is the devil. For what are the riches, the wealth possessed by the inhabitants of the earth? Why, they are a phantom, a mere shadow, a bubble on the wave, that bursts with the least breath of air. Suppose I possessed millions on millions of wealth of every description I could think of or ask for, and I took a sudden pain in my head, which threw me entirely out of my mind, and baffled the skill of the most eminent physicians, what good would that money do me, in the absence of the power to say to that pain, "Depart?" But suppose I possessed power to say to the pain, "Go thou to the land from whence thou camest;" and say, "Come, health, and give strength to my body;" and when I want death, to say, "Come you, for I have claim upon you, a right, a guarantee deed, for this body must be dissolved;" says death, "I want it, to prey upon;" but again I can say to death, "Depart from me, thou canst not touch me;" would I not be rich indeed. How is it now? Let the slightest accident come upon one of the human family, and they are no more. Do we then possess true riches in this state? We do not.

What shall we do to secure the true riches? "*Seek first the kingdom of God, and its righteousness.*" Lay up for ourselves treasures in heaven, where moth cannot eat, rust corrode, nor thieves break through and steal them. If we find the pearl of great price, go and sell all we have to purchase it, and secure to ourselves the friendship of God, and our Elder Brother Jesus Christ, and walk humbly before God, and obey those whom He has told us to obey, all the days of our lives, and He will say, "*These are my friends, and I will withold nothing from them.*"

And is it indeed possible that we can come into that power, while we are in this mortality, to say to death, "Touch me not?" Were it possible, I for one do not want it, I would not accept it were it offered to me. If the Lord Almighty proffered to revoke the decree, "Dust thou art, and to dust thou shalt return," and say to me, "You can live for ever as you are;" I should say, "Father, I want to ask you a few questions upon this point. Shall I still be subject to the tooth-ache, to the head-ache, to the chills and fever, and to all the diseases incident to the mortal body?" "O yes, but you can live, and never die." "Then I would have you, Father, to let the old decree stand good; I find no fault with your offer, it may be a good one; but I have the promise of receiving my body again—of this body coming up in the morning of the resurrection, and being re-united with the spirit, and being filled with the principles of immortality and eternal life. Thank you, Father, I would rather take a new body, and then I shall get a good set of new teeth. My sight, too, is failing; if I want to read, I cannot do it without using glasses; and if I wish to walk a few miles, I cannot do it without making myself sick; if I wish to go out on a journey, I am under the necessity of taking the utmost care of myself for fear of injuring my health; but when I get a new body, this will not be so; I shall be out of the reach of him that hath the power of death in his hands, for Jesus Christ will conquer that foe, and I shall receive a new body, which will be filled with eternal life, health, and beauty."

What more? Why, to him that overcometh shall be glory, immortality, and eternal life. What more? Jesus says, as it was said yesterday, Except ye are one, ye are not mine. Again, he says, I pray thee, Father, to make these, my disciples, one, as thou, Father, art in me, and I in thee, that they also may be one in us, I in them, and thou in me, that they may be made perfect in one. This is a curiosity that ranks among the mysteries that the people do not understand. The Father and I are *one*, you disciples and I are *one*; it is quite a curiosity, but it is as true as it is curious. It is nothing more than a key-word to exaltation, glory, power, and excellency, by which principalities, kingdoms, dominions, and eternal lives will surround us.

That will give you true riches, and nothing else will. The only true riches in existence are for you and I to secure for ourselves a holy resurrection; then we have command of the gold and the silver, and can place it where we please, and in whose hands we please. We can place it here and there, where it can be found, and in abundance, when we say the word. We can say then to the flies, and to the grasshoppers, "Be ye extinct," and it will be so; and again say, "Go ye, and make a work of devastation," and at our word clouds of them darken the sun, and cover the ground, the crops are destroyed in a day. We can then say to the hail-storm, "Stay thou thy rage, and hurt not the fields and fruit trees of the servants of God;" and we are obeyed. On the other hand, when they need a little chastisement, we can say to the rain, to the lightnings, and to the thunders, "Chasten ye the people;" and the elements are at once in a state of agitation, and they are chastened by the destruction of their crops, and cities are swallowed up in the yawning earthquake, when God can bear their wickedness no longer. He does not want to slay His children who love and serve him, He is not a hard master, nor a severe Father, but when He chastens, it is because He wishes to bring His children to understanding, that they may know *where* the true riches are, and *what* are the true riches of eternity, and rejoice with Him in His presence, being made equal with Him.

These are some of my reflections upon *true riches*. Why will the Latter-day Saints wander off after the things of this world? But are they not good? We cannot do very well without them, for we are of the world, we are in the world, we partake of the elements of which it is composed; it is our mother earth, we are composed of the same native material. It is all good, the air, the water, the gold and silver; the wheat, the fine flour, and the cattle upon a thousand hills are all good; but, *why do men set their hearts upon them in their present organized state?* Why not lay a sure foundation to control them hereafter? Why do we not keep it continually before us that all flesh is grass; it *is* today, and to-morrow *it is not*; it is like the flower of the grass when it is cut down, it withers, and is no more? Why do the children of men set their hearts upon earthly things? They are to be used, but not to the abusing of yourselves. They are to be used to make us comfortable. Suppose all the good things of this world should be given to us, the gold and the silver, the cattle and the horses, and all the flocks of a thousand hills; it would be for the express purpose of building mansions and temples, of feeding the poor that cannot feed themselves, of succouring the tried and the tempted, of sending Elders to preach the Gospel from nation to nation, from island to island, and of gathering Israel from the four quarters of the globe. But that moment that men seek to build up themselves, in preference to the kingdom of God, and seek to hoard up riches, while the widow and the fatherless, the sick and afflicted, around them, are in poverty and want, it proves that their hearts are weaned from their God; *and their riches will perish in their fingers, and they with them.*

Where are the true riches—the pearl of great price? They are here. How can we secure them? By being obedient, *for the willing and obedient will eat the good of the land by and bye;* but those who heap to themselves riches, and set their hearts upon them, *where will they be by and bye?* There are men in our midst who will quarrel for five dollars, and have their trials before Bishops and other tribunals if it costs all they possess. They say, "I will have my rights." They tell about their rights, *when they know nothing about rights; in this they are governed solely by the influence of former traditions.* Why do they not say, "*I will satisfy my hellish will, if it destroys me for time and all eternity.*" If they would say that, they would say the truth. If a man says, "It is my right to have this or that," *he knows nothing about rights,* so never say anything more about rights. But if you can find *one individual* who knows what right is, ask him, and then say, "That is right, and I will do it." Take that course, and rejoice that you have found somebody to tell you what right is. When my heart trembles with rage, and my nervous system becomes irritated to knock down and kill, it is for me to say, Brigham, hold on, you should not do this. Do you wish me to tell you what right is? I will point out the way if you will walk in it. If your neighbor or your brother should sue you at the law for your coat, give it to him, and your cloak also, and not turn round and say, "It is my right; are you going to rob me?" The instructions of the Saviour of the world, which I have quoted, are right; and I could prove it so by philosophical reasoning, and make you believe it, and you would be satisfied it is the best course you could pursue. I will give you the key to it, which is this—it gives you an influence you never can obtain by contending for your rights. You say, "Take it, it is no matter whether it is my right or not." If a man asks you to go with him one mile, go two, and then you can say, "You only asked me to go one mile, but I have gone two." That is the counsel Jesus Christ gave. If you sit down and calmly reason the case, you cannot but discover that it gives you an influence over that man, which you could not gain by contending with him in anger. All the power which is gained by contending with people is usurped power.

The power which belongs to the true riches is gained by pursuing a righteous course, by maintaining an upright deportment towards all men, and especially towards the household of faith, yielding to each other, giving freely of that which the Lord has given to you, thus you can secure to yourselves eternal riches; and gain influence and power over all your friends, as well as your enemies. "If you want anything I have, here, take it, and I will have influence and power over you;" this is a key word to gain the true riches; that is the amount of it.

I want to hint at the negative of the question again. I have, from time to time, said many things to you in this tabernacle, and so have my brethren, and the people are much inclined for the mysteries of the kingdom. I can tell you what they are, in some degree. The idea appears very foolish to me when we are talking about it, but we are obliged to use the English language as it is, which is scarcely a similitude of what we want. Again it is first rate to communicate our ideas, and good to enable us to talk one way, and mean another, when we have a disposition to do so. Brother Hyde preached us a good discourse on mystery yesterday.

What is a mystery? *We do not know, it is beyond our comprehension.* When we talk about mystery, we talk about eternal obscurity; for that which is known, ceases to be a mystery; and all that is known, *we* may know as we progress in the scale of intelligence. That which is eternally beyond the comprehension of all our intelligence is mystery, yet this word is used by the translators of the Bible. They write about mystery, and talk about mystery; what are they talking about? I do not know what they mean, nor what they wish to convey by that word, and they do not know themselves. This langauge is made use of in the Bible, because they have nothing better. Things transpire almost every day in our lives which we class under the term mystery, for want of a better term. What does it mean, in reality? *Why, nothing at all.* But for the accommodation of those who speak the English language, we will continue to use the term, and proceed to examine the negative of true riches.

Here are the earth and the inhabitants upon its face, organized for the express purpose of a glorious resurrection. The *terra firma* on which we walk, and from which we gain our bread, is looking forth for the morning of the resurrection, and will get a resurrection, and be cleansed from the filthiness that has gone forth out of her. This is Bible doctrine. What filthiness has gone forth out of her? *You and I*, and all the inhabitants of the earth; the human body, and all earthly bodies, both animal and vegetable; are composed of the native element that we breathe, that we drink, and that we walk upon; we till the earth for our bread, which is one of the materials of which your body is composed, it comes forth from the native elements into an organized state; what for? To be exalted, to get a glorious resurrection. We are of the earth, earthy, and not only will the portion of mother earth which composes these bodies get a resurrection, but the earth itself. It has already had a baptism. You who have read the Bible must know that that is Bible doctrine. What does it matter if it is not stated in the same words that I use, it is none the less true that it was baptized for the remission of sins. The Lord said, "I will deluge (or immerse) the earth in water for the remission of the sins of the people;" or if you will allow me to express myself in a familiar style, to kill all the vermin that were nitting, and breeding, and polluting its body; it was cleansed of its filthiness; and soaked in the water, as long as some of our people ought to soak. The Lord baptized the earth for the remission of sins, and it has been once cleansed from the filthiness that has gone out of it, which was in the inhabitants who dwelt upon its face.

The earth is organized for a glorious resurrection, and life and death are set before the people, true riches and false riches; and the whole world are gone after false riches; after that which is not life, after decomposition, after that which perishes, and passes away like the twilight of evening. The Lord has set before the inhabitants of the earth, true riches, from the days of Adam until now. In olden times, in the ages we call "the dark ages of the world," men could talk to the Lord face to face, and He looked like another man. When He had a mind to do so, He could walk into the assemblies of the people, and none of them would know him, only they knew He was a stranger that had visited their meeting. He understands the difference between true riches and the bogus which passed current in the days of Pharoah in Egypt. We see the bogus power again exhibited in the days of Saul the king of Israel, by the witch of Endor, who, at the request of Saul, brought forth the spirit of Samuel, or some other spirit. They understood the principles of life, for the Lord had set life and death before them, true riches and false riches, or in other words, composition and decomposition, and the laws, principles, and powers of the eternal world; and the people of the early ages of this world understood them.

The people in this age, are like the old miser, whose latter end was drawing nigh; he had saved a good purse of gold, but he was blind and could not see it, so he requested the attendants to bring him the gold that he might put his hand on it; when he laid his hand upon it, he could go to sleep. He possessed the negative of true riches. Again, they are like the man who found a lump of gold which weighed 100 pounds, the last that was heard of him was, he was sitting upon it, offering a great price to the passers by for something to eat, and swearing that if he had to starve to death, he would stick by the gold, and die a rich man. If he had understood the principles of life—the principles of true riches, he could have commanded that gold in California, in England, or anywhere else;

but he had no power over it, and died like a fool, no doubt. What good was his gold to him? He had not the power of endless life in him, and he will be decomposed, and the particles which compose his body and spirit will return to their native element. I told you some time ago what would become of such men. But I will quote the Scriptures on this point, and you can make what you please of it. Jesus says, he will DESTROY *death* and *him* that hath the power of it. What can you make of this but decomposition, the returning of the organized particles to their native element, after suffering the wrath of God until the time appointed. That appears a mystery, but the principle has been in existence from all eternity, only it is something you have not known or thought of. When the elements in an organized form do not fill the end of their creation, they are thrown back again, like brother Kimball's old pottery ware, to be ground up, and made over again. All I have to say about it is what Jesus says—I will *destroy* Death, and him that hath the power of it, which is the devil. And if he ever makes "*a full end* of the wicked," what else can he do than entirely disorganize them, and reduce them to their native element? Here are some of the mysteries of the kingdom.

On the other hand, let us take the affirmative of the question; and inquire what is life and salvation? It is to take that course wherein we can abide for ever and ever, and be exalted to thrones, kingdoms, governments, dominions, and have full power to control the elements, according to our pleasure to all eternity; the one is life, and the other is death, which is nothing more or less than the decomposition of organized native element. There can be no such thing as power to annihilate element. There is one eternity of element, which can be organized or disorganized, composed or decomposed; it may be put into this shape or into that, according to the will of the intelligence that commands it, but there is no such thing as putting it entirely out of existence.

I never studied philosophy to any great extent, but on one occasion I had a kind of a confab with Professor Orson Pratt, who endeavoured to prove that there was empty space, I supposed there was no such thing. He thought he had proved it; but I thought he had not proved a word of it, and told him the idea was folly. After hearing a good many arguments from him, and other men, his colleagues in learning, I wished them to tell me where empty space was situated, that I might tell the wicked, who wish to hide themselves from the face of him that sitteth upon the throne, where to go, for they will then be *where God is not,* if they can find empty space. To argue such a question as that, would be, to confute my own arguments in favor of other truths I have advocated, and oppose my own system of faith. We believe that God is round about all things, above all things, in all things, and through all things. To tell about empty space is to tell of a space where God is not, and where the wicked might safely hide from His presence. There is no such thing as empty space.

Remember, that true riches—life, happiness, and salvation, is to secure for ourselves a part in the first resurrection, where we are out of the reach of death, and him that hath the power of it; then we are exalted to thrones, and have power to organize element. Yes, they that are faithful, and that overcome, shall be crowned with crowns of eternal glory. They shall see the time when their cities shall be paved with gold; for there is no end to the precious metals, they are in the native element, and there is an eternity of it. If you want a world of the most precious substance, you will have nothing to do but say the word, and it is done. You can macadamize streets with it, and beautify and make glorious the temples. We can then say to the elements, "Produce ye the best oranges, lemons, apples, figs, grapes, and every other good fruit." I presume we do not draw a single breath that there are not particles of these things mingled in it. But we have not the knowledge now to organize them at our pleasure. Until we have that power we are not fully in possession of the true riches, which is the affirmative of the question, and the negative of the question is no riches at all in reality.

Well, brethren, I think I have stood out first rate. When I rose I did not think I could speak over ten minutes. May the Lord God bless you, and have mercy upon the world, and upon this people, that we may be saved in His kingdom. Amen.

{8}

"When I Contemplate the Subject of Salvation," A Sermon Delivered on 12 February 1854

(from *The Teachings of President Brigham Young*, Vol. 3, 1852-1854 [Salt Lake City: Collier's Publishing Co., 1987], 230-45)

When I contemplate the subject of Salvation, and rise before a congregation to speak upon that all-important matter, it has been but a few times in my life that I could see a beginning point to it, or a stopping place. There is such a multiplicity of principles, and circumstances all interwoven so closely that it seems to be one eternity. I suppose this is the case in reality. To be Saved, to be Redeemed, and to have a right to the Celestial Kingdom of God is to be infinitely connected with the principles of Eternity.

I recollect once when I was preaching, a question was asked me: "What is Priesthood?" The answer was ready, and perfectly simple in its nature, plain to be understood, and is *couched in a short sentence (viz.): Priesthood is a perfect system of Government that rules and reigns in Eternity.*

A question at once arises in the mind: "Where is Eternity?" The answer is at hand: *Eternity* is here:—we are in Eternity just as much so as any other beings in Heaven or on Earth. Heavenly beings are no more in Eternity than we are. We are in the midst of Eternity; and when we become acquainted with the system of government and the laws that rule in Eternity, we shall then know [that] it [is] calculated to endure; to govern and control all things which are in Heaven, and on the Earth.

The Eternal Priesthood of God—the Government of God—the Laws of Eternity—is a pure and perfect system of government!

While meditating this morning upon what we are here for—why man is acted upon as he is, and the cause of what we see continually exhibited before us—which is referred to in hundreds of passages of scripture, for the ancient prophets and apostles could see the darkness, ignorance, wickedness and blindness of mankind in the midst of Eternity. Made as they are, they seem to be governed and controlled—or were we to speak without reflection, at a glance over the face of the living masses of the human family, we might say with some show of truth: "they are compelled to do as they do, and be what they are by some power unknown to them, and over which they have no control." Men in general seem not to know what is the cause of action, and why it is we do as we do. While these thoughts pass through my mind, the question:

"What are we here for," was answered very nigh as Brother Taylor spoke this morning. We came here to serve God, to be Saints, and help build up the Kingdom of God. Yet we see many things that do not tend to righteousness; we then consider the Lord must be the controller of all things, and it is His hand that rules and overrules, that He has His way, fulfilling the counsels of His own will, setting bounds to man that he cannot pass. Though He governs, and controls the children of men, it is but to a certain extent; for numerous powers, principles, and spirits operate in as great a variety of ways upon them which is seen in their actions, feelings and impressions. The variety is very great. We behold this variety not only in the human creature but in all the other works of God. We may examine the Earth, the elements in which it floats, the planetary system, the starry heavens, and a thousand other things common to natural philosophy, and the same principle of endless variety presents itself to our notice.

What is natural philosophy? We may illustrate this question by saying: If we plow the ground, and properly prepare it for the reception of seed, and then sow it with good wheat it will produce wheat. This is natural philosophy. Every seed will bring forth its own kind. All the reasonable doings, and labors of man have been performed upon the principles of natural philosophy.

While we see this great variety in nature we ask philosophers how many elements they count, for they say the elements can be numbered with ease. This is vain philosophy. I do not believe that any man by the science of natural philosophy has discovered *all* the elements, and numbered them. They are so interspersed, and operate in such an endless variety of ways; creating an endless variety of new forms, and results. It has not come within the capacity of the most able philosopher to arrange, number, and classify them, to do which is the province of natural philosophy.

When we read the scriptures we read the letter, or that which we know naturally, that we see with our eyes, hear with our ears, handle with our hands, and understand with our natural mind as natural beings. The Apostles when speaking of a certain class of unbelievers, wisely said, "They were like brute beasts made to be taken and destroyed." That is, they (the beasts) know naturally as we do when they are hungry; when they want to eat and drink, when they are uneasy from the effects of cold, or over much heat.

What we can see, hear, smell, taste, feel, and understand is embraced in natural philosophy. But without something more than we can gather from natural philosophy—from the natural organization of the human system it all tends to death. As it is written the letter killeth but the spirit giveth life.

That God fills immensity is a true principle to me. There is no portion of space where He is not. There is no element in existence that does not contain Him; no matter whether it be in its primitive, or in an organized state, He is through it and round about it. God fills immensity.

Can any person make it plain to our understanding why things are as they are? What produces that which seems natural, and rational to us, and perfectly congenial to our feelings? But our feelings are wholly the result of tradition. As a general thing, what we individually see and understand appears right to us, though we come in contact with things we call wrong—like men's acts, and thoughts, we are very apt to call wrong—but that which we do, and that which *we* think, and that which *we* consider to be right, to us is perfectly right. People can be traditionated to think, and act, in every possible way, and justify themselves therein. For instance, refer to the traditions of the world, and ask those who profess Christianity if they can believe it is right for a wife to go on to the funeral pyre to be burnt alive with her dead husband. In some parts of the world, if a husband dies they make what they call a "funeral pyre," which is composed of fine dry wood mingled with other inflammable combustibles, which they set fire to, and the beautiful healthy young woman is consumed with the dead body of her husband? Does the Christian consider this right? It appears almost impossible for us to believe that any human being could be traditionated to do what we often read in history. I will relate another circumstance that transpired upon one of the southern islands. A missionary who had made some considerable progress in his labors on one of these islands, was much annoyed by the practice of polygamy among the natives. One of them who had become a member of the Church told his priest that he had two wives. This, of course, appeared to the clergyman [as] an unpardonable sin, who told the savage if he remained a member of the Church he must have but one wife. The native went from the presence of the priest and in a while returned again saying, "Me good Christian, me one wife." The priest inquired what he had done with the other one. "Me kill her and eat her up." He believed he had done just right. Is it not strange how people can be traditionated to believe and practice such enormities. That is, to us it appears strange. Some of the old people in this Church, who have been brought up in what we call the blue states, or the Eastern States, are influenced continually by the habits of their youth. To this day the old woman of 80 years of age considers it decidedly wrong to take up her knitting after sundown on Saturday evening. Were she to do it under any pretext whatever, her conscience would be stung with guilt, while another individual would not consider it wrong to run his mill on Sunday but feel perfectly justified in the act. But the good old lady could not take up her knitting after sundown on Saturday night without feeling condemned. Why is this? Because her father, and her mother, and her priest taught her so. They told her it was not right to work after sundown on Saturday. The influence of this teaching follows her to this day.

Mormonism rubs off a great deal of this old rust, and causes them to judge, and think for themselves.

Again, I ask this congregation a question, which if I do not answer, I want you should sometime, when you choose, or I should like some of the Elders [to] answer it when they preach to us here. I shall not try to answer it myself. The question is, "How many spirits has the Lord got?" Many spirits are gone out into the world. We hear of spirits that rap, and spirits that knock, and spirits that write, and numerous others that perform as great a variety of other things. Who can tell how many spirits the Lord has? Perhaps the rapping spirit is one the Lord has sent. The Apostle in one place enumerates up spirits of God. In another place he says, "Try the spirits for many false prophets are gone out into the world." He also speaks of three spirits like frogs, that are the spirits of devils working miracles, which go forth to the kings of the Earth, and of the whole world, to gather them to the battle of that great day of God Almighty. Add to these another quotation, (viz.) "And then shall that wicked be revealed, whom the Lord shall consume with the spirit of his mouth, and shall destroy with the brightness of his coming; even him whose coming is after the working of Satan, with all power, and signs, and lying wonders. For this cause God shall send them strong delusion, that they should believe a lie, that all might be damned who believe not the truth, but had pleasure in unrighteousness." How many spirits the Lord has sent into the world I do not pretend to say, but if any man among you knows, let him tell the number.

You may now inquire if the Lord has any spirits but what are good spirits. Are they not all good that He controls, and sends forth to do His pleasure? How shall we answer this question? Shall we say they are all good, or that some are good, and some are evil? Were I to answer it and leave out all modifications, I would say at once, the Lord has control over all spirits, influences, and powers within the confines of His dominions, whether these dominions extend throughout eternal space, or only occupy a portion of it. All within His dominions, good, and bad, clean, and unclean, noble and ignoble, great or small, every spirit in His dominions is controlled by Him. He gives them their ability, He endows them with the knowledge, power, understanding, and every other attribute they possess according to their worthiness, or unworthiness; all they possess they have received from that God who owns, governs, and controls these dominions of which we form a part. I have answered the question in part.

A thousand different queries will arise in the minds of the people upon this and other subjects, each shade of thought being prompted by the spirit they have received from some quarter. All people have received intelligence, either more or less, or a spirit, or an impression that causes the variety in manner, expression, thought, and action which we see manifested among the multitudes that compose the nations of the Earth. This variety is caused, chiefly, by the spirit they have received.

I observe that natural philosophy, or in other words, the letter killeth, but the spirit giveth life. Now, it is clear to the mind, by the external operations of spirits, there is a tangible something that is invisible to the natural eye. But if a person has the gift of seeing spirits, they see a body, or the body of a spirit. They however do not see with the natural eye. Many are endowed with this natural gift. They are natural seers, and if the spirit should present itself behind them, in an opposite direction to the natural vision, they can see it there as well as in any other position, although they may not turn round to see it. In the visible operations of spirits, we see the affects of an invisible agency. And as varied are the effects we see as the spirits that produce these affects. Among the many spirits that are sent into the world, we read that the Lord God sent his seven spirits into all the Earth—it confounds and puzzles the children of men to know what spirit to follow to secure to themselves the object of their pursuit. Have you ever felt yourselves in a quandary to know the right from the wrong; the course you ought to pursue, and the one you ought to avoid, in order to gain the object of your pursuit, whatever it might be? Your own minds will echo an affirmative to this question, and each one of you can judge of it for yourselves. It is certain that we see, know, and understand that spirits operate upon the people, and there are spirits that operate upon the brute creation. That evil spirits operate upon them you can discover by their actions—by what is manifested through their bodies. The same animals are subject to entirely different operations at different times according to the disposition of the spirit that influences them. Some spirits are so well schooled at the present day, and have obtained so much influence over certain individuals as to take the entire control of their hands and cause them to write in the handwriting of Washington, George the Fourth, Phillip of France, or Joseph Smith the Prophet. Or they can cause a table to move about from place to place; and rap on doors, on casements, or on tables.

Are these the spirits of the Lord, sent forth into all the Earth, or are they not? Are the people governed, and controlled by good spirits or evil ones? Can they tell? These are intricate matters to the human family. It is hard for them to discriminate between the good and the evil. It is impossible for them to know the spirits unless the Lord opens the vision of their minds, to give them understanding of things that are not seen with the natural eye. See the present commotions, and hear the loud rumors of war that are spreading like a dark cloud over the world! Who can understand it? No man or woman that now lives or that ever did live can understand the operations of spirits, why things are as they are, and the cause of the endless variety and the sentiments, feelings, and actions of the inhabitants of the Earth, unless God opens the visions of their minds, and unveils eternity to them, revealing what is in the next, or in the previous world if you please.

But I said we are in eternity. It is true, but could we look beyond this mortality we should see that which is unclothed. We are now clothed upon with mortal flesh which veils the vision of the eternal spirit, that we cannot perceive what is going on in those eternal elements that have passed through a routine of changes until they have secured to themselves an eternal organization both in body and spirit, in the tabernacle, and out of it. Who can understand these deep matters unless the Lord reveals them? No one!

Then Brethren and Sisters it is all important that we make this the subject of our consideration, and deep thought, when we rise from our couch, and it ought to be the last thing contemplated when we retire to rest. Our God—our religion—the Way of Life and Salvation—what the Lord wishes of us, to learn our daily actions, thoughts and feelings, to ascertain if we are pursuing the right path, should be the first and foremost, and most prominent thing in our minds. And for this very potent reason, except the Lord is continually with us, guiding us by the light of His Holy Spirit, we are liable to be overtaken by the enemy, drawn away from the right path, lose our faith and confidence in God, and be led captive by the Devil at his will. How important it is that every Latter-day Saint should live their religion. Is it not necessary that every person should know for themselves that they are governed, and controlled by the spirit of the Lord Jesus?

I will make a remark here that will perhaps reflect a little light on the minds of some. We are taught to ask the Father when we pray, in the name of Jesus Christ. The ancients as well as the modern revelations ascribe honor, praise, and glory to Christ. We render praise, and honor, and thanksgiving to the Fathers, and the Son, and the Holy Ghost; or in other words, *Holy Spirits*. This idea may give you a particle of light. I do not, however, pretend to say how many spirits the Lord has sent forth; but the Holy Spirit that Jesus promised to his disciples, the ancients enjoyed, and so does every man who understands the way of the Lord and has had committed to him the Keys of the Everlasting Priesthood; they are exhorted to seek and enjoy a Holy Spirit. It is not a matter of moment to me how many other spirits there are; but, brethren and sisters, let you and I seek diligently to possess the Holy Spirit of the Lord Jesus, and then if there are myriads of unholy spirits around us we are prepared

79

to discern the difference.

As I observed in the beginning of my remarks, I never know where to begin, or where to leave off in the subject of Salvation. But I wish to say touching the mysterious presentations that are made in this day, let no man marvel at them. If Joseph Smith is a prophet he has told us the truth, and Mormonism is the work of the Most High. We believe the time is fast approaching, according to the words of other prophets, as well as Joseph Smith; and according to the words of Jesus Christ, and His Apostles, when the veil of the covering will be taken from the nations of the Earth, for there has been a veil of darkness and ignorance over them. It will be taken off, and all flesh will behold the glory of God, Saint and Sinner, the righteous and the unrighteous; those that believe in Jesus Christ, and those who do not believe in him, all flesh must see the glory of God, and the hand of God manifested to the degree that every knee shall bow, and every tongue confess to the glory of the Father, and that His son Jesus Christ whom He sent into the world is the Savior of the world. Therefore do not be astonished at the marvelous manifestations from the spirit world, nor be afraid, but let your feelings be calm, for you will see every kind of spirit that ever was in the world manifested among the children of men in the last days. The Priesthood of God is no sooner revived, and in operation, in every age of the world, than the Devil introduces his priesthood in opposition to it; for the Devil has got a priesthood, which many of you have seen illustrated here. He says, "I have got power, and the Earth is mine, and I rule." So he will as long as he can; but there are bounds set to his power. He has power to take natural life, and there his power is at an end. Death will yet be driven from the Earth and him that hath the power of it which is the Devil.

When you see spiritual manifestations that you do not understand be quick to see, quick to hear, and then be quick to understand, but slow to judge. I give you this advice for a safeguard, that you may always be upon safe ground, and not be led away, when you may be distant from the body of the Church. The Elders of Israel in their travels may see a great many mysterious things. A table for instance moving about in a room by means of an invisible force would be a mystery to an Elder uneducated in the principle of spiritual agencies. One of our Elders in St. Louis last summer went to see the operations of the spirit rappers. When he saw a table moving, says he, "That is of the Devil." The table made a bound at him, and he narrowly escaped injury. Had I been placed in his situation I should have commanded it in the name of Jesus Christ to stand still, and I am persuaded it would have obeyed me. I do not know but I might, however, have felt somewhat timid and tried to get out of the way.

It is all right. The Lord will suffer the priesthood of the Devil, and every specious of his hidden mysteries to work. He intends the Devil shall exercise himself, to let the people see his power. So when you see the manifestation of a spirit, never judge whether it is of God or not, unless you understand the spirit.

There is a great deal to be done that might be considered absolutely wrong, but the wrong alone abides with the actors, as for instance, in the case of Judas Iscariot. It was necessary Jesus should be slain, and his blood shed to atone for the sins of the world; but is there any credit due to the man who perpetrated the deed? No, they are cursed for it, because they had the spirit and disposition to commit such an atrocity. They wanted to do it, and they are reaping their reward. So it is in this day, a great many do things that are opposed to every principle of righteousness, and humanity, but it is necessary to purify the Saints. The actors have an evil design, but the design of the Lord is good to His people. In the case of the brothers of Joseph who was sold into Egypt, their design was evil. Had the cause of the jealousy of Joseph's brothers, the dreams Joseph dreamt been left out of his history, it would have been a marvel to following generations why his brethren wished to destroy him. They had evil in their hearts in seeking his destruction, but God designed by that means to save the house of Jacob.

Do I find fault and complain? No. But I say rap away, and write away, and go to all lengths you please for God controls the whole of it. Do you inquire how you are to know whether it is of God or not? You are told here every Sabbath what you must do in order to be saved. Cling close to the Lord; keep His law faithfully, and do as your leaders instruct you continually, and rest not until you get the spirit of the Lord Jesus sufficiently to know and understand things that are out of sight to the natural eye; then nothing can move you.

There is a danger all the time of your being led away from the path of righteousness. There was a few words dropped here this morning which I agree with and yet I would alter them a little. It was concerning men's faith and integrity in serving God, and being determined to serve him though the devil should stand at the door; and that he would not give the ashes of a rye straw for those who would not hold on to the cause of truth whatever should be the consequence. When a man is instructed then is the time to consider him a good Saint, and always on hand to do right, not withstanding the consequences. But wait until he is instructed. There are Elders in this Church, though they cannot be considered unfaithful to their God; yet they are asking for things that is as inconsistent for them to have, as it would be to open a chest of joiner's tools for your little children to play with. Wait brethren until we have time to instruct you, and do not plead like a child for a razor, for you will only cut your fingers if you should get what you ask for. When the child looks upon a finely polished razor, he is dazzled with its shining exterior, and before he knows he draws it through his hand. It is precisely so with many of the Latter-day Saints, they are so anxious to obtain this thing and the other thing which if they could obtain would prove their destruction. Wait until you know how to handle sharp-edged tools. Joseph used to talk about people handling edged tools.

Let me make the application of this to the Elders that go abroad. Brethren do not undertake to handle that [which] you do not understand. There are multitudes of spirits in the world. Everything we see, and have a knowledge of has got its own peculiar spirit, or else there is no life in it. The spirit constitutes the life of everything we see. Is there life in these rocks, and mountains? There is. Then there is a spirit peculiarly adapted to those rocks and mountains. We mark the progress of the growth of grass, flowers, and trees. There is a spirit nicely adapted to the various productions of the vegetable kingdom. There is also a spirit to the different ores of the mineral kingdom, and to every element in existence. And there is a spirit in the Earth. I am inclined at this stage of my remarks to expose my ignorance. I am not aware that any of the philosophers, or astronomers have told you that the Earth is a living creature and breathes as much as you and I do. It is the breathing of the Earth that causes the ebbing and flowing of the tide, and not the moon as some have vainly supposed. The moon has nothing to do with this natural phenomenon. The motion is natural to the Earth and independent of the moon's influence. It is the life in the Earth that forces the internal waters to the summits of some of the highest mountains which often gush out forming lakes, and springs. I am now exposing my ignorance to you astronomers, but I boast not, when I say I know as much about it as you do, and then a little more.

There is no philosopher that can tell how many elements there are, for there is an eternity of them. Go to the forests of Europe and America, and see if you can find two leaves alike. Go into the meadows and see if you can find two blades of grass exactly alike. We can see an eternity of variety, and there is an eternity of elements to cause that variety, and an eternity of spirits and lives to those elements.

Who is the giver of all these—who the proprietor, and controller of them? Let the Lord speak, and He would say it is I the Lord Almighty who governs and controls, and am in and round about all things. As we heard this morning the wealth of this world is nothing for it passeth away. The Lord suffers His creatures to gather together riches to try them, that He may see if they will set their hearts upon them in preference to the more enduring substance. In the end of this life, the rich man, and the king upon his throne with all their splendor will be brought to the same level with the begger [sic]. The Lord throws down kingdoms and governments, but He does not do it as you and I would, in anger. When we look upon the outrages of the wicked upon the innocent and helpless, had we the power and should give way to the impulse of our resentment, we should blast them, and everything around them with utter desolation. But He has His own way of producing their destruction. He establishes a cause that is sure to bring about the affect desired. There is always a cause for every affect we see. For instance, If I were to operate upon that table as the table movers do, and it should move from place to place without any visible assistance, you might be inclined to take off your hats to me and feel awe struck in my presence as a being of superior power—and some might, in their enthusiasm, believe me a god, and might inquire of me when I left the upper regions. The table moves by the force of animal magnetism. That is the term applied to it. No table can move unless it is charged with the life that is in the operators. Animal magnetism is a true principle. It is called by this name because the term belongs to earthly beings, but we should call it the Spirit of Life, the power of the Holy Ghost, or the Life of God in the creature. When the Lord sheds the Holy Ghost upon His children, by means of bringing their bodies in contact with other bodies according to the order established by Him, it is transmitted from one person to another; this you may, if you please, call animal magnetism. When the Lord touches a person, that person is filled with life. The very principle the philosophers call animal magnetism was taught and practiced by Jesus and his Apostles. It has always been taught and you teach it continually to your families, though you may not be aware of it. It is taught largely in the scriptures for instance in the Epistle of James it is said, "Is any sick among you? Let him call for the Elders of the Church, and let them pray over him, anointing him with oil in the name of the Lord" etc. The Lord in the Gospel by Mark, among other things that believers should do, said, "They shall lay hands on the sick and they shall recover." You are full of Life; and if you have the power of God upon you, you are filled with still more Life than the person who has not the power of God upon them. If a person filled with the power of God comes in contact with another person who has a disease upon him, it can be overpowered by the laying on of his hands commanding it at this same time to depart in the name of Jesus Christ; and the sick person will immediately rise from his bed made whole. I have seen instances of this kind a great many times in my life, and so have you. This is what the world calls animal magnetism. It is the Life, that is in everything, and God is the author of it, and in this way He is in everything, and round about everything. This does not refer to his personal tabernacle, it is not in you nor in this room. He is at home; or else on a visit to some of His friends; He is where He wishes to be in His personal tabernacle, but His power is in everything. Devils are as much

83

indebted to Him for their being, as you and I are, both the devils on the Earth, and the devils of Hell; they are all under obligations to Him for their life and being, as any other being there is in Heaven or on Earth. They have made an evil use of the knowledge they have.

When I was young, a Methodist priest whom no person would fellowship because he taught so many new things in his preaching, made a remark that I believe is true. Says he, "Evil is inverted good." Now for Methodists to talk such things was indeed strange; they did not know *that the Devil is as eternal as God*, and coequal with Him in this respect. Evil is inverted good. If you receive the Priesthood, and make an evil use of it, it will make devils of you. If I am a righteous man, I acknowledge the hand of God in all things, that I owe my life and all I am to Him. Suppose I become a devil, do I owe Him any less? No! A perfect trim mounted devil is one who has had the Eternal Priesthood upon him, or else he has not got his proper character. That is the way devils become what they are. Evil must have an end. It may be painful to endure it for the present, but when it has reached its bounds the Lord will put a stop to it. All evil is bounded. The Devil cannot transcend his bounds. Wicked men are bounded in their operations, and they cannot go beyond them. We used to hear Orthodox ministers say [that] when a person died in their youth, that bounds was set to their lives, and they could not live any longer. That is a mistaken idea. The life of man was not to exceed one thousand years, for saith the Lord, in the day you eat of the Tree of the Knowledge of Good and Evil you shall die: and according to the reckoning of the Lord's time, one day with Him is as a thousand years of our time. Men may live if they can until they are as old as Methuselah, but they must die within the thousand years, or in the Lord's day. It is your privilege to live as long as you can in time, within a thousand years, if you can fight the devils, and successfully keep them at bay from taking your body away by death. So it is with everything else, in these lower possessions of our Father in Heaven, and they cannot be passed.

With regard to spirits, I wish to say further. The Lord is taking the covering from the face of the Earth. Joseph Smith commenced the opening of the last dispensation by giving revelation direct from Heaven when the whole world denied the principle. There was not a single orthodox Church or individual that acknowledged it, except here and there a poor out cast, forlorn person, who was considered lunatic, or one led about by the Devil because he believed in the principle. Joseph Smith gave to the world the revelations of God [which were given] to him; but, the world would not receive them. A few favoured ones did. We have had testimony since, sufficient to satisfy both Saint and Sinner that the Devil can make them believe his revelations. I think Andrew Jackson

Davis is a very eminent instrument in this work of the Devil, and there are thousands besides. Revelation from the other world is no new thing. Brother Waterhouse and his family came to this valley by the revelations of a rapping spirit; and I will say the same spirit took him away. If any spiritual rapping brings people into this Church, the same spirit will take them out of it. How are we to know the truth but by keeping the commandments of God. Judge not, brethren but be ready and quick to hear, and discern. Judge no man but cling to the Lord, and to the Holy Spirit of Christ, for the letter killeth, but the spirit giveth life. I would rather a man would only speak five words whose heart is melted under the influence of the Spirit of Truth, than hear a man talk two hours with the eloquence of Cicero. It is not the sounds that issue from the mouth that convinces the people, but it is when the Lord breathes through the man that stands up in His name that produces a convincing, and winning affect upon the people, so as to carry them away in favor of the man, and the principles He advocates. It is your eternal (I dislike to use the term) magnetism that you carry with you, that does the good, even if you never open your mouth.

Vain philosophy, or philosophy without the Spirit of God, will carry you to the Devil. Let us therefore cling to the Lord our Father, and to Jesus Christ our Elder Brother. I have spoken enough at this time. May God bless you. Amen.

"I Propose to Speak Upon a Subject that does not Immediately Concern Yours or My Welfare," A Sermon Delivered on 8 October 1854

(from *The Teachings of President Brigham Young*, Vol. 3, 1852-1854 [Salt Lake City: Collier's Publishing Co., 1987], 343-68)

I propose to speak upon a subject that does not immediately concern yours or my welfare.

I expect in my remarks I shall allude to things that you search after as being absolutely necessary for your salvation in the Kingdom of God. It is true if you are faithful, and diligent there are things that will be fully made known to you in due time—at the proper time, according to the will of the Lord. But so many among us are preaching, lecturing, contemplating upon, and conversing about things away beyond our reach, sometimes I wish to gratify the people by speaking upon these subjects; for I think upon them as well as you; I meditate upon the future and the past as well as you, and I now gratify myself by gratifying the people.

In the first place, I wish to say to all men and women who believe in the Lord Jesus Christ, in the Holy Bible, and in the revelations that have been given at sundry times from the days of Adam to the present, I request that I may have your faith and prayers united with mine that whatever the Lord is pleased to give to the Latter-day Saints through your humble servant this afternoon, He may give it, and that He does not wish to give He may retain, and keep from you. I make this request of the Saints for this reason; I know by my experience, by the visions of eternity that God reveals things to individuals that does not belong to the Church at large at present, or that does not yet belong to the Mass. That I know.

It is natural for the people to desire that which is not beneficial to them. It is so in temporal things, and it is so in things that are spiritual. That I know.

Again, the Lord blesses His people with temporal things in abundance, and wishes to bless them with knowledge and understanding that is not for the world of mankind who do not believe in Him. That I also know.

I may say things this afternoon that does not belong to the world. What if I do? I know the Lord is able to close up every person's mind who have eyes but see not, hearts but do not understand; so I may say what I please with regard to the Kingdom of God on the Earth, for there is a veil over the wicked that they cannot understand the things which are for their peace.

Jesus said at one time, "It is not meet to take the children's bread and give it to dogs." This saying applies to all the dispensations that has been brought forth to the children of men from the days of Adam until now.

I wish the congregation to understand in connection with my sayings thus far, that the Latter-day Saints believe in God the Father, in Jesus Christ His son, in the Holy Ghost[,] God's minister, and in the Celestial Law, or, in other words, the ordinances of the House of God, which, if obeyed, are calculated to save intelligent beings, exalt them, and bring them back into the presence of their God.

I will tell you what I believe still further than this; though I do not pretend to say that the items of doctrine, and ideas I shall advance are necessary for the people to know, or that they should give themselves any trouble about them whatever. I believe in the eternities of worlds, saints, angels, kingdoms, and gods: In eternity without beginning. I believe the gods never had a beginning, neither the formation of matter, and it is without end; it will endure in one eternal round swimming in space, basking, living, and moving in the midst of eternity. All the creations are in the midst of eternity, and that is one eternity, so they move in one eternal round.

Consequently, when you hear philosophers argue the point how the first god came, how intelligence came, how worlds came, and how angels came, they are talking about that which is beyond their conception; about that which never was, and never will be worlds without end. It manifests their folly. It shows they know nothing of such matters; and if they do know some things they have a right to know, there are things they have no right to know. This applies to all classes of mankind.

These are my views with regard to the gods, and eternities. Do you wish I should particularize?

Then, can you by any process of reasoning or argument, tell whether it was an apple that bore the first seed of an apple, or an apple seed that made the first apple? Or, whether it was the seed of a squash that made the first squash, or a squash that bore the first squash seed? Such abstruse questions belong to the philosophy of the world; in reality there never was and never will be a time when there was not both the apple and the apple seed.

(You must be patient with me, as I am not well enough to preach to such a large congregation in the open air, and labor onward without ceasation; you must allow me to take my own time.) I will proceed a little further with my preliminaries before I commence my subject.

Inasmuch as I have taken the ground that there never was a beginning, nor end—I wish to say further; there is an eternity of elements, and an eternity of space and there is no space without a kingdom; neither is there any kingdom without a space. Were the best mathematician to multiply figures from the time he first commenced to learn at five or ten years of age, until he is one hundred years old, or until he has exhausted the capacity of figures known to man, he can then tell no more about the number of the creations of God in comparison than a mere child who knows nothing whatever of figures. There is no beginning, no end; there is no bounds, no time, when the elements will cease to be organized into bodies with all the variety you have a faint specimen of on this Earth.

There are philosophers who believe that this Earth upon which we stand has been in existence for millions of ages. I wish to advance a few items that will open the minds of these philosophers, that they may be like well instructed scribes who treasure up in their hearts the mysteries of the Kingdom of God, the Principles of Eternity. Those who wish to be taught eternal principles, and become true philosophers[,] their minds can reach forth into the unlimited fields of eternity and still discover no end to the boundless expanse, and to its fullness.

There is no necessity of creating a world like this and keeping it in one unalterable state or condition for the express purpose of bringing intelligent beings upon it, while there is an eternity of matter yet to be organized; and when we have lived as long as the best mathematicians among you can figure by millions, billions, trillions, etc., when [you have] exhausted all your wisdom and knowledge, and figures[,] you are then in the midst of eternity where you began.

A true philosopher wishes to grow, and increase continually; he wishes his mind to expand and reach forth, until he can think as God thinks; as angels think, and behold things as God beholds them.

You recollect I told you in the commencement, I should talk about things that did not particularly concern you and me; but the people want to hear something in advance of their present knowlege; they want to find out if there is anything more for us to learn. When you have lived through eternities to come, learning continually, you may then inquire, "Brother Brigham, is there anything more for me to learn." My reply to such an inquiry would be, yes there is an eternity of knowlege yet to learn.

Search after wisdom, get knowlege, and understanding, and forget it not; and be not like the fool whose eyes are in the ends of the Earth, or like the misers who are around us here; they are so craving, and anxious after property, that if they saw a picayune on the wall opposite to me there, they would run over forty dollars to secure that picayune; their eyes are on earthly riches to the neglect of riches that are more enduring.

There are a great many persons who are so anxious to learn about eternity, gods, angels, heavens, and hells, that they neglect to learn the first lessons preparatory to learning the things they are reaching after. They will come short of them.

I wish to speak a few words about the Bible as I have hinted at it. The Ordinances of the Kingdom of God on the Earth are the same to the children of Adam from the commencement to the end of his posterity pertaining to the carnal state on this Earth, and the winding up scene of this mortality. With regard to the Bible we frequently say, we believe the Bible, but circumstances alter cases, for what is now required for the people may not be required of a people that may live a hundred years hence. But I wish you to understand, with regard to the Ordinances of God's House to save the people in the Celestial Kingdom of our God, there is no change from the days of Adam to the present time, neither will there be until the last of his posterity is gathered into the Kingdom of God.

Those who are not acquainted with our doctrine are astonished, and say, "That is strange indeed; we thought no such thing as preaching faith, repentance, and baptism was practiced in ancient, or Old Testament times." I can tell you that no man from the days of Adam, no woman from the days of Eve to this day, who have lived, and who are now living upon the Earth will go into the Kingdom of their Father and God, to be crowned with Jesus Christ, without passing through the same Ordinances of the House of God, you and I have obeyed. I wish you distinctly to understand that.

There are many duties, and callings spoken of in the scriptures, and there are many not written, those for instance which are handed out to you by your President as circumstances require. Those imposed by the President of the Church of God, or by the president of any portion of it, are duties as necessary to be observed as though they were written in the Bible; but these requirements, duties, callings etc. change with the circumstances that surround the people of God. But when you speak of the system of Salvation to bring back the children of Adam and Eve into the presence of our Father and God, it is the same in all ages, among all people, and under all circumstances worlds without end[.] Amen.

I think these preliminaries will satisfy me, and I feel prepared to take my text; it is the words of Jesus Christ, but where they are in the Bible I cannot tell you now, for I have not taken pains to look at them. I have had so much to do, that I have not read the Bible for many years. I used to be a Bible student; I used to read and study it, but did not understand the spirit and meaning of it; I knew well enough how it read. I have read the Book of Mormon, the book of Doctrine [and] Covenants, and other revelations of God which [He] has given to His people in latter times; I

89

look at them, and contrast the spirit and power of them with my faithfulness. My clerks know how much time I have to read, it is difficult for me to snatch time enough even to eat my breakfast and supper, to say nothing of reading. I tell you my text is in the Bible and reads as follows. "And this is Life Eternal, that they might know Thee the only true God, and Jesus Christ whom thou hast sent." I will now put another text with this and then offer a few remarks, it is one of the sayings of the Apostle Paul. "For though there be that are called gods, whether in Heaven, or in Earth (as there be gods many and lords many) but to us there is but one God, the Father, of whom are all things, and we in Him; and one Lord Jesus Christ, by whom are all things, and we by him." This God is the Father of our Lord Jesus Christ and the Father of our spirits. I feel inclined here to make a little scripture. (Were I under the necessity of making scripture extensively I should get Brother Heber C. Kimball to make it, and then I would quote it. I have seen him do this when any of the Elders have been pressed by their opponents, and were a little at a loss; he would make a scripture for them to suit the case, that never was in the Bible, though none the less true, and make their opponents swallow it as the words of an Apostle, or one of the Prophets. The Elder would then say, "Please turn to that scripture, gentlemen and read it for yourselves." No they could not turn to it but they recollected it like the Devil for fear of being caught.) I will venture to make a little [scripture]. This God is the God and Father of our Lord Jesus Christ precisely as He is our Father varying from mortality to immortality, from corruptible to incorruptible, and that is all the difference. He is the God and Father of our Lord Jesus Christ, both body and spirit; and He is the Father of our spirits, and the Father of our flesh in the beginning. You will not dispute the words of the Apostle, that He is actually the God and Father of our Lord Jesus Christ, and the Father of our spirits[.] You may add these words to it, or let it alone, it is all the same to me, that He is not only the Father of our spirits, but also of our flesh, He being the founder of that natural machinery through which we have all obtained our bodies.

Do you wish me to simplify it? Could you have a father without having a grandfather; or a grandfather without having a great grandfather? I never heard of [but] one circumstance that varied from this rule, and that was a son of the Emerald Isle who said he was born of one of his aunts. Does this unlock to your understandings how the Lord Almighty is our natural Father; He set the great machine to working. If you cannot see this truth now, you will if you are faithful, and patient.

I will now quote another scripture. "And hath made of one blood all nations of men for to dwell on all the face of the Earth, and hath determined the times before appointed, and the bounds of their habitations." From these words we understand that God has made of one blood all the inhabitants that are upon the Earth [—all] that has been, and that will be in the future will be of the same blood as those that have been. Do you believe that scripture? I do with all my heart. I believe we are all of one flesh, blood, and bones. We are made of the same matter, the same elements, we have sprung from one mother, Earth. Matter was brought together from the vast eternity of it that exists, and this terra firma upon which we stand was organized, then comes the world of mankind, the beasts, fishes, fowls, and every living thing to dwell upon the Earth after its kind; and vegetation of every kind to support the animal life upon it, until the organization of this world was perfected in all its variety; being brought from the eternity of matter, and prepared for intelligent beings to dwell upon, wherein to prepare themselves to dwell eternally in the presence of their Father and God. Those who keep this their second estate, and do honor to their being, and answer the design of their creation, shall be exalted to inhabit the Earth, and live upon it when it shall be Celestial, and brought back into the presence of God, there to dwell forever and ever.

Before I proceed any further, I will ask a question. And I would like the men, and women of intelligence, to understand and watch well, to see if I keep the thread of truth, whether I preach to you according to the law, and the testimony, according to the words of the Prophets, of Jesus Christ and his Apostles, and according to the words of angels. Mark ye well my sayings, and see if you can pick any flaw in them. If you think you can so do, when you come to the proper place to be corrected, you may then receive instructions that will do you good. The question I wish to ask is simply this; and I put it to all the Elders of Israel, and to all the men and women of intelligence in Israel which pertains to the Kingdom of God on Earth; and if the whole world were before me I would ask them the same question. Can any man, or set of men officiate in dispensing the laws, and administering the ordinances of the Kingdom of God, or of the kingdoms and governments of the world legally, without first obeying those laws, and submitting to those ordinances themselves. Do you understand me? If a foreigner wishes to become a citizen of the United States he must first become subject to this government; must you not first acknowlege and obey the laws of this government? Certainly you must.

Then, to apply this to the Kingdom of God on Earth, and ask yourselves if any man has the power, the influence[,] the right, the authority, to go forth and preach this gospel, and baptise for the remission of sins unless he himself has, in the first place, been baptised, ordained and legally called to that office? What would the Elders of Israel and every other sensible man say to this? They would all decide at once with me, that no man can lawfully officiate in any office in the Kingdom of God, or in the governments of men, he has not been called to, and the authority of which has not been bestowed upon him. I am not going to talk a thousand things to you, but I wish to tell you a few, and desire you to understand them, and connect them together.

There are a few more questions I would like to ask, for the simple reason of bringing the minds of the people to bear upon certain items of principle, and the philosophy of the Kingdom of God on Earth, that they may know how heavenly things are. But I will pass on, and notice some of the texts I have quoted. Before I proceed however, I will put one more question, at the same time I wish you [to] bear in mind the one I have just asked, do not forget th[at] no man has authority to officiate in the ordinances of heavenly or earthly governments only so far as he has obeyed them himself. Now to know the only wise God and Jesus Christ whom He has sent, will put the man, woman[,] congregation, or nation in possession of Eternal Life. Are the hearts of the Latter-day Saints prepared to have Eternal Life given to them in mass, and say there shall be no more apostasy, but bring them all up that they may know and understand the Gods, Eternities[,] Creations, Heavens, Hells, Kingdoms, Thrones, Principalities, and Powers? It cannot be done. The sheep and goats are together; the wheat and the tares are growing together; the good and the bad are mixed; and they must so remain until the time when Jesus Christ will say, "gather my sheep into my fold; gather my wheat into my garner, and let the tares, and chaff, and stubble be burned.["] That is not yet.

Now if you believe what you have heard me say you will believe there is lords many, and gods many; and you will believe that unto us, the inhabitants of this Earth there is but one God with whom we have to do; and according to the tenor of the Bible, we believe there are many[,] very many who have entered into Power, Glory, Might, and Dominion, and are gathering around them Thrones, and have power to organize elements, and make worlds, and bring into existence intelligent beings in all their variety, who if they are faithful and obedient to their calling and creation will in their turn be exalted in Eternal Kingdoms of the Gods. Do you believe that? You and I have only one God to whom we are accountable, so we will let the rest alone, and search after the one we have to do with; let us seek diligently after Him, the very being who commenced this creation. (asked blessing on bread)

We will now make our inquiries with regard to our position with the God with whom we have to do. You will please recollect all ye Elders in Israel, for I want you to be instructed, by my remarks, that you may not fall into errors, that you have tested the question in your own minds with regard to the rights of officiating in ordinances. Now I wish to ask you if you have any conception or idea as to the creation of the world?

"Oh yes," you reply, "A great many of us have a tolerable idea of it, but still there are mysteries we do not understand; there are some things in the Bible about the creation that seem to be dark: we have learned some things in this Kingdom we do not understand, and that do not correspond with the reading of the Bible." Let me open the eyes of your understanding.

There has never been a time when the creations of worlds commenced, they are from eternity to eternity in their creations and redemption. After they are organized they experience the good and the evil; the light, and the dark, the bitter and the sweet, as you and I do. There never was a time when there were not worlds in existence as this world is, and they pass through similar changes in abiding their creation preparatory to exaltation. Worlds have always been in progress, and eternally will be.

Every world has had an Adam, and an Eve: named so, simply because the first man is always called Adam, and the first woman Eve; and the Oldest Son has always had the privilege of being Ordained, Appointed and Called to be the Heir of the Family, if he does not rebel against the Father, and he is the Saviour of the family. Every world that has been created, has been created upon the same principle. They may vary in their varieties, yet the eternity is one; it is one eternal round. These are things that scarcely belong to the best of this congregation. There are items of doctrine, and principles, in the bosom of eternity that the best of the Latter-day Saints are unworthy to receive. If the visions of their minds were opened to look into the vast creations, and gaze upon the Power, and Glory, and Goodness, and Exaltation of the Gods they would exclaim; "Wo is me[,] I am undone, I am of unclean lips."

But we will look at it a little. Do any of you know anything about the creation of this world? "Oh yes, we understand a good deal about it from the account given in the Bible." So you read in the Bible of there being three persons in one god; many religionists in the world believe in a three [in] one god, however, I do not wish to spend time to deliberate upon the notions adopted by the sectarians, the world is full of them. There are lords many and gods many according to the Bible; it does not contradict the doctrine, neither can you find a single passage that does away with that idea.

But let us turn our attention to the God with which we have to do. I tell you simply, He is our Father; the God and Father of our Lord Jesus Christ, and the Father of our spirits. Can that be possible? Yes, it is possible, He is the Father of all the spirits of the human family.

All things are first made spiritual, and brought forth into His kingdom. The spirits of all the human family were begotten by one Father. Now be watchful, for if I have time, and feel able, I shall communicate something in connection with this you are not expecting.

Yes, every son and daughter of Adam according to the flesh can claim one parentage; the Heathen, and the Christian, the Jew and the Gentile, the high and the low, the king and the beggar, the black and the white, all who have sprung from Adam and Eve have one father. "Then you make it out we are brethren and sisters." Certainly for the whole human family are made of one blood of the same material; they are all begotten and brought forth by one parentage, and from one generation to another they are of one flesh and blood, and of one kindred. The God and Father [of] our Lord Jesus Christ is the Father of our spirits.

I began at the end, and shall probably finish at the beginning of my discourse; but it is no matter which end a man begins at, for the first shall be last, and the last first; which proves it is one eternal round; it is one eternity. Eloheim looks round upon the eternity of matter, and said to His associates, and *those* that He was pleased to call upon at that time for His counselors, with regard to the Elements[,] Worlds, Planets, King-doms and Thrones; said He, "Yahovah Michael, see that Eternal Matter on all sides, this way and that way; we have already created Worlds upon Worlds, shall we create another world? Yes, go and organize the elements yonder in space"; not empty space for there is no such thing, once in a while, earth quakes, and the extensive destruction of combustible matter by fire will come nigh making empty space for perhaps the millionth part of a second. "Yahovah Michael go and create a world, make it, organize it, form it; and then put upon it everything in all the variety that you have see[n], that you have been in the habit of being associated with in other worlds, of beasts, birds, fowls, fish, and every insect, and creeping thing, and finally, [when] the whole eternity of element is full of life, bring it together and make of it living creatures."

Yahovah Michael goes and does as he is told. What I am now going to tell you, will no doubt astonish the whole of you. When Yahovah Michael had organized the world, and brought from another kingdom the beasts[,] fish, fowl, and insects, and every tree, and plant with which we are acquainted, and thousands that we never saw, when He had filled the Earth with animal and vegetable life, Michael or Adam goes down to the new made world, and there he stays.

Do you suppose he went there alone. Moses made the Bible to say his wife was taken out of his side, was made of one of his ribs. I do not know anything to the contrary of my ribs being equal on both sides. The Lord knows if I had lost a rib for each wife I have, I should have had none left long ago. Some try to say how many wives the Governor of Utah has, but if they can tell, they can tell more than I can, for I do not know how many I have; I have not counted them up for many years. I did not know how many I had before I left the United States I had so many. I heard that I had ninety. Why bless your souls, ninety is not a

94

beginning. You might ask me if I have ever seen them all; I answer no; I see a few of them I pick up myself here. I have lots, and scores I never see nor shall not until the morning of the resurrection.

Now about the rib. As for the Lord taking a rib out of Adams side to make a woman of, He took one out of my side just as much.

"But, Brother Brigham, would you make it appear that Moses did not tell the truth?"

No not a particle more than I would that your mother did not tell the truth, when she told you that little Billy came from a hollow toad stool. I would not accuse your mother of lying, any more than I would Moses; the people in the days of Moses wanted to know things that was not for them, the same as your children do, when they want to know where their little brother came from, and he answered them according to their folly, the same as you did your children.

Now some will be ready to say, "We always heard these Mormons did not believe the Bible." I believe all the truth that is there and that is enough for me, and for you to believe.

"Then the Lord did not make Adam out of the dust of the earth."

Yes he did, but I have not got to that part of my discourse yet. Adam was made of the dust of the earth.

"Was he made of the dust of this earth."

No[,] but of the dust of the earth where on he was born in the flesh; that is the way he was made; he was made of dust.

"Did the Lord put into him his spirit."

Yes, as the Lord put into you your spirit, he was begotten of a father, and brought forth as you and I were; and so are all intelligent beings brought forth from eternity to eternity. Man was not mad[e] the same as you make an adobe to put in a wall. Moses said Adam was made of the dust of the ground, but he did not say of what ground. I say he was not made of the dust of the ground of this Earth, but he was made of the dust of the earth where he lived, where he honored his calling, believed in his Saviour, or Elder Brother, and by his faithfulness, was redeemed, and got a Glorious Resurrection. All creatures that dwell upon this Earth are made of the elements that compose it; which are organized to see if they will abide their creation, and be counted worthy to receive a resurrection. "What[,] every flesh."

Yes every flesh, for all flesh pertaining to this world is made of the dust of this Earth; it is all made from the same material, according to the will and pleasure of Him who dictates all things. Our bodies are composed of the same material that composes this Earth; they are composed of the water, air, and solid earth, either of which will resolve back to their native fountain.

How many elements are there I do not know anymore than you.

They have never all been classified by science, though scientific gentlemen have tried to do it.

I tell you more, Adam is the Father of our spirits. He lived upon an earth; he did abide his creation, and did honor to his calling and Priesthood; and obeyed his Master or Lord, and probably many of his wives did the same, and they lived, and died upon an earth, and then were resurrected again to Immortality and Eternal Life.

"Did he resurrect himself," you inquire. I want to throw out a few hints upon the resurrection as it seems to come within the circuit of my ideas whether it ought to come within the circuit of my remarks or not. I believe we have already acknowledged the truth established that no person can officiate in any office he has not been subject to himself and been legally appointed to fill. That no person in this Kingdom can officiate in any ordinance he himself has not obeyed; consequently no being who has not been resurrected posesses the Keys of the Power of Resurrection. That you have been told often. Adam therefore was resurrected by some one who had been resurrected.

I will go a little further with this lest some of you will be querying, doubting, and philosophizing this away. It is true, Jesus said "I lay down my life that I might take it again. No man taketh it from me, but I lay it down of myself. I have power to lay it down, and I have power to take it again." I do not doubt the power of Christ; but did he prove that in his resurrection? No. But it is proved that an angel came and rolled away the stone from the door of the sepulchre, and did resurrect the body of the Son of God.

"What angel was this."

It is no[t] for me to say. I do not know him. If I ever did know him it is so long since I have entirely forgotten who it was. That Jesus had power to lay down his life, and power to take it up again I do not dispute. Neither do I dispute, but what an angel came, that was sent by the Father of our Lord Jesus Christ, to roll away the stone from the sepulchre, and resurrect the Son of God. Suffice it to say that he was some character who had himself been resurrected.

"Is there any further proof with regard to this sacred order of the Kingdom of God on the Earth."

Oh yes, you can find it in all the scriptures. For instance when the Saviour appeared to Paul of Tarsus, on the road, in answer to the question, "Lord what wilt thou have me do," he was told to go into the city of Damascus, and it should be told him there what to do. In the mean [time] one Ananias was sent to him, who Baptized and Ordained him. Jesus would not do this, because he had servants on Earth whose special duty it was to administer these ordinances.

Again the angel that appeared to Cornelius would not operate in the ordinances of the Gospel, but told him to send men to Joppa to the house of one Simon the Tanner, and call for one Peter etc. whose duty it was to do it, he being called and ordained to that power. Many more instances of this kind might be quoted but the above will suffice to illustrate the principle.

Now, many inquiries will be made about the Saviour, such as, "Who is he? Is he the Father of Adam? Is he the god of Adam? [']When Christ has finished his labor and presented it to his father, then he, Adam will recieve a fullness.['"] That is all easily understood by me. He cannot receive a fullness of the kingdoms He has organized until they are completed. If He sends His servants off to the right and to the left to perform a certain labor[,] His kingdom is not complete, until His ministers have accomplished everything to make His kingdom complete and returned home again.

Many inquire, who is this Saviour? I will tell you what I think about it, and as the [Southerners] say I reckon, and as the Yankees say I guess; but I will tell you what I reckon. I reckon that Father Adam was a resurrected being, with his wives and posterity, and in the Celestial Kingdom they were crowned with Glory[,] Immortality and Eternal Lives, with Thrones, Principalities and Powers: and it was said to him[, "]It is your right to organize the elements; and to your Creations and Posterity there shall be no end, but you shall add Kingdom to Kingdom, and Throne to Throne; and still behold the vast eternity of unorganized matter.["]

Adam then was a resurrected being; and I reckon,

Our spirits and the spirits of all the human family were begotten by Adam, and born of Eve.

"How are we going to know this?"

I reckon it.

And I reckon that Adam came into the Garden of Eden, and did actually eat of the fruit that he himself planted; and I reckon there was a previous understanding, and the whole plan was previously calculated, before the Garden of Eden was made, that he would reduce his posterity to sin, misery, darkness, wickedness, wretchedness, and to the power of the Devil, that they might be prepared for an Exaltation, for without this they could not receive one.

I reckon that all things were first made spiritual preparatory to the natural organization. "What was the use of all this[,] could not spirits be happy?" Yes as far as they could. These Indians that roam upon the plains, and upon the mountains are comparatively happy in their degraded condition, because they do not know the comforts of civilized life. They can lay upon the ground; pull up sage brush to form a temporary shield against the cold, and get plenty of lizards, and crickets to eat, and they are happy. We would want a comfortable house to live in and something comfortable to eat; something that is suited to our nature, ability, taste, and appetite. We would not be happy and satisfied short of that. So our spirits are as happy as they know how to be. Were you now to live without a house you could not be happy; neither could the spirit be happy without a tabernacle which is the house of the spirit. Whe[n] the spirit enters the body it is pure, and good, and if the body would be subject to the spirit it would always be taught to do the will of the Father in Heaven. But the spirit is interwoven with the flesh and blood; it is subjected to the body, consequently Satan has power over both. I reckon the Father has been through all this.

Do you recollect what I told the brethren who came across the plains this season, when they were perplexed by their oxen; and were calling upon God to give you grace to perform the labor which lay before you, He could not sympathize with you, or know the nature of your trials if He had not passed through the same Himself. He knew just as much about crossing the plains, and the trials connected with it as any of us.

The inquiry will arise, among those who are strenuous, and tenacious for the account given by Moses, as to Adam.

"Did not Adam die."

Yes he died.

"Does not the Bible say he died."

I do not know nor care, but I think it would be hard I think to find where he died; or where Moses died though I have no doubt Moses died, and Adam also; how? Just as you and I have to die, and be laid away in the bowels of Mother Earth; that, however, Moses did not see fit to tell us.

Adam planted the Garden of Eden, and he with his wife Eve partook of the fruit of this Earth, until their systems were charged with the nature of Earth, and then they could beget bodies, for their spiritual children. If the spirit does not enter into the embryo man that is forming in the womb of the woman, the result will be false conception, a living, intelligent being cannot be produced. Adam and Eve begat the first mortal bodies on this Earth, and from that commencement every spirit that was begotten in eternity for this Earth will enter bodies thus prepared for them here, until the winding up scene, and that will not be until the last of these spirits enters an earthly tabernacle.

Then I reckon that the children of Adam and Eve married each other; this is speaking to the point. I believe in sisters marrying brothers, and brothers having their sisters for wives. Why? Because we cannot do otherwise. There are none others for me to marry but my sisters.

"But yo[u would] not pretend to say you would marry your father and mothers daughter."

If I did not I would marry another of my sisters that lives over in another garden; the material of which they are organized is just the same; there is no difference between them, and those who live in this garden. Our spirits are all brothers and sisters, and so are our bodies; and the opposite idea to this has resulted from the ignorant, and foolish traditions of the nations of the Earth. They have corrupted themselves with each other, and I want them to understand that they have corrupted their own flesh, blood, and bones; for they are of the same flesh, blood, and bones, as all the family of the Earth.

I am approaching the subject of our marriage relations Brother Hyde lectured upon, but I shall not have time, or strength to say much about this. But, I reckon that Father Adam, and Mother Eve had the children of the human family prepared to come here and take bodies; and when they come to take bodies, they enter into the bodies prepared for them, and that body gets an exaltation with the spirit, when they are prepared to be crowned in Father[']s Kingdom.

"What, into Adam's Kingdom?"

Yes.

As to my talking what I want to say at this time I shall not do it. I am exhausting myself; I have to speak loud, and it is hard labor.

I tell you, when you see your Father in the Heavens, you will see Adam; when you see your Mother that bear your spirit, you will see Mother Eve. And when you see yourselves there you have gained your Exaltation; you have honored your calling here on the Earth; your body has returned to its mother Earth; and somebody has broken the chains of death that bound you, and given you a resurrection.

How are you going to get your resurrection? You will get it by the President of the Resurrection pertaining to this generation, and that is Joseph Smith Junior. Hear it all ye ends of the Earth; if ever you enter into the Kingdom of God it is because Joseph Smith let you go there. This will apply to Jews and Gentiles, to the bond, and free; to friends and foes; no man or woman in this generation will get a resurrection and be crowned without Joseph Smith says so. The man who was martyred in Carthage Jail [in the] State of Illinois holds the Keys of Life and Death to this generation. He is the President of the Resurrection in this Dispensation and he will be the first to rise from the dead. When he has passed through it, then I reckon the Keys of Resurrection will be committed to him. Then he will call up his Apostles. You know I told you last conference I was an Apostle of Joseph Smith; and if faithful enough I expect Joseph will resurrect the Apostles; and when they have passed through the change, and received their blessings, I expect he will commit to them the Keys of the Resurrection, and they will go on resurrecting the Saints, every man in his own order.

I want to say a little more about marriage relations, so that you may understand what my views are. When you get your resurrection, you are not yet exalted; but by and by, the Lord Jesus Christ, our Elder Brother, the Saviour of the world, the Heir of the Family; when he has put down Satan, and destroyed death; then he will say, come let us go home into the presence of the Father.

What will become of the world then? It will be baptized with fire. I[t] has been baptized with water, and it will then be cleansed by fire, and become like a sea of glass, and be made Celestial; and Jesus Christ our Elder Brother will take the whole Earth, with all the Saints and go with them to the Father even to Adam; and you will continue to receive more and more Intelligence, Glory, Exaltation, and Power.

I want to tell you a thing with regard to parents, wives, brothers and sisters etc. The time will come when it will be told where this man, and that woman shall be placed; The real blood of Joseph will be selected out from among the tribes of Israel, and every man, and woman will be put in their places, and stand in their order where the Lord designs them to be. When you get back into the presence of God, and the Lord should say ["]Who have you brought with you?["] Your reply would be, ["]My wife and children;" but in reality you have only with you your brothers and sisters. The Father would say, "These are my children.["] When you meet your Father in Heaven you will know Him, and realize that you have lived with Him, and rested in His bosom for ages gone passed, and He will hail you as His sons and daughters, and embrace you, and you will embrace Him, and ["]Hallelujah[,] thank God I have come to Father again, I have got back home["] will resound through the Heavens. There are ten thousand things connected with these ideas. You see the human family of every shade of color between black and white. I could stand here and tell you what I reckon but it would take an age for me to tell you all there is about it.

We have all come from one father even Adam, both the black and the white, the grizzled and the gray; the noble, and the ignoble; and the time will come, when they will all come back again into His presence. When they have behaved themselves, and proved faithful to their calling, and to their God the curse will be removed, from every class, and nation of men that desires to work the work of God. This [has] been told you[,] that saviours would come upon Mount Zion, and judge the Mount of Esau. Let me read it for you, ["]There shall saviours come upon Mount Zion, and *Save* the Mount of Esau.["] What does gentile signify? Disobedience. What does Israel signify? Obedience. What is the name of the first man[?] Adam, which signifies first man, and Eve signifies first woman. And when Michael the Archangel shall sound his trumph and the Ancient of Days shall come, all things that we have once been familiar with will come back again to our memory.

100

In our marriage relations here we are marrying our brothers, and our sisters. As to a man having more wives than one, this is startling indeed to the traditions of the people. With regard to it being the law of the Lord for a man to have only one wife, or for a man to have no wife[,] it is no such thing, all that rests in the traditions of the people, and in the doings of legislative bodies; that is all there is about wives in the world as to their having many or none. It is corruption for men to deny the truth; for men to work iniquity, to defile themselves, and to betray the innocent.

If there are any of my friends who do not belong to the Church here, I want to tell you one thing. I will take all the sin there is before God and angels in men having one wife, two wives, ten, or fifty wives, that will use them well, upon my own shoulders, if they will acknowledge them, support them, raise children by them, and bring them up as well as they know how; I say I will take all the sins there is in this, of the whole of the Latter-day Saints, and place them with one sin of you poor devils, who when you were young men courted that poor innocent girl, and made her believe you would marry her, then got her in the family way and left her to the wide world, you poor curses. This one sin of yours will weigh down all the sins of the Latter-day Saints together, and go down about enough for you to be damned in the bottomless pit; while the *Elders of Israel* will be exalted among the Gods. There are scores, and hundreds, and thousands of these poor girls upon the streets of the cities of the United States.

["]Why Governor did you ever see any of them?["] Yes lots of them; in that neighborhood, and in the other neighborhood[.] I have found respectable families, where a young mechanic, a merchant, a lawyer, or a farmer, or some other poor miserable wretch fit for nothing but the fire of Hell, would insinuate themselves into the family[,] court the daughter, win her affections, deceive her, and then forsake her, and then boast of your achievements and rejoice over your success; but weep and howl for the miseries that shall come upon you, you poor damned wretches. I want to cut their damned throats and I will if I catch any of them doing it here. I should hold myself guilty before God and angels if I did not sweep the Earth of such a wretch. I will not ask the Lord to do a dirty trick I would not do myself. Let them prowl around my daughters, and I will slay them, yes, as fast as I can come to them. What more will I do? When I find a young woman caught in this snare, I will take her to my house, and say, you shall have a home with me and my family.

I only know these iniquities by observation[.] I was never of such sins; the wickedest day I ever saw I would not betray an innocent female, but instead of prostituting them, I would tell them how to do right, and teach them the way of Life and Salvation, and see them safe in the

Kingdom of God if they would obey my counsel. But you will take a poor helpless, innocent creature, and lead the unsuspecting victim nigh to the alter of marriage, and then ruin the innocent lamb[,] you poor cursed gentiles, go and weep, and howl. In New York alone there is over eighteen hundred prostitutes licensed in that city, to corrupt themselves for Hell; and I want to tell every man that is going to Hell, that it is full of such creatures, so full that their elbows stick out of the windows.

Instead of creating such an awful state of society as this presents, we take to ourselves wives, acknowlege them, raise their children, school them, and try to teach them the way of Salvation. Let me tell you what they should [do] in the city of New York, that holy, that righteous city, and to other cities, where there are thousands of licensed house[s] of ill fame, besides thousands of private ones that are not licensed but go under different appel[l]ations. They should set fire to every poor filthy debaucher, and collect, the illegitimate children, as the[y] are called, that are running the streets, and wash them, and school them, and teach them righteousness, and not suffer them to mingle with those that mingle unlawfully together. Also take the women, and wash them, clean, and put them to work, at spinning[,] weaving, and at other useful employment in the country. As they now exist they want to die[,] they have lost their character, and nothing appears in the future for them but a life of wretchedness of the lowest grade. There are thousands of these poor women who would bless the first person who would kill them. They do not wish to kill themselves, but live they must and disguise their real feelings.

Let the world cleanse themselves before they talk about Utah; and when they get sanctified, and become purer than we are, they may come and give us a few [lessons] upon purity. It is a subject I do not wish to name, but in my remarks I seemed to run on to it, and could not well avoid it.

I wish you to understand well the position I have taken, and the nature of the remarks I have made. Profit by them, both saints and sinners. You have had things laid before you that does not belong to the world, nor to men and women, who calculate to apostatize. They belong to the wise; to those who are serving God with all their hearts. Now let me say to the wicked in heart, you cannot remember a word of this discourse unless you remember it in the Lord. I might reveal all there is in eternity, and those who have not their hearts on righteousness would know nothing about it, nor be in the least instructed.

I commenced with Father Adam in his resurrected state, noticed our spiritual state, then our temporal, or mortal state, and traveled until I got back to Father Adam again. After considering all this[,] what have you seen that make[s] it appear we are not brethren and sisters[?] Does it appear that we are not because we are commanded to multiply and replenish the Earth? You think when you run into grand children and great grand children etc. that by and by there will be no connection. They are just as much connected in spirit and body, in flesh, blood, and bone, as your children are that you bear off your own body.

This is something pertaining to our marriage relation. The whole world will think what an awful thing it is. What an awful thing it would be if the Mormons should just say we believe in marrying brothers and sisters. Well we shall be under the necessity of doing it, because we cannot find anybody else to marry. The whole world are at the same thing, and will be as long as man exists upon the Earth.

I feel as though I had said enough. I have talked long enough for my own good; and we shall bring our conference to a close. If there is anything to be done.

I would bless you all so that you would be saved if I had the power—I have the power to bless all the faithful and I do bless you in the name of Jesus Christ. Amen.

{10}

"To Know God is Eternal Life—
God the Father of Our Spirits and Bodies—
Things Created Spiritually First—
Atonement by Shedding of Blood,"
A Sermon Delivered on 8 February 1857

(from *Journal of Discourses*, 26 vols.
[Liverpool: Latter-day Saints' Book Depot, 1855-86], 4:215-21)

I feel myself somewhat under obligations to come here and talk to the people, inasmuch as I have absented myself for some time, and others have occupied this stand.

Perhaps I will not talk to you long, but I desire to pursue some of the ideas that brother Cummings has just laid before you. I can testify that every word he has spoken is true, even to the advancement of the Saints at a "snail gallop." Though that is rather a novel expression, still it is true, as well as all the rest which he advanced.

The items that have been advanced are principles of real doctrine, whether you consider them so or not. It is one of the first principles of the doctrine of salvation to become acquainted with our Father and our God. The Scriptures teach that this is eternal life, to "know Thee, the only true God, and Jesus Christ whom thou hast sent;" this is as much as to say that no man can enjoy or be prepared for eternal life without that knowledge.

You hear a great deal of preaching upon this subject; and when people repent of their sins, they will get together, and pray and exhort each other, and try to get the spirit of revelation, try to have God their Father revealed to them, that they may know Him and become acquainted with Him.

There are some plain, simple facts that I wish to tell you, and I have but one desire in this, which is, that you should have understanding to receive them, to treasure them up in your hearts, to contemplate upon these facts, for they are simple facts, based upon natural principles; there is no mystery about them when once understood.

I want to tell you, each and every one of you, that you are well acquainted with God our heavenly Father, or the great Eloheim. You are all well acquainted with Him, for there is not a soul of you but what has lived in His house and dwelt with Him year after year; and yet you are seeking to become acquainted with Him, when the fact is, you have merely forgotten what you did know. I told you a little last Sabbath about forgetting things.

There is not a person here to-day but what is a son or a daughter of that Being. In the spirit world their spirits were first begotten and brought forth, and they lived there with their parents for ages before they came here. This, perhaps, is hard for many to believe, but it is the greatest nonsense in the world not to believe it. If you do not believe it, cease to call Him Father; and when you pray, pray to some other character.

It would be inconsistent in you to disbelieve what I think you know, and then to go home and ask the Father to do so and so for you. The Scriptures which we believe have taught us from the beginning to call Him our Father, and we have been taught to pray to Him as our Father, in the name of our eldest brother whom we call Jesus Christ, the Saviour of the world; and that Saviour, while here on earth, was so explicit on this point, that he taught his disciples to call no man on earth father, for we have one which is in heaven. He is the Saviour, because it is his right to redeem the remainder of the family pertaining to the flesh on this earth, if any of you do not believe this, tell us how and what we should believe. If I am not telling you the truth, please to tell me the truth on this subject, and let me know more than I do know. If it is hard for you to believe, if you wish to be Latter-day Saints, admit the fact as I state it, and do not contend against it. Try to believe it, because you will never become acquainted with our Father, never enjoy the blessings of His spirit, never be prepared to enter into His presence, until you most assuredly believe it; therefore you had better try to believe this great mystery about God.

I do not marvel that the world is clad in mystery, to them He is an unknown God; they cannot tell where He dwells nor how He lives, nor what kind of a being He is in appearance or character. They want to become acquainted with His character and attributes, but they know nothing of them. This is in consequence of the apostacy that is now in the world. They have departed from the knowledge of God, transgressed His laws, changed His ordinances, and broken the everlasting covenant, so that the whole earth is defiled under the inhabitants thereof. Consequently it is no mystery to us that the world knoweth not God, but it would be a mystery to me, with what I now know, to say that we cannot know anything of Him. We are His children.

To bring the truth of this matter close before you, I will instance your fathers who made the first permanent settlement in New England. There are a good many in this congregation whose fathers landed upon Plymouth Rock in the year 1620. Those fathers began to spread abroad; they had children, those children had children, and their children had children, and here are we their children. I am one of them, and many of this congregation belong to that class. Now ask yourselves this simple question upon natural principles, has the species altered? Were not the people who landed at Plymouth Rock the same species with us? Were they not organized as we are? Were not their countenances similar to ours? Did they not converse, have knowledge, read books? Were there not mechanics among them, and did they not understand agriculture, &c. as we do? Yes, every person admits this.

Now follow our fathers further back and take those who first came to the island of Great Britain, were they the same species of beings as those who came to America? Yes, all acknowledge this; this is upon natural principles. Thus you may continue and trace the human family back to Adam and Eve, and ask, "are we of the same species with Adam and Eve?" Yes, every person acknowledges this; this comes within the scope of our understanding.

But when we arrive at that point, a vail is dropt, and our knowledge is cut off. Were it not so, you could trace back your history to the Father of our spirits in the eternal world. He is a being of the same species as ourselves; He lives as we do, except the difference that we are earthly, and He is heavenly. He has been earthly, and is of precisely the same species of being that we are. Whether Adam is the personage that we should consider our heavenly Father, or not, is considerable of a mystery to a good many. I do not care for one moment how that is; it is no matter whether we are to consider Him our God, or whether His Father, or His Grandfather, for in either case we are of one species—of one family—and Jesus Christ is also of our species.

You may hear the divines of the day extol the character of the Saviour, undertake to exhibit his true character before the people, and give an account of his origin, and were it not ridiculous, I would tell what I have thought about their views. Brother Kimball wants me to tell it, therefore you will excuse me if I do. I have frequently thought of mules, which you know are half horse and half ass, when reflecting upon the representations made by those divines. I have heard sectarian priests undertake to tell the character of the Son of God, and they make him half of one species and half of another, and I could not avoid thinking at once of the mule, which is the most hateful creature that ever was made, I believe. You will excuse me, but I have thus thought many a time.

Now to the facts in the case; all the difference between Jesus Christ and any other man that ever lived on the earth, from the days of Adam until now, is simply this, the Father, after He had once been in the flesh, and lived as we live, obtained His exaltation, attained to thrones, gained the ascendancy over principalities and powers, and had the knowledge and power to create—to bring forth and organize the elements upon natural principles. This He did after His ascension, or His glory, or His eternity, and was actually classed with the Gods, with the beings who create, with those who have kept the celestial law while in the flesh, and again obtained their bodies. Then He was prepared to commence the work of creation, as the Scriptures teach. It is all here in the Bible; I am not telling you a word but what is contained in that book.

Things were first created spiritually; the Father actually begat the spirits, and they were brought forth and lived with Him. Then He commenced the work of creating earthly tabernacles, precisely as He had been created in this flesh himself, by partaking of the course material that was organized and composed this earth, until His system was charged with it, consequently the tabernacles of His children were organized from the coarse materials of this earth.

When the time came that His first-born, the Saviour, should come into the world and take a tabernacle, the Father came Himself and favoured that spirit with a tabernacle instead of letting any other man do it. The Saviour was begotten by the Father of His spirit, by the same Being who is the Father of our spirits, and that is all the organic difference between Jesus Christ and you and me. And a difference there is between our Father and us consists in that He has gained His exaltation, and has obtained eternal lives. The principles of eternal lives is an eternal existence, eternal duration, eternal exaltation. Endless are His kingdoms, endless His thrones and His dominions, and endless are His posterity; they never will cease to multiply from this time henceforth and forever.

To you who are prepared to enter into the presence of the Father and the Son, what I am now telling will eventually be no more strange than are the feelings of a person who returns to his father's house, brethren, and sisters, and enjoys the society of his old associates, after an absence of several years upon some distant island. Upon returning he would be happy to see his father, his relatives and friends. So also if we keep the celestial law when our spirits go to God who gave them, we shall find that we are acquainted there and distinctly realize that we know all about the world.

Tell me that you do not know anything about God! I will tell you one thing, it would better become you to lay your hands upon your mouths and them in the dust, and cry, "unclean, unclean."

Whether you receive these things or not, I tell you them in simplicity. I lay them before you like a child, because they are perfectly simple. If you see and understand these things, it will be by the Spirit of God; you will receive them by no other spirit. No matter whether they are told to you like the thunderings of the Almighty, or by simple conversation; if you enjoy the Spirit of the Lord, it will tell you whether they are right or not.

I am acquainted with my Father. I am as confident that I understand in part, see in part, and know and am acquainted with Him in part, as I am that I was acquainted with my earthly father who died in Quincy, Illinois, after we were driven from Missouri. My recollection is better with regard to my earthly father than it is in regard to my heavenly Father; but as to knowing of what species He is, and how He is organized, and with regard to His existence, I understand it in part as well as I understand the organization and existence of my earthly father. That is my opinion about it, and my opinion to me is just as good as yours is to you; and if you are of the same opinion you will be satisfied as I am.

I know my heavenly Father and Jesus Christ whom He has sent, and this is eternal life. And if we will do as we have been told this morning, if you will enter into the Spirit of your calling, into the principles of securing to yourselves eternal lives, eternal existence, eternal exaltation, it will be well with you. But if, after being put into a carriage and placed upon the road, after having everything prepared for the journey that infinite wisdom could devise, this people stroll into the swamp, get into the woods among the brambles and briars, and wander around until night overtakes them, I say, shame on such people.

I am ashamed to talk about a reformation, for if you have entered into the spirit of your religion, you will know whether these things are so or not. If you have the spirit of your religion and have confidence in you, walk along and continue to do so, and secure to yourselves the life before you, and never let it be said, from this time henceforth, that you have wakened out of your sleep, from the fact that you are always awake.

We talk about the reformation, but recollect that you have only just commenced to walk in the way of life and salvation. You have just commenced in the career to obtain eternal life, which is that which you desire, therefore you have no time to spend only in that path. It is straight and narrow, simple and easy, and is an Almighty path, if you will keep in it. But if you wander off into swamps, or into brambles, and get into darkness, you will find it hard to get back.

Brother Cummings told you the truth this morning with regard to the sins of the people. And I will say that time will come, and is now nigh at hand, when those who profess our faith, if they are guilty of what some of this people are guilty of, will find the axe laid at the root of the tree, and they will be hewn down. What has been must be again, for the Lord is coming to restore all things. The time has been in Israel under the law of God, the celestial law, or that which pertains to the celestial law, for it is one of the laws of that kingdom where our Father dwells, that if a man was found guilty of adultery, he must have his blood shed, and that is near at hand. But now I say, in the name of the Lord, that if this people will sin no more, but faithfully live their religion, their sins will be forgiven them without taking life.

You are aware that when brother Cummings came to the point of loving our neighbours as ourselves, he could say yes or no as the case might be, that is true. But I want to connect it with the doctrine you read in the Bible. When will we love our neighbour as ourselves? In the first place, Jesus said that no man hateth his own flesh. It is admitted by all that every person loves himself. Now if we do rightly love ourselves, we want to be saved and continue to exist, we want to go into the kingdom where we can enjoy eternity and see no more sorrow nor death. This is the desire of every person who believes in God. Now take a person in this congregation who has knowledge with regard to being saved in the kingdom of our God and our Father, and being exalted, one who knows and understands the principles of eternal life, and sees the beauty and excellency of the eternities before him compared with the vain and foolish things of the world, and suppose that he is overtaken in a gross fault, that he has committed a sin that he knows will deprive him of that exaltation which he desires, and that he cannot attain to it without the shedding of his blood, and also knows that by having his blood shed he will atone for that sin, and be saved and exalted with the Gods, is there a man or woman in this house but what would say, "shed my blood that I may be saved and exalted with the Gods?"

All mankind love themselves, and let these principles be known by an individual, and he would be glad to have his blood shed. That would be loving themselves, even unto an eternal exaltation. Will you love your brothers or sisters likewise, when they have committed a sin that cannot be atoned for without the shed[d]ing of their blood? Will you love that man or woman well enough to shed their blood? That is what Jesus Christ meant. He never told a man or woman to love their enemies in their wickedness, never. He never intended any such thing; his language is left as it is for those to read who have the Spirit to discern between truth and error; it was so left for those who can discern the things of God. Jesus Christ never meant that we should love a wicked man in his wickedness.

Now take the wicked, and I can refer to where the Lord had to slay every soul of the Israelites that went out of Egypt, except Caleb and Joshua. He slew them by the hands of their enemies, by the plague, and by the sword, why? Because He loved them, and promised Abraham that He would save them. And He loved Abraham because he was a friend to his God, and would stick to Him in the hour of darkness, hence He promised Abraham that He would save his seed. And He could save them upon no other principle, for they had forfeited their right to the land of Canaan by transgressing the law of God, and they could not have atoned for the sin if they had lived. But if they were slain, the Lord could bring them up in the resurrection, and give them the land of Canaan, and He could not do it on any other principle.

I could refer you to plenty of instances where men have been righteously slain, in order to atone for their sins. I have seen scores and hundreds of people for whom there would have been a chance (in the last resurrection there will be) if their lives had been taken and their blood spilled on the ground as a smoking incense to the Almighty, but who are now angels to the devil, until our elder brother Jesus Christ raises them up—conquers death, hell, and the grave. I have known a great many men who have left this Church for whom there is no chance whatever for exaltation, but if their blood had been spilled, it would have been better for them. The wickedness and ignorance of the nations forbid this principle's being in full force, but the time will come when the law of God will be in full force.

This is loving our neighbour as ourselves; if he needs help, help him; and if he wants salvation and it is necessary to spill his blood on the earth in order that he may be saved, spill it. Any of you who understand the principles of eternity, if you have sinned a sin requiring the shedding of blood, except the sin unto death, would not be satisfied nor rest until your blood should be spilled, that you might gain that salvation you desire. That is the way to love mankind.

Christ and Belial have not become friends; they have never shaken hands; they never have agreed to be brothers and to be on good terms; no, never; and they never will, because they are diametrically opposed to each other. If one conquers, the other is destroyed. One or the other of them must triumph and utterly destroy and cast down his opponent. Light and darkness cannot dwell together, and so it is with the kingdom of God.

Now, brethren and sisters, will you live your religion? How many hundreds of times have I asked you that question? Will the Latter-day Saints live their religion? I am ashamed to say anything about a reformation among Saints, but I am happy to think that the people called Latter-day Saints are striving now to obtain the Spirit of their calling and religion. They are just coming into the path, just waking up out of their sleep. It seems as though they are nearly all like babies; we are but children in one sense. Now let us begin, like children, and walk in the straight and narrow path, live our religion, and honour our God.

With these remarks, I pray the God of Israel to bless you forever and ever, for you are the best people on earth. I can say that I am happy that you are doing so well as you are. Continue to increase in all the graces of God's Spirit until the day of His coming, which I desire with all my heart, in the name of Jesus Christ. Amen.

11

A Series of Instructions and Remarks by President Brigham Young, at a Special Council, Tabernacle, March 21, 1858

(Great Salt Lake City, 1858)

I do not know but what I would correctly portray the minds and feelings of many of the people by saying that they do not take much thought in regard to the situation and circumstances we are under, nor of the propriety and policy of our movements.

God has led this people; he has sent forth the new and everlasting covenant. He restored the priesthood to the children of men, and called upon Joseph Smith, jun., to be the first Elder in this church and upon Oliver Cowdery to be the second. From that time until now all persons that have the Spirit of this work have seen and can now see and understand that the hand of the Lord has been with this people and that he has led them all the time. But when men and women so neglect their duty that their minds run into darkness, they are almost universally impressed that this work has been produced by the wisdom of men. Those who have the Spirit of the Lord Jesus Christ: constantly acknowledge the hand of God in leading this people.

We esteemed Joseph our leader. He truly was our leader in one sense,—the leader that we conversed with face to face, but he was not our invisible Leader, for that Leader was and is the Lord Jehovah.

For almost fourteen years this people have been led and directed by the Twelve Apostles, and this people acknowledge that they have been their leaders. This was the universal acknowledgment of the church before we left Nauvoo. When there was a Presidency selected they were taken from the Quorum of the Twelve. They have not left the Quorum, neither have they been cut off, and I am their President. I have never left the Quorum of the Twelve, but have advanced a step in duty and given place to others to act as Apostles, until we come to where Joseph is. The people now and for some years past have acknowledged the First Presidency to be their leaders, and yet there is not a man or woman in this kingdom, who has the Spirit of it, but what fully understands that it is not man that leads them, but it is the Lord Almighty who directs their movements through His servants.

We have the privilege of seeing and speaking to each other, and how easily we can behold the glow of the countenances while we are looking at each other and can get the expression of the eye and receive of the Spirit from each other, to what we can realize when we hold communion or converse with an invisible being. If the First Presidency are led by the Holy Ghost our associates receive of that Spirit, of which you are witnesses, when you converse or associate with us, whether you receive a good spirit or a bad one. You can understand, when you meet a brother or a sister, whether they are possessed of a meek and quiet spirit—of the spirit of intelligence—or not. That is the Spirit of the Lord—that is actually holding communion with the Lord, although it is through a tabernacle.

We acknowledge that we are led by the hand of the Lord, and if he does not lead us we may expect to fall into the ditch. Now the question arises, what is the best policy for this people to adopt? We exclaim at once, it is policy to follow the Lord and his dictations. We acknowledge that, and that is what we wish to do; consequently, according to the best light and intelligence we are in possession of, we will tell you what we think the Lord wishes of us and his policy concerning this people.

I need not now rehearse our drivings, the loss of property, the sufferings of men, women and children, and the waste of life that has occurred in consequence thereof in times past. This is understood. The history of this church is before us and is also before the world, and you can call to mind, at your pleasure, the facts that relate to our past transactions and drivings, our being hunted, killed, peeled, smitten, scattered and finally driven from the Christian world by the Christians.

The policy that I believe the Lord designs concerning this people we can learn by referring to several passages that are written and given to us for our instruction concerning the last days. The word of the Lord to us is, "I will fight your battles, saith the Lord." He has done so, thus far; and he will do so, if we take his counsel. Although we have had to leave our homes several times, and a great many lives have been lost in consequence of the sufferings, yet the Lord has fought our battles. True, he did not preserve Joseph and Hyrum when in the hands of the mob, he has not preserved the lives of all the faithful, but I have acknowledged his hand in the dissolution of our brethren and sisters, and it is right.

I will deviate from my subject a little, and say a few words with regard to br. Joseph that some, perhaps, have not understood. If Joseph Smith, jun., the Prophet, had followed the Spirit of revelation in him he never would have gone to Carthage. Do you understand that? [Voices, 'Yes.'] A great many do, and some do not. Many of the first Elders of this church have a different understanding; they are under the impression that he went there according to his own choice. Joseph intended to go West; he designed to raise a company to come to the very country we now occupy.

112

He said, "I can see life and liberty and salvation in that course, but if I return to give myself up, it is death and darkness to the full; I am like a lamb led to the slaughter," and never for one moment did he say that he had one particle of light in him after he started back from Montrose to give himself up in Nauvoo. This he did through the persuasion of others. I want you all to understand that.

With regard to myself I cannot say what I will do. I do not know precisely in what manner the Lord will lead me, but were I thrown into the situation Joseph was, I would leave the people and go into the wilderness, and let them do the best they could. Will I run from the sheep? No. Will I forsake the flock? No. But if Joseph had followed the revelations in him he would have been our earthly shepherd to-day, and we would have heard his voice and followed the shepherd instead of the shepherd's following the sheep. When the shepherd follows the sheep it reverses the natural order, for the sheep are to follow the shepherd.

I want you to understand that if I am your earthly shepherd you must follow me, or else we shall be separated. As I told the people after Joseph's death, they might cling to the Twelve and receive salvation and be led in the way of truth and holiness, or go to hell if they pleased, for we asked no odds of them. I feel so to-day.

That is the way I feel about many families in the church. A great many parents follow off their children, and men follow their women. For a man to follow a woman is, in the sight of heaven, disgraceful to the name of a man. It is a disgrace for parents to follow their children. I am your leader, Latter Day Saints, and you must follow me; and if you do not follow me you may expect that I shall go my way and you may take yours, if you please. I shall do as the Spirit dictates me. What does it now direct me to dictate to you?

Our enemies are determined to blot us out of existence if they can. Have they done so? No. Long before the Book of Mormon was printed, when Joseph first obtained the plates and commenced the translation of that book, all hell was moved against him, as it is against us to-day. He was but one man, and to oppose him required but a small power of the enemy compared to what it now requires. And as the kingdom of God grows, the enmity of the wicked will increase and extend broader and broader until we shall see the day when the whole wicked portion of mankind is as much opposed to us as any portion of them is now. "We are to be killed," is the constant feeling and cry of our enemies. "You 'Mormons' must be used up, or else you must bow down to the Christianity of the 19th century," say the world. You can further examine, if you choose, and at your leisure, the religions that they profess. You were more or less brought up in them from your youth, and they make me think of a young man's reply in Connecticut to a reformation preacher who was passing by. The young man was splitting wood, and the preacher asked him if he did not wish to get religion. The young man replied, that "he did not know that he did." The preacher then asked him whether he had got religion; he replied, "I do not know whether we have any now, but mother makes the best kind; will you get off from your horse and taste a little?" "Of what does your mother make your religion?" asked the preacher. "She makes it out of New England rum and molasses, and that is the best religion I know of." That is the religion of the day—that is their Christianity.

In connection with this anecdote I will relate a recent statement of modern degeneracy in Berlin, in the kingdom of Prussia. Recruits were wanted for the army, and out of over 12,000 young men who were drafted, only a trifle over 800 were found fit for the service. And yet that is one of the first Christian states that was organized and became a Christian kingdom after the days of the Savior; that is what their religion has done for them.

With respect to keeping men in ignorance I have said to some of the officers of our Government that I wished my brethren to know as much as I do, and as quick as I learn a little more I wish to impart it unto them. I wish this people to know what I know, and I wish that you knew a little more. I not only wish that you were all prophets, but I wish that you were greater prophets than I am, or even br. Heber, and had more than we have of the revelations of Jesus Christ. I have charged the brethren with stupidity, though I do not know that I should complain of them in the least, but really I would like to have this people wake up and know for themselves the things that are of God and the things that are not of God, and know whether they are led in the path of truth and righteousness or in some other way.

Should I take a course to waste life? We are in duty bound to preserve life—to preserve ourselves on the earth—consequently we must use policy and follow in the counsel given us, in order to preserve our lives. Shall we take a course to whip our enemies? or one to let them whip themselves? or shall we go out and slay them now? We have been preparing to use up our enemies by fighting them, and if we take that course and shed the blood of our enemies, we will see the time, and that too not far from this very morning, when we will have to flee from our homes and leave the spoil to them.—That is as sure as we commence the game. If we open the ball upon them by slaying the United States soldiery, just so sure they would be fired with anger to lavishly expend their means to compass our destruction, and thousands, and millions if necessary, would furnish means, if the Government was not able, and turn out and drive us from our homes, and kill us if they could.

The policy the Lord pursued is the reason we were not killed in

Nauvoo. Joseph's going to Carthage did not save this people. I have acknowledged the hand of the Lord in it from the beginning, and say it was right, it was all well enough, but the people would have been just as well off if Joseph had left the country. They succeeded in killing him, and thought they could kill me and br. Kimball and br. Hyde and all the Twelve and Elders of this church, but I told them that they must keep their hands off from Brigham. I promised them that if they put their hands on me to take me prisoner I would send them to hell across lots, God being my helper: I feel so this morning. They have not done that, neither have I employed lawyers; I do my own pleading. With my God and my brethren I am enabled to defend myself, and they dare not put their hands on me.

If they should succeed in slaying a few more of the Elders of this people, they would say, "let us go ahead, we have succeeded in killing Joseph and Hyrum, now let us kill the Twelve." In seeking my life they will have to wait until they kill me, will they not? If they cannot kill me, they would naturally say, "take care how you try to handle the rest of them."

If they do not succeed in killing the first Elders of this church, they will be cautious how they try to put their hands on you. But if they can kill us with impunity they would take you by the hair of the head and draw a knife across your throats, as they wished to serve me after the death of Joseph. But I carried a little tooth-pick with a blade some 18 or 20 inches long and a little over two inches wide, and I said come on, if you want to take me a prisoner. I am ready for you; and I intend to be always on the guard against my enemies. But let us begin a fight with the Government troops, and we shall have to leave our buildings and they will possess them, and I am in favor of leaving them before I am obliged to.

Br. George A. Smith has told us that he loved to come to the mountains—that it was a pleasure trip and as fine a journey as he ever had—and how pleased he was to leave his home in the States, and how he liked this country, and why? Because he was obliged to. Now let us leave before we are obliged to.

A large majority in this congregation have never been driven five times, as some of us have been, and I presume that I could pick out a large number that have never been driven from their homes, and have never been compelled to leave their property. I have had to leave mine five times. 'Did you leave wealth?' Yes, every time. The first time I left the least, the second time I left more, the third time still more, and so on; and now I have more to leave than I left in all the five times.

'Where are you going?' To the deserts and the mountains. There is a desert region in this Territory larger than any of the Eastern States, that no white man knows anything about. Can you realize that? What is the reason you do not know any thing about that region? It is a desert country with long distances from water to water, with wide sandy and alkali places entirely destitute of vegetation and miry when wet, and small, scattering patches of greasewood, and it is a region that the whites have not explored, and where there are but few Indians. There are places here and there in it where a few families could live.

Four years ago this spring we sent Bishop David Evans and a company to go to that desert, for we then had too long neglected to explore it. We wanted to plant settlements there in preparation for this day, for we have had foreshadowings and a promise of the scenery now before us. That company did not accomplish the object of their mission; they were absent a few weeks and went to the first mountain, but they did not go to the mountain where they were sent, and made no settlement. Now we are going to try it again.

Probably there is room in that region for 500,000 persons to live scattered about where there is good grass and water. I am going there, where we should have gone six or seven years ago. Now we are going to see whether the sheep will follow the shepherd. I do not care whether they follow me or not. I am like the man who said he was going to Zion. After br. Hyde had done preaching in a certain place in the East, a Presbyterian priest rose to oppose him, but he could not induce the congregation to be still until he opposed 'Mormonism' though he did not know any more about it than a red dog. Br. Hyde went out, and the people also began to go out, and the priest shouted out, 'those who want to hear "Mormonism" exposed, take your seats, and those who are going to Zion, go out of the door.' The congregation still kept going out and a young man as he neared the door, halloed to the priest, 'we are all going to Zion.' The people may go to Zion, or stay and hear "Mormonism" exposed.

'When are you going to start?' As soon as this snow is off I am going to start part of my family. I am going to a place that I can say to our enemies, 'whither I go you cannot come.' They may come here, and then they will find themselves a great many miles from home and will not want to go much further.

'How many are you going to call?' Only five hundred families to leave this city immediately, though more may go now, if they wish to. 'But,' says one, 'I have no team.' That is so much the better—you have so much less to care for. The only difficulty I can see is that we have too much provisions and goods to be convenient for us at this time. Says one, 'I would like to go, but I have a wife and three or four children, and nothing else.' All the better for that; you and your wife can take a handcart, and let the children walk. 'How can we go without provision?'

We are going to send that. Br. Wells and br. Sharp will take all the teams that have been drawing rock, and we are going to get as many more as we can, and send out an ox train. John, William, Harry, etc., say, 'we have no provision.' I will relieve your minds on that point. We have received only a small amount of the tithing wheat from Box Elder and Weber counties, a very little from Utah county, not any from the counties south of that, and how much do you think we now have in the General Tithing Store, from this and Davis county? We have enough to load 1,200 teams, 40,000 bushels of wheat. And I say to the Bishops to-day, report immediately to Bishop Hunter what your Wards need, for we are going to distribute that wheat to the people through the Bishops, and they can pay for it when they are able. We are going to forward this tithing wheat and flour with Church teams and all the other teams we can procure.

Another says, "I have no cow." I have two, you may strip mine part of the time. I know that the complaints among the poor will be trifling when compared to what they will be among the rich. I have so much property around me that I am really plagued. I want to cache the doors and the windows, and the frames, and casings; and my chairs, tables, secretaries and the articles that belong to the Historian's Office and the Tithing Office, etc., and I have so much property to look after that I hardly know what to do. The caches should be made in safe and dry localities, and looking glasses, clocks, musical instruments, and perhaps some other articles should be taken with you. If I had nothing but a little day book in my pocket, I could start and run. I know that it will be troublesome to men who possess fine houses and good orchards, and you now can perceive that the rich have cares once in a while. It makes me think of the old saying, "God bless the rich, the poor can beg." God bless the rich and help them to get their property out of the way, for the poor can pick up and start when they please.

That is the policy I suggest to you, and it is the best policy I can now see to make our enemies whip themselves, as they have thus far. Have we killed any of them? No. But to hear them tell the story, they have killed many 'Mormons' this winter, for they say they have been shooting at 'Mormons' through the winter, and the 'Mormons' have not fired a single gun at them. They are whipped so far, without our fighting them.

I will now say a few words with regard to politics. Pledges to the Democratic platform are what brought James Buchanan into the Presidential chair, and the main plank in that platform is the principle of popular sovereignty, as established in '76. When the Republicans saw that he would be elected President, what plan did they adopt? They went to work to spoil his Administration by causing him to disgrace himself. They so managed the affair as to induce him, in the case of Kansas and

Utah, to take steps to trample upon the rights of the people, in violation of the very principle upon which he gained his election. If you want to know his present position, I will explain it to you in my own way by saying that he and his party were walking straight-forward on the plank of popular sovereignty, and the Republicans succeeded in making him throw himself directly across that plank; and now every Democrat that comes along says, "Buchanan, what are you doing here? I am going ahead," and they have to step over him. In his acts touching Utah and Kansas he has disregarded the fundamental principles of the Constitution. The Republicans managed to have him pledge himself and induced him to take a course in opposition to that pledge, that they might destroy his Administration. And now, if James Buchanan had never given orders for an army to march to this country, he might have flung up his hat, but as it is he is whipt and is a disgrace before the nation. He is becoming a hiss and a by-word. You can scarcely read a newspaper, even those brought by the last mail, and what the next will bring we do not know, without learning that such is the case. He is becoming a stink in the nostrils of every honorable person throughout the nation, and is so obnoxious to the people that I do not know but that they will kill him. They killed some thirty persons, about the time of his inauguration, at the National Hotel in Washington, in trying to kill him; and I do not know but what they will succeed in killing him yet, if the Lord don't let the devil kill him in some other way. He is a disgrace to the Democratic party. Br. George A. Smith was in Washington at the time of the poisoning at the National Hotel, and he says that nearly all then stopping at that hotel were nasty, stinking office seekers, and if so it is a pity that they did not keep on poisoning.

There are now two prominent parties in the nation; the Democratic, which professes to follow the Declaration of Independence and the Constitution of the United States in strictness, and the Republican, as they style themselves, or Black Republican, as termed by the Democrats. The Republicans have succeeded in flooring Buchanan, and they are now rejoicing over his downfall and expect to come into power at the next Presidential election in 1860.

If Buchanan can be eased down, his own party wish to accomplish it so as not to break his neck. His edicts must be fulfilled, whether they are right or wrong, to preserve the DIGNITY of the Government. He has given orders to the soldiery to build a station 'at or near Salt Lake City' in Utah Territory. Those orders must be fulfilled, or both political parties of the nation are disgraced, so I am for letting them come and take 'Sebastopol.'

We want five hundred families to go south forthwith, and be ready to raise corn, potatoes, squashes, beans, etc., etc., this season. In these valleys we now have more grain in the ground that we know what to do with. Instead of planting the sugar cane seed here, plant it there, and you can make your sweet unmolested. I am not going to plant any potatoes nor corn here; and I have sown all the small grain that I shall sow here this season. I will let the rest of my ground lie untilled, and then I will do all I can to gather the crop that I have caused to be put into the ground, if we can get the chance, and we think we shall. Some of you may think I am imprudent in making these statements here, lest our enemies hear of them and start to come here before we are ready for them. If they do that, while we are doing all we can to get away, we shall kill the infernal scoundrels. They may have 'Sebastopol' after it is vacated, but they cannot have it before, according to my present feelings.

No doubt some of the brethren will be a little surprised at this move, and think it hard. Who should be the first to volunteer, in all the settlements of the Saints? You who have never been driven, or those who have been driven twice, thrice, or four or five times? Were I to call for volunteers, generally those who have suffered the most would be soonest on hand and say, "we care no more about our property than we do about the ashes of a rye straw, for we can accumulate more." You may ask whether I am willing to burn up my houses? Yes, and to be the first man that will put the torch to my own dwellings.

If any one sends out word that the army may come in, and that we are not going to fight them, send word at the same time that if they come in to annoy us while we are hastening away, we will send them to hell, God being our helper. We have just as much as we can do to get ready to—what? Waste this city? this beautiful city? What was it twelve years ago? Not much. Once in a while an Indian would come and camp in the bushes, and a few wolves would be howling around. There were also crickets in abundance. Suppose that this whole city is laid in ashes and the troops occupy its site, they will or should be withdrawn as soon as the credit and dignity of the Government is supposed to be saved.

Our Elders are willing and many are over-anxious to fight, and I also should be for killing, if I was crowded into a corner and could not back out. But I would sooner see this city laid in ashes, than to lose one good Elder. We are not obliged to go and endanger our lives. Every time we have left our homes before, it has been in the fall and winter, but now it is spring and we have the pleasant part of the season before us.

This is a different country to what we have heretofore lived in. As I have told you often, if people lived in their old log houses, in their tents and wagons for years, and if we had lived here until now in wickeups you would not hear one cough where you now hear a hundred. It is the worst country in the world to be housed up in close air, and it would be still worse if you would go up on Mount Nebo to sleep for you could not live there long in a tight house.

I never permit myself to sleep in a house, since I have been in this valley, without a door or window open; and if I am in a place the least close, I feel it at once and know it will injure my health. I must have the air here. Turn this people out of doors, if you want to make them healthy. When we sent off a little company a week ago last Wednesday, I called upon br. Free to go, knowing that he had been very ill, and believing that it would improve his health. He has since sent word that his health has improved every day, and he begins to feel quite strong and hearty. Send out these women and children, many of whom are not in health, and let them sleep in wagons and they will become healthy.

Such property as you do not need to or cannot remove, but which will keep in a cache, where you please in any dry and safe place. I would cache window and door frames and casings, etc., and thus save all that we can; we may come back here. And let us go to diligently and remove the women and children and the aged and infirm and the wheat and flour and meat, to as far south as Provo, to begin, and retain the able bodied men as much in the vacated settlements as possible, to look after our enemies and the growing crops, &c., and when we get ready to let them, our enemies may come in, in welcome. If this city was vacated and the army here, they would not dare to go to any place only where Government has ordered them to build a station. Let them whip themselves; they are at this time whipt in a masterly manner, and they have done it themselves. Did you ever see any man get so angry and full of revenge that he would be glad to be able to jump up and bite his own nose, and jump until he was tired, and after all find his nose still unhurt on his face, and then begin to curse and rip about it, having nobody to spite himself upon? Our enemies are precisely in that situation. We used to say, when wishing to describe hell, that it was "to want to and can't." They "want to and can't."

If we are obliged to remove, cache and lay waste, it is for our good, it is not for our injury. "The earth is the Lord's and the fullness thereof," and he that cannot take joyfully the spoiling of his goods, whenever the Lord requires it to be done and it seems to be necessary, is not worthy to be a follower of the Lamb; and when the moving is over I will have just as much better a house than my present one, than it is better than the old row of log cabins we used to live in. The buildings I now have do not begin to satisfy me, for I mean to keep improving so that I will know how to help build up Zion, when I have the privilege. So also will your buildings be as much better than the ones you now occupy, as they are better than your old shanties which you first lived in, and the earth will be more productive than it has been. If we take the right track, the Lord will bless us accordingly.

Many may say, "br. Brigham, perhaps you are mistaken; you are liable to err, and if the mob should not come, after all, and we should burn up our houses and learn that the Government had actually countermanded their orders and that no armies are coming to Utah, it would be a needless destruction. We have all the time felt that there was no need of leaving our houses.—How easy it is for men to be mistaken, and we think a Prophet may be mistaken once in a while." I am just as willing as the Lord, if he is disposed to make me make mistakes, and it is none of the business of any other person. If a people do the best they know, they have the power to ask and receive, and no power can prevent it. And if the Lord wants me to make a mistake, I would as soon be mistaken as anything else, if that will save the lives of the people and give us the victory. If you get such feelings in your hearts, think of what my conclusion on the subject is, and do not come to my office to ask me whether I am mistaken, for I want to tell you now perhaps I am.

Do I want to save you? Ask that question. But John, what are you doing? Are you now an Elder in Israel? "Yes, I am a High Priest." What is the office of an High Priest? John replies, "I do not know, without it is to whip my wife, knock down my children and make everybody obey me; and I believe a High Priest presides over an Elder." You will find some Elders just about that ignorant. Let me tell you what the office of a High Priest and an Elder is. It holds the keys of the revelation of Jesus Christ; it unlocks the gates of heaven. It opens the broad windows of revelation from eternity. John, what are you about, imagining that I may be mistaken? or that br. Heber may be mistaken? Why do you not open the windows of heaven and get revelation for yourself? and not go whining around and saying, "do you not think that you may be mistaken? Can a Prophet or an Apostle be mistaken?" Do not ask me any such question, for I will acknowledge that all the time, but I do not acknowledge that I designedly lead this people astray one hair's breadth from the truth, and I do not knowingly do a wrong, though I may commit many wrongs, and so may you. But I overlook your weaknesses, and I know by experience that the Saints lift their hearts to God that I may be led right. If I am thus borne off by your prayers and faith, with my own, and suffered to lead you wrong, it proves that your faith is vain. Do not worry. I have opened the subject and I will now sit down and let others unfold a little more. My mind is too full this morning to come to close points.

May God bless you. Amen.

12

"Intelligence, Etc.,"
A Sermon Delivered on 9 October 1859

(from *Journal of Discourses*, 26 vols.
[Liverpool: Latter-day Saints' Book Depot, 1855-86], 7:282-91)

I shall address you this morning upon a subject that is more interesting to me than any other pertaining to the life of man. It is a subject of deep study and research, and has been from age to age among the reflecting and philosophical portions of the human family. The intelligence given to the children of men is the subject to which I allude, and upon which has been expended more intellectual labour and profound thought than upon any other that has ever attracted the attention of man.

The Psalmist has written, "What is man, that thou art mindful of him? and the son of man, that thou visitest him? For thou hast made him a little lower than the angels, and hast crowned him with glory and honour." This passage is but one of many which refer to the organization of man as though it were a great mystery—something that could not be fully comprehended by the greatest minds while dwelling in earthly tabernacles. It is a matter of vital interest to each of us, and yet it is often farthest from the thoughts of the greater portion of mankind. Instead of reflecting upon and searching for hidden things of the greatest value to them, they rather wish to learn how to secure their way through this world as easily and as comfortably as possible. The reflections what they are here for, who produced them, and where they are from, far too seldom enter their minds.

Many have written upon this great subject, and there exists a great variety of reflections, views, and opinions which I have not time to dwell upon in detail. I will merely give you a few texts, or what you may term a text-book. Nor shall I now take time to minutely elaborate any particular point, but will present such views as shall come into my mind, trusting that I shall have your faith and prayers to be able to edify both Saint and sinner, believer and unbeliever.

If the inhabitants of the earth thoroughly understood their own being, their views, feelings, faith, and affections would be very different from what they now are. Many believe in predestination, while others of the Christian world oppose that doctrine and exclusively advocate free grace, free will, free offering, etc.; and each party of Christians has its pet theory or doctrine, upon which it builds its hopes of eternal salvation.

Such a course is like five or six hundred men each selecting and running off with a piece of the machinery of a cotton mill, and declaring that he had the cotton mill entire. This comparison may be truly applied to the Christian world as it now is with regard to the holy and divine principles which have been revealed pertaining to eternal life and salvation.

Many of you, no doubt, have concluded that the doctrine of election and reprobation is true, and you do so with propriety, for it is true; it is a scriptural doctrine. Others do not believe this doctrine, affirming with all their faith, might, and skill that free grace and freewill are or ought to be the foundation of man's faith in his Creator. Very well. I can also say to them that free grace and freewill are scripturally true. The first-named doctrine is as true as the second, and the second as the first. Others, again, declare that mankind have no will, neither free nor restrained, in their actions; for instance, the Rationalists or Freethinkers, who deny the existence and divinity of the Gods that we believe in. But so far from their believing their own theory, Mr. Neil, of Boston, while in prison for having no religion, wrote an essay, in which he declared that "All is God."

I might enumerate many more instances, and say that they are all right so far as they go in truth. The doctrine of freewill and conditional salvation, the doctrine of free grace and unconditional salvation, the doctrine of foreordination and reprobation, and many more that I have not time to enumerate, can all be fully and satisfactorily proved by the Scriptures, and are true.

On the other hand, many untrue doctrines are taught and believed, such as there being infants, not a span long, weltering in the flames of hell, there to remain throughout the countless ages of eternity, and the doctrine of total depravity. Some have gone so far as to say that a man or woman who wishes to be saved in the kingdom of God—who wishes to be a servant or handmaid of the Almighty, must feel that deep contrition of heart, that sound repentance, and such a sense of his or her unworthiness and nothingness, and of the supremacy, glory, and exaltation of that Deity they believe in, as to exclaim before God and their brethren and sisters that they are willing to be damned. To me that is one of the heights of nonsense; for if a person is willing to be damned, he cares not to make the efforts necessary to secure salvation. All this confusion is in the world—party against party—communities against communities—individuals against individuals. One sets out with five truths and fifteen errors, making the articles of his faith twenty; another dissents from him, rejects those five truths, selects perhaps five more, and adds as many errors as did the former one, and then he comes out a flaming reformer. Men, in dissenting from one another, have too often exercised no better judgment than to deny and dissent from many truths because their ancestors cherished and believed them, which has produced numerous parties, sects, and articles of faith, when, in fact, taking them in mass, they have an immense amount of true principles.

It was the occupation of Jesus Christ and his Apostles to propagate the Gospel of salvation and the principles of eternal life to the world, and it is our duty and calling, as ministers of the same salvation and Gospel, to gather every item of truth and reject every error. Whether a truth be found with professed infidels, or with the Universalists, or the Church of Rome, or the Methodists, the Church of England, the Presbyterians, the Baptists, the Quakers, the Shakers, or any other of the various and numerous different sects and parties, all of whom have more or less truth, it is the business of the Elders of this Church (Jesus, their elder brother, being at their head,) to gather up all the truths in the world pertaining to life and salvation, to the Gospel we preach, to mechanism of every kind, to the sciences, and to philosophy, wherever it may be found in every nation, kindred, tongue, and people, and bring it to Zion.

The people upon this earth have a great many errors, and they have also a great many truths. This statement is not only true of the nations termed civilized—those who profess to worship the true God, but is equally applicable to pagans of all countries, for in their religious rights and ceremonies may be found a great many truths which we will also gather home to Zion. All truth is for the salvation of the children of men—for their benefit and learning—for their furtherance in the principles of divine knowledge; and divine knowledge is any matter of fact—truth; and all truth pertains to divinity.

When we view mankind collectively, or as nations, communities, neighbourhoods, and families, we are led to inquire into the object of our being here and situated as we find ourselves to be. Did we produce ourselves, and endow ourselves with that knowledge and intelligence we now possess? All are ready to acknowledge that we had nothing to do with the origin of our being—that we were produced by a superior Power, without either the knowledge or the exercise of the agency we now possess. We know that we are here. We know that we live, breathe, and walk upon the earth. We know this naturally, as the brute creation knows. We know that our food and drink come from the elements around us: by them we are nourished, cherished, refreshed, and sustained, with the addition of sleep. We live and breathe, and breathe and live. Who can define and point out the particularities of the wonderful organization of man?

It enters into the minds of but few that the air we inhale is the greatest source of our life. We derive more real nourishment to our mortal tabernacles from this element than from the solid food we receive into our stomachs. Our lungs expand and contract to sustain the life which

God has given us. Of the component parts of this great fountain of vitality I have not time to treat; but this interesting information you may gather in part from numerous works on natural philosophy. I will, however, say that the air is full of life and vitality, and its volume fills immensity. The relative terms height, depth, length, and breadth do not apply to it. Could you pass with the velocity of the electric fluid over telegraphic wires, during the continuation of more years than you can comprehend, you would still be surrounded by it and in the bosom of eternity as much as you now are; and it is filled with the spirit of life which emanates from God.

Many have tried to penetrate to the First Cause of all things; but it would be as easy for an ant to number the grains of sand on the earth. It is not for man, with his limited intelligence, to grasp eternity in his comprehension. There is an eternity of life, from which we were composed by the wisdom and skill of superior Beings. It would be as easy for a gnat to trace the history of man back to his origin as for man to fathom the First Cause of all things, lift the veil of eternity, and reveal the mysteries that have been sought after by philosophers from the beginning. What, then, should be the calling and duty of the children of men? Instead of inquiring after the origin of the Gods—instead of trying to explore the depths of eternities that have been, that are, and that will be,—instead of endeavouring to discover the boundaries of boundless space, let them seek to know the object of their present existence, and how to apply, in the most profitable manner for their mutual good and salvation, the intelligence they possess. Let them seek to know and thoroughly understand things within their reach, and to make themselves well acquainted with the object of their being here, by diligently seeking unto a superior Power for information, and by the careful study of the best books.

The life that is within us is a part of an eternity of life, and is organized spirit, which is clothed upon by tabernacles, thereby constituting our present being, which is designed for the attainment of further intelligence. The matter composing our bodies and spirits has been organized from the eternity of matter that fills immensity.

Were I to fully speak what I know and understand concerning myself and others, you might think me to be infringing. I shall therefore omit some things that I would otherwise say to you if the people were prepared to receive them.

Jesus Christ says, "And this is life eternal, that they might know thee the only true God, and Jesus Christ whom thou has sent." We are not now in a capacity to know him in his fulness of glory. We know a few things that he has revealed concerning himself, but there are a great many which we do not know. When people have secured to themselves eternal life, they are where they can understand the true character of their Father and God, and the object of the creation, fall, and redemption of man after the creation of this world. These points have ever been subjects for speculation with all classes of believers, and are subjects of much interest to those who entertain a deep anxiety to know how to secure to themselves eternal life. Our bodies are organized from the eternity of matter, from such matter as we breathe, and from such matter as is found in the vegetable and mineral kingdoms. This matter is organized into a world, with all its appendages, by whom? By the Almighty; and we see it peopled by men and women who are made in the image of God.

All this vast creation was produced from elements in its unorganized state; the mountains, rivers, seas, valleys, plains, and the animal, vegetable, and mineral kingdoms beneath and around us, all speaking forth the wonderful works of the Great God. Shall I say that the seeds of vegetables were planted here by the Characters that framed and built this world— that the seeds of every plant composing the vegetable kingdom were brought from another world? This would be news to many of you. Who brought them here? It matters little to us whether it was John, James, William, Adam, or Bartholomew who brought them; but it was some Being who had power to frame this earth with its seas, valleys, mountains, and rivers, and cause it to teem with vegetable and animal life.

Here let me state to all philosophers of every class upon the earth, When you tell me that father Adam was made as we make adobies from the earth, you tell me what I deem an idle tale. When you tell me that the beasts of the field were produced in that manner, you are speaking idle words devoid of meaning. There is no such thing in all the eternities where the Gods dwell. Mankind are here because they are the offspring of parents who were first brought here from another planet, and power was given them to propagate their species, and they were commanded to multiply and replenish the earth. The offspring of Adam and Eve are commanded to take the rude elements, and, by the knowledge God has given, to convert them into everything required for their life, health, adornment, wealth, comfort, and consolation. Have we the knowledge to do this? We have. Who gave us this knowledge? Our Father who made us; for he is the only wise God, and to him we owe allegiance; to him we owe our lives. He has brought us forth and taught us all we know. We are not indebted to any other power or God for all our great blessings.

We see man upon the earth, and discern that he is endowed with great intelligence, which displays its scope and power in various ways to meet and provide for the exigencies and wants of the human race. Wise statesmen know how to devise and plan for a kingdom, and can closely calculate the results of the policies they adopt. They understand the course to be pursued to induce the people to submit to a wholesome government or to a despotic rule as may please the will of the rulers. There are historians of various grades, philosophers wise and simple, and an exceedingly great variety of capacities and tastes. In our Republican government we see some who are acute politicians, but that seems to be the extent of their knowledge. You may find others who are good statesmen, but poor politicians. Some are excellent mathematicians, and understand and care for but little outside that science. Still, if a man is capable of learning the geography of the earth, he is also capable of learning the laws of the nations that inhabit it, if you will give him time according to his capacity. One scholar in a school may far outstrip the rest; but give them sufficient time, and they can learn what the quick, bright scholar has learned so easily and quickly. If we are capacitated to learn one thing to-day, we can learn another to-morrow. It is the height of folly to say that a man can only learn so much and no more. The further literary men advance in their studies, the more they discern there is to learn, and the more anxious they are to learn. This is made manifest before us day by day, and is observed upon the face of the whole earth.

The principle of intelligence is within us. Who planted it there? He who made us. That which you see developed in the children of men (you may call it disposition, or whatever else you please,) is the force of the mind or the spirit, and the body is a tabernacle organized for its temporary habitation.

It is written of the Saviour that he descended below all things. If he did, he descended in capacity. I will merely tell you what I believe on this point. I believe that there never was a child born on this earth with any less capacity than dwelt in the child that was born in a manger of his mother Mary. I believe, according to the natural ability which he received from his mother and from his supposed father Joseph, that there never was a child that descended lower in capacity, or that knew less. Yet, according to the history given of him, his power of mind developed with such wonderful rapidity that when he was but a few years old he propounded questions to the learned doctors of his day which they could not answer, and answered questions propounded to him which the querists could not answer. He increased in wisdom and knowledge, and came into communication with his Father. The Being whom we call Father was the Father of the spirit of the Lord Jesus Christ, and he was also his Father pertaining to the flesh. Infidels and Christians, make all you can of this statement. The Bible, which all Christians profess to believe, reveals that fact, and it reveals the truth upon that point, and I am a witness of its truth. The Apostles who were personally acquainted with Jesus Christ did know and understand what they wrote, and they wrote the truth.

He was endowed with capacity to receive intelligence. We, his brethren, are also endowed with capacity to receive intelligence. And what some would call the volition of the creature—the will of the creature—the disposition, the power of willing or determining, is bequeathed to us in like manner as it is to the Son of God; and it is as independent as it is inherited by the angels or Gods—that is, the will to dispose of this intelligence at our pleasure in doing good or evil. It is held by the followers of Robert Owen that men are more or less influenced entirely in their actions by the force of circumstances: but is there a man or woman in this house that could not walk out, if you wanted to—if your will was set in you to do it? or sit here until meeting is out, if you are disposed? The volition of the creature is made independent by the unalterable decree of the Almighty. I can rise up or sit still—speak or be silent. Were this not so, I would at once request parents never to correct a child for another disobedient act.

We are organized to be so independent in this capacity as to determine and act for ourselves as to whether we will serve God and obey him in preference to serving ourselves. If we serve ourselves and evil principles, we do not subserve the object of our creation. This element of which our tabernacles are organized is calculated to decompose and return to its mother earth, or to its native element. This intelligence, which might be called divine intelligence, is implanted in mortal or human beings; and if we take a course to promote the principles of life—seek unto our Father and God, and obtain his will and perform it, the spirit will become purified, sanctified, cleansed, and made holy in the body, and the grave will cleanse the flesh. When the spirit overcomes the evil consequences of the fall, which are in the mortal tabernacle, it will reign predominant in the flesh, and is then prepared to be exalted, and will, in the resurrection, be reunited with those particles that formed the mortal body, which will be called together as with the sound of a trumpet and become immortal. Why? Because the particles composing these bodies have been made subject and obedient, by the law of the everlasting Priesthood, and the will and commandment of the Supreme Ruler of the universe, who holds the keys of life and death. Every principle, act, and portion of the lives of the children of men that does not tend to this will lead to an eternal dissolution of the identity of the person.

"Why," some say, "we thought that the wicked were to be sent to hell to dwell with eternal burnings for evermore." They go to hell and will stay there until the anger of the Almighty consumes them and they become disorganized, as the elements of the fuel we burn are disorganized by the action of fire and thrown back again to their native element. The wicked will endure the wrath of God and be "turned into hell, with all the nations that forget God." What will be done with them there? Those who did not persecute the Son of God in the flesh while acting for themselves and following the direction of their own will—those who did not persecute the holy Priesthood of the Son of God—those who did not consent to the shedding of innocent blood—those who did not seek to obliterate the kingdom of God from the earth, will, by-and-by, be sought after.

You read about a first resurrection. If there is a first, there is a second. And if a second, may there not be a third, and a fourth, and so on? Yes; and happy are they who have a part in the first resurrection. Yes, more blessed are they than any others. But blessed also are they that will have part in the second resurrection, for they will be brought forth to enjoy a kingdom that is more glorious than the sectarian world ever dreamed of.

The "Mormon" Elders will tell you that all people must receive this Gospel—the Gospel of Jesus Christ, and be baptized for the remission of sins, or they cannot be saved. Let me explain this to you. They cannot go where God and Christ dwell, for that is a kingdom of itself—the celestial kingdom. Jesus said, "In my Father's house are many mansions," or kingdoms. They will come forth in the first, second, or some other resurrection, if they have not been guilty of the particular sins I have just mentioned; and they will enjoy a kingdom and a glory greater than they had ever anticipated. When we talk about people's being damned, I would like to have all understand that we do not use the term "damnation" in the sense that it is used by the sectarian world. Universal salvation or redemption is the doctrine of the Bible; but the people do not know how or where to discriminate between truth and error. All those who have done according to the best of their knowledge, whether they are Christians, Pagans, Jews, Mohammedans, or any other class of men that have ever lived upon the earth, that have dealt honestly and justly with their fellow-beings, walked uprightly before each other, loved mercy, tried to put down iniquity, and done as far right as they knew how, according to the laws they lived under, no matter what the laws were, will share in a resurrection that will be glorious far beyond the conceptions of mortals.

How many times have I been asked, "Do you believe that such a man as John Wesley will be damned?" I could answer the question either way, for they do not know what it is to be saved or damned. John Wesley is in the spirit-world. He did not receive the ordinances of the everlasting Gospel in the flesh, and consequently is not prepared to hold the keys of the kingdom and be a minister of the great work of God in the last dispensation, but is dependent upon others to attain a celestial glory. Has he gone to hell? No. When the spirit leaves the body, it goes into the spirit-world, where the spirits of men are classified according to their own wills or pleasure, as men are here, only they are in a more pure and refined state of existence. Do you suppose that John Wesley is lifting up his eyes in hell, being in torment? No; he is talking to those who heard and would not believe him when he was on the earth. He may be asking them whether they do not now see the justice of a reformation from the Church of England mode of religion—whether they do not now see that that Church had gone astray from the true religion, and that he was right. Yes; and they, no doubt, see it as John Wesley does, and are willing to worship God according to the best knowledge they have. As death left him, so judgment will find him, trying to worship God in the best manner he was acquainted with. John Wesley and his true followers will receive a glory far surpassing what they ever thought or dreamed of while under the influence of their greatest inspirations, and they will be saved. Are they also damned? Yes, because they have not attained the victory over the enemy of all righteousness. It is the holy Priesthood of God that gives man the victory in this world, and he begins to reign over the power of the enemy here. The keys of the kingdom of the Son of God outreach and circumscribe the power of the Enemy.

Much has been said about the power of the Latter-day Saints. Is it the people called Latter-day Saints that have this power, or is it the Priesthood? It is the Priesthood; and if they live according to that Priesthood, they can commence their work here and gain many victories, and be prepared to receive glory, immortality, and eternal life, that when they go into the spirit-world, their work will far surpass that of any other man or being that has not been blessed with the keys of the Priesthood here.

Joseph Smith holds the keys of this last dispensation, and is now engaged behind the vail in the great work of the last days. I can tell our beloved brother Christians who have slain the Prophets and butchered and otherwise caused the death of thousands of Latter-day Saints, the priests who have thanked God in their prayers and thanksgiving from the pulpit that we have been plundered, driven, and slain, and the deacons under the pulpit, and their brethren and sisters in their closets, who have thanked God, thinking that the Latter-day Saints were wasted away, something that no doubt will mortify them—something that, to say the least, is a matter of deep regret to them—namely, that no man or woman in this dispensation will ever enter into the celestial kingdom of God without the consent of Joseph Smith. From the day that the Priesthood was taken from the earth to the winding-up scene of all things, every man and woman must have the certificate of Joseph Smith, junior, as a passport to their entrance into the mansion where God and Christ are—I with you and you with me. I cannot go there without his consent. He holds the keys of that kingdom for the last dispensation—the keys to rule in the spirit-world; and he rules there triumphantly, for he gained full power and a glorious victory over the power of Satan while he was yet in the flesh, and was a martyr to his religion and to the name of Christ, which gives him a most perfect victory in the spirit-world. He reigns there as supreme a being in his sphere capacity, and calling, as God does in heaven. Many will claim—"Oh, that is very disagreeable! It is preposterous! We cannot bear the thought!" But it is true.

I will now tell you something that ought to comfort every man and woman on the face of the earth. Joseph Smith, junior, will again be on this earth dictating plans and calling forth his brethren to be baptized for the very characters who wish this was not so, in order to bring them into a kingdom to enjoy, perhaps, the presence of angels or the spirits of good men, if they cannot endure the presence of the Father and the Son; and he will never cease his operations, under the directions of the Son of God, until the last ones of the children of men are saved that can be, from Adam till now.

Should not this thought comfort all people? They will, by-and-by, be a thousand times more thankful for such a man as Joseph Smith, junior, than it is possible for them to be for any earthly good whatever. It is his mission to see that all the children of men in this last dispensation are saved, that can be, through the redemption. You will be thankful, every one of you, that Joseph Smith, junior, was ordained to this great calling before the worlds were. I told you that the doctrine of election and reprobation is a true doctrine. It was decreed in the counsels of eternity, long before the foundations of the earth were laid, that he should be the man, in the last dispensation of this world, to bring forth the word of God to the people, and receive the fulness of the keys and power of the Priesthood of the Son of God. The Lord had his eye upon him, and upon his father, and upon his father's father, and upon their progenitors clear back to Abraham, and from Abraham to the flood, from the flood to Enoch, and from Enoch to Adam. He has watched that family and that blood as it has circulated from its fountain to the birth of that man. He was foreordained in eternity to preside over this last dispensation, as much so as Pharaoh was fore-ordained to be a wicked man, or as was Jesus to be the Saviour of the world because he was the oldest son in the family.

Abraham was ordained to be the father of the faithful,—that is, he was ordained to come forth at a certain period; and when he had proved himself faithful to his God, and would resist the worship of idols, and trample them under his feet in the presence of their king, and set up the worship of the true God, he obtained the appellation of "father of the faithful." "For whom he did foreknow he also did predestinate to be conformed to the image of his son." He knew, millions of years before this world was framed, that Pharaoh would be a wicked man. He saw—he understood; his work was before him, and he could see it from the beginning to the end. And so scrutinizing, penetrating, and expanded are his visions and knowledge, that not even a hair of our head can fall to the ground unnoticed by him. He foreknew what Joseph, who was sold into Egypt, would do. Joseph was foreordained to be the temporal saviour of his father's house, and the seed of Joseph are ordained to be the spiritual and temporal saviours of all the house of Israel in the latter days. Joseph's seed has mixed itself with all the seed of man upon the face of the whole earth. The great majority of those who are now before me are the descendants of that Joseph who was sold. Joseph Smith, junior, was foreordained to come through the loins of Abraham, Isaac, Jacob, Joseph, and so on down through the Prophets and Apostles; and thus he came forth in the last days to be a minister of salvation, and to hold the keys of the last dispensation of the fulness of times.

The whole object of the creation of this world is to exalt the intelligencies that are placed upon it, that they may live, endure, and increase for ever and ever. We are not here to quarrel and contend about the things of this world, but we are here to subdue and beautify it. Let every man and woman worship their God with all their heart. Let them pay their devotions and sacrifices to him, the Supreme, and the Author of their existence. Do all the good you can to your fellow-creatures. You are flesh of my flesh and bone of my bone. God has created of one blood all the nations and kingdoms of men that dwell upon all the face of the earth: black, white, copper-coloured, or whatever their colour, customs, or religion, they have all sprung from the same origin; the blood of all is from the same element. Adam and Eve are the parents of all pertaining to the flesh, and I would not say that they are not also the parents of our spirits.

You see some classes of the human family that are black, uncouth, uncomely, disagreeable and low in their habits, wild, and seemingly deprived of nearly all the blessings of the intelligence that is generally bestowed upon mankind. The first man that committed the odious crime of killing one of his brethren will be cursed the longest of any one of the children of Adam. Cain slew his brother. Cain might have been killed, and that would have put a termination to that line of human beings. This was not to be, and the Lord put a mark upon him, which is the flat nose and black skin. Trace mankind down to after the flood, and then another curse is pronounced upon the same race—that they should be the "servant of servants;" and they will be, until the curse is removed; and the Abolitionists cannot help it, nor in the least alter that decree. How long is that race to endure that dreadful curse that is upon them? That curse will remain upon them, and they never can hold the Priesthood or share in it until all the other descendants of Adam have received the promises and enjoyed the blessings of the Priesthood and the keys thereof.

132

Until the last ones of the residue of Adam's children are brought up to that favourable position, the children of Cain cannot receive the first ordinances of the Priesthood. They were the first that were cursed, and they will be the last from whom the curse will be removed. When the residue of the family of Adam come up and receive their blessings, then the curse will be removed from the seed of Cain, and they will receive blessings in like proportion.

I have but just commenced my remarks, and have presented you a few texts; and it is not time to adjourn. The exertion required to speak to you somewhat at length seems to injure me. I will therefore stop.

I bless you all, inasmuch as you have desired and striven to do right, to revere the name of Deity, and to exalt the character of his Son on the earth. I bless you in the name of Jesus Christ! Amen.

13

"I Take the Liberty of Preaching to the People, Wishing to do so for the Benefit of the Saints," A Sermon Delivered on 14 July 1861

(from *Brigham Young Addresses, 1860–1864,
A Chronological Compilation of Known Addresses
of the Prophet Brigham Young,* Vol. 4
[Salt Lake City: Elden J. Watson, 1980])

I take the liberty of preaching to the people, wishing to do so for the benefit of the saints. If we could but understand the economy of heaven in our organization and in the dealings of God with his people, if we had eyes to see, ears to hear, hearts to understand facts as they are, all mankind would seek for eternal life. In the economy of heaven every person that is experienced, as the saints very well know, that life, eternal life, is not obtained by every fancy and fanatasism conjured up by men. There are certain principles that pertain to life everlasting, those principles will, and those alone, abide the day that is to come, abide the scrutinies of Jehovah, abide the presence of him who dwells in eternal burnings. Those principles are as pure as pure can be. That that is impure tends to the dissolving or separation of the particles of matter that are organized. I frequently contemplate the saying of Brother Joseph when he said the Twelve Apostles did not understand the first principles of the Gospel. I should be most happy if I understood the first principles of the Gospel, the first principles of life, perfectly, for myself. Then I would delight in possessing language that I could convey the same to others. To see these human faces before me, these intelligent beings, we may traverse the earth around and behold the intelligence of mankind, behold that eternal variety in this intelligence, circumscribe it, philosophize upon it, have ability really to understand its origin. Ask intelligent beings, "where is your origin? Can you print it before us that we can see it? Can you tell it to us?" It is in obscurity. It is beyond the comprehension of the people and eternally would remain so if God did not reveal it. Look at the people before us this day. Behold the millions of human faces that many of you, perhaps, have seen. Who can tell their origin? Can the philosopher? A great many have tried, but they all sink into the conclusion that man is a mystery to himself and is past finding out. These intelligent beings that I now see, that I behold as we say with the natural eye, Br. Kimball would call it the natural eye, the eye of the spirit, very well, the eye that God has given me and the power of sight: How long is it since they were in chaos? all that pertains to man independent of the intelligence that dwells within his body, independent of that spirit of life, light and intelligence? I see the faces of these, my brethren and sisters. How long is it since you and I were mingled with the native element that now fills the atmosphere, the sea, the earth? The apostle says we are of the earth, earthly. The human organization tends to the earth, bends to it, inclines to it, clings to it and the decree is, "dust thou art and unto dust thou shalt return." To hear these very intelligent beings that could rise and speak were we in social conversation, the intelligence that would be imparted by the organs of speech that we behold with our eyes, but a few days since was swimming in native element. God has organized this. He has his own way and that way is not changed. All beings are here upon the same principle; all that ever was and all that ever will be are upon the same principle. Here we are. If we could understand the first principles of our organization and see the multitudes, the vast work, I say the boundless space, to see the particles of matter organized by the decree and the law of Jehovah and the machine that he has set in order, giving it its bounds, this matter is constantly organizing. Generations come and they pass away. Now see the mountains of solid rock? They have their time for organizing and they have their time for decay. You see one generation come and go and another take their place and we see the vast creations coming into existence, and when we call for our fathers and our mothers, our progenitors, where is the nations that has lived a hundred years ago? They are in eternity, and their bodies are in the dust. Where is that intelligence they possessed? It is gone. Where? Into the invisible world. Where are the generations that preceeded them? From the days of Adam until now all flesh, till the ones that now live, are mouldering in the dust. There is a design in all this. The organization that you see in yourselves and in one another, organized expressly to continue, to endure, to develop the power of the Almighty, the glory, the intelligence of our Father and our God. Where are these people, the nations of the earth that have sunk like Babylon? They are no more upon the earth. We look upon the inhabitants of the earth and we inquire, "Can you tell me, ye men, ye skillful, ye philosophers and divines that study perhaps three score years to find out, what man is made for? Can you tell me what you were sent here for on this earth? Do you understand your origin? Do you know the design of your being, why you are here?" "I am here and that is all I can tell about, know, or understand." "Why not understand your origin?" "It is beyond the conception of man, beyond the power of all the divines on the earth in our day. It is past finding out." You may go to our mother church and then you may follow down through all the days of the reformation until this day, and until the Prophet Joseph arose,

135

they was as dark as midnight darkness, not a man upon the earth that was capable of delineating the character of himself, was capable of telling his origin. Now if we did but understand things as they are, the first principles of life is to organize this course material. We see it organized into intelligent man, that is capable of receiving little upon little, here a little and there a little, line upon line, line upon line. He reads one verse in the bible and commits it to memory. It does not deprive him of the privilege of commiting [sic] another verse, and chapter after chapter and book after book. It does not deprive him of commiting [sic] to memory the history of the nations, and he treasures up in the storehouse God has organized within him. He treasures up wisdom, knowledge upon knowledge. Here is the intelligence we see. Then we see the inferior, and from it we trace the highest degrees of intelligence we behold in man and follow it down to the brute, and from the brute to the vegetable, and it is impossible for the philosopher to distinguish and draw the line between them. You see that eternal variety? God has organized it. There is no philosophy or divine, but what will tell you, "I did not organize myself. I did not possess power to produce myself. I am here, and it was a superior power by which I am, and all the human family." It is a superior power to many that we are here upon the earth. The trees that grow, the leaves that shoot forth, the flowers, the grass that comes from the earth, it is all beyond the power and capacity of man to produce. We are here. We see we are here. We know we are here. How come we are here? Did we come by chance? You know some of our philosophers that have lived previous to our day and some that are now living, that deny the existence of a supreme being. I will confess they are more consistent than many that pretend to believe in a supreme being. Old Adam Neil of Boston, that was thrust into prison for being an infidel wrote an essay and sent it forth to the people. He said he was so far from believing in a God that he believed we were all gods and saw that supreme divinity in everything he saw. He believed all was God and yet he was imprisoned by the christians, he did not believe in one character. The christians say "we believe in God the Father, God the Son and God the Holy Ghost." What next? Have they a body? "Not at all." Have they any parts, a hand, an arm that they can stretch forth? "Not at all." An eye that they can see out of? (we will reduce them to one person) Then has this being got feet, limbs? "No." Stomach, ears, any senses about him? "No, he is without body parts and passions." And of course he is without principle or power. This is the God that the infidel, Adam Niel was thrust into prison for not believing in. He was more consistant [sic] than the christians. He believed in that supreme divinity that fills immensity, that was in all intelligent beings, in the brute, in the vegetables, that is, all over and round about. So far from believing there was no God, he believed in many gods. I say he was more consistant [sic] than the christians. But from the days of the apostacy of the church, who has been able to tell the origin of mankind, to know the relationship that exists between the divine and the natural, to converse with gods and angels and bring the knowledge of the gods to man's capacity and teach them how to converse together and chat together until the eyes of man was open to see as they are seen? Nobody has been able to do this until Joseph Smith arose. I was not very religious myself in my youthful days in my outward profession, though I had all that reverence in my heart that any man should have, yet I was called an infidel. I heard no man that could delineate, exhibit, print before the people, the least idea of man or the origin of his being upon the earth. I heard the great and the good. I searched, endeavored to learn for myself where the wisdom of God was if it ever was on the earth. I found it not. One of the greatest speakers that America ever offered: I heard him speak upon the soul of man. When he had exhausted over three hours in trying to tell his evidence, what the soul of man is, he labored like a balloon under the pressure of confined gas that goes up, up, up, and is drifted hither and thither by every current of air, until the gas is exhausted, when it suddenly drops to the ground by its own weight. His discourse suddenly came to an end, when our friend, the expounder of the mysteries of the kingdom of God, after exhausting all his ability and strength, all his mental and physical power, to tell what the soul of man is, he concluded with these profound remarks: "Brethren, it is beyond the capacity of any human being to understand this great mystery, but I came to the conclusion that the soul of man is an *immaterial substance*." Did every any such thing exist? That term carries with it a flat contradiction. But this is the knowledge of the world. When they have exhausted all their philosophy, they know nothing of these matters. Do we know? Yes, we do, and in this consists our comfort and consolation. As pertaining to our bodies, they were organized from the coarse material, from the rude element that we live in. We breathe it, eat it, drink it, it is all around us, in us, and through everything. The materials that organize this world is the same of which our bodies are organized. Br. Kimball told us this morning, Jesus was begotten of the Father, born of the virgin Mary, and he possessed a body like you and I. A great many have talked about it Divines have exhausted all the powers of their minds upon it in the days of the Reformation. You can read their writings, and no doubt you have read them, and what do they know about it? Nothing at all. Ask the divinity of this age how Jesus came upon the earth, and can they tell? No. They tell you a thousand things, and they are all wrong. Jesus Christ came here because his Father came here and he was begotten of the Father, and he was born of the virgin Mary as my mother bore me and as my father begot me and as you begot your children. What, is it possible that the Father of Heights, the Father of our spirits, could reduce himself and come forth like a man? Yes, he was once a man like you and I are and was once on an earth like this, passed through the ordeal you and I pass through. He had his father and his mother and he has been exalted through his faithfulness, and he is become Lord of all. He is the God pertaining to this earth. He is our Father. He begot our spirits in the spirit world. They have come forth and our earthly parents have organized tabernacles for our spirits and here we are today. That is the way we came. Do the divines of christendom know anything about it? Can all the philosophers of the nineteenth century detail one point intelligently concerning this? They can not, and if they should happen to make a true point by the aid of the truth they already possess, it appears so wonderful to them they are at a loss to know whether it is true or not. All this pertains to the first principles of the gospel. You must get the people where you can save them before you can save them. If you want to find out what the people are here for, how did you come here, and if we are here (and it is a fact that we are living), what we are living for. If we can find out how we came to live, the next step is to find out what we came for. We are living to live, we endure to endure, exist to an eternal existance, live to live for ever more and never die. One path leads to life, to continue this organization, the other to dissolving this matter, separating the particles one from the other until they return to their native element, and that is called death. Is there any such principle as annihilation? No. There is no such principle in heaven or on earth or under the earth. There is an eternity of matter before us, there ever was and there ever will be, there is no bounds to it. Does the scriptures teach the doctrine I am now teaching you? It is taught in the Old and New Testament, perhaps not precisely as I am wording it, but I can read the fact. The human family is here and we came here upon natural principles, upon the natural principle that God has placed in the people. The foolishness of men and through their traditions they have taken away the truth and introduced something else and the people do not know whether they have knowledge or not. They do not know by what power they exist, whether they are made human beings or divine beings, or belong to the brute creation. We have something to say about our christian brethren and we sometimes talk as I did this morning. I am thankful that I am so far from the christians. What do I mean by the word "christian?" That we must be like Christ, christlike, that is what we understand by christian. A man that is filled with the power of God, that knows and understands the revelations of the Lord Jesus Christ and observes the commandments of the Father, one that bows humbly to his requirements and delights himself in them, that is the christian. We call the present sectarian order of christians, "christians," but they do not know what it means. Have we a scripture for this? Yes, it can be read in the bible. Here we are, intelligent beings, and we are called to be christians. We are calling upon the human family to be christians. We have travelled the world around to call upon the people to be christians. Do they hearken to the words of wisdom? Some do once in a while, but they are one here and one there, they are like the gathering of grapes after the vintage is done. They are one of a city and two of a family, one here and another there, they are like the gathering of grapes after the vintage is done. They are one of a city and two of a family, one here and another there from the vast multitudes of the earth. Once in a while one embraces the truth and they practice it in their lives and they are trying to be christians, or christlike. Compare the wisdom of the world, and do they know anything about their origin, the errand for which they were sent here unto this world? No, they do not. They are here, a world of intelligent beings, made to endure forever. Every iota of the creations of God pertaining to mankind, the brute creation, the vegetable creation and everything else God has organized pertaining to this world is made expressly to endure for ever and ever. The gospel of the Son of God is to purify this matter. There is certain ordeals for it to pass through. The gospel is a set of laws and ordinances. In the beginning when the earth was cursed, the water was not cursed, the water was held sacred and is to this day except through the wickedness of the children of men. You get into the bowels of the earth where the water is not contaminated by the wickedness of the people that lives on the surface and you will find the pure water. That water will wash your body clean. Then we will use it as an emblem of purity as we now use the sacrament to commemorate the death and suffering of the Savior. As the water purifies the body externally by the obedience of the commandments of God, the spirit is made pure and they go forth as Jesus did. He was baptized to fulfil righteousness. It was required of him to do so. He did it to set the pattern for his brethren, to mark out the steps they should take. When John objected Jesus said, "Suffer it so to be now." John said he needed to be baptized of him. "I understand that," said the Savior, "but suffer it to be so now." It is necessary for you and I to go and be baptized because the Lord commanded it. If the water purifies the body externally, so does the commandments of the Lord and the words of eternal life purify the spirit of man. No man can be made pure without obeying the ordinances of the gospel. As I said this morning, it is not all that were going to be cast into hell to dwell eternally with the devils. There are only a few who will go into everlasting pain and they are they that reject the gospel. Who will be saved in the celestial kingdom of God? They that have the oracles of truth and obey them. Where will the rest go? Into kingdoms that God has and will prepare for them and there are millions of such kingdoms.

There is as many degrees of glory as there are degrees of capacity and to them will be meted out according to their faith, and goodness and the truth that abides in them and according to the light God has imparted to them. Those nations have lived and died, millions and millions of them, and have had no knowledge of the Son of God. Will they be condemned and cast into hell? No, but they will be judged without law. They that have had the Old and New Testament, will they be cast into that place they say has no bottom to it? No, all they that have [lived] according to the best light they have will have all the glory they anticipate. Who will go into the presence of the Father and the Son? Those who have had the priesthood on the earth, those who have enjoyed the oracles of divine truth, possess the keys and power of this priesthood that God has revealed in this day, those that live so that can prepare themselves to dwell with the Father and the Son. Can anybody else? Let me pause and ask this question: can any other person come into the presence of the Father and the Son? It would take a year to tell all that is in the gospel and then we stop and say we only just commenced. Yes, millions live on the earth that will come up in the morning of the first resurrection. What are those people trying to do? They are trying to learn the position they occupy and the relationship in which they stand to God and to one another. We are trying to build up Zion, first in the hearts, then in our houses, and in our neighborhoods, and by and bye we expect to return to the place where God built the garden of Eden. Do you know where that is? It is in Jackson County, Missouri. Now don't any of you run crazy about it and be scared, and do not jump up so high in the air that you will fall down and hurt yourself. Be careful, be modest, mild, sincere with yourselves, and let the Lord have his own, and come to the conclusion that if he built it there it is none of my business. Can any of the divines of the day tell where it will stand? No. Where will it stand? On Jackson County, Missouri, North America. Here the people are trying to build up Zion in their hearts, in their houses and in their neighborhoods. Are we saints yet? We are trying to be and when we are instructed enough and have purified ourselves enough we will return to that place where the Lord commenced his work and where he will finish it. We will build up Zion and holy temples unto the Lord and we will enter therein and be baptized for our forefathers and our mothers, they that were good, that loved truth, that lived according to the light they had, they that would have received the gospel if they had the opportunity. We will attend to all the ordinances of the gospel for them, for the men and women that have lived in the flesh and died without the benefits arising from the gospel and the living priesthood. Thousands and millions of these will come up in the first resurrection by thousands and millions. This may appear strange to talk to the people, but it is true. We will go and build up temples. We started a temple here. Shall we finish it? I don't know whether we shall or not before we go back to Jackson County, but it will be finished by and bye, and we will enter into this temple and receive the ordinances for the just. How will we find out who to administer for? By revelation. Jesus will visit his disciples and inform them that such a man lies so and so, go through with the ordinances for him and prepare him for the resurrection. And then here comes the apostle Peter, James, John, Joseph, Hyrum and somebody that has this power who will lay on hands on these men and give them power to resurrect this man and that man and they will go all over the world resurrecting the people. These are some of the first principles of the gospel. Do the Twelve Apostles understand them all? I do not and I am one of the Twelve. I have an eternity before me in which to learn. I have learned a great deal already. All that can be saved in the celestial kingdom will be saved there, and all that can be saved in the terrestrial kingdom will be saved there, and also in the telestial kingdom. And there are other kingdoms, multitudes of them to meet the capacity of the people that we are in the habit of seeing and conversing with every day. Will the Lord destroy this earth? No, he is going to baptize it with fire and with the Holy Ghost to prepare it to come into his presence again. Will he destroy the animal creation? No, they are made by him and they have abided their creation, and everything he has created has abided their creation except man, the lord of the soil of all the earth, to whom the Almighty committed the earth and the fullness thereof, to Adam and his posterity, to the kings of the earth, but they have forefited their right and title, and they are the only ones that have transgressed. The brute creation has kept the law by which they were made; the vegetable kingdoms, the animal kingdom has kept the law by which they were made and the earth has kept the law by which it was made, and it has honored God and will be baptized and brought forth in the resurrection. We find out what we are and what we are here for, and how we are here to live forever. This is the object and design of the creator. Those intelligent eyes I now see sparkle with eternal life; they are made to exist forever. The human family are endowed with the most precious attributes God could bestow on any being in the world. They are endowed with attributes like unto himself to improve upon; to improve upon every fine feeling, upon every right and judgment, and upon every moment of time; to improve all to the glory of God, to prepare to dwell with him in his presence. Do you suppose that we have a father?

Don't you see that this tends to destroy the beautiful organization of man and it goes back to the dust? Let the passions of man be ungoverned by any influence and the result would ultimately be the disaffection of the whole human race and they would return to original matter and it would have to wait millions of ages before another particle of it would be found in another organization. The spirit of peace, love, union, tends to life instead of cutting off a man's nose. If he was born without a nose we would want to put one on if we had the skill, so as to make him a comely person, excuse me for this expression. You see, one course tends to an eternal duration, the other tends to destruction or decomposition and a return to native element.

14

"True Character of God—
Erroneous Ideas Entertained Towards Him,"
A Sermon Delivered on 23 February 1862

(from *Journal of Discourses*, 26 vols.
[Liverpool: Latter-day Saints' Book Depot, 1855-86], 9:386-89)

We certainly should be extremely knowing, did we know everything; but, as we do not, we will be satisfied with what we do know and can still learn. This people know much. Their experience and their knowledge, coupled with that which has been revealed to them from the Fountain of all knowledge, are far beyond the capacities of those who have not heard and received the Gospel.

I have a few words to say touching our present existence, and in reference to the remarks made to-day by brother Kimball pertaining to the body. Our mortal bodies are all important to us; without them we never can be glorified in the eternities that will be. We are in this state of being for the express purpose of obtaining habitations for our spirits to dwell in, that they may become personage of tabernacle. Our former religious traditions has taught us that our Father in heaven has no tabernacle, that his centre is everywhere and his circumference nowhere. Yet we read that "God came from Teman, and the Holy One from Mount Paran." "Before him went the pestilence, and burning coals went forth at his feet." "And the ancient of days did sit, whose garment was white as snow, and the hair of his head like the pure wool." "Hast thou an arm like God? Or can'st thou thunder with a voice like him?" "And I will take away mine hand and thou shalt see my back parts; but my face thou shalt not see." "The eyes of the Lord are upon the righteous, and his ears are open to their cry." The idea that the Lord our God is not a personage of tabernacle is entirely a mistaken notion. He was once a man.

Brother Kimball quoted a saying of Joseph the Prophet, that he would not worship a God who had not a Father; and I do not know that he would if he had not a mother; the one would be as absurd as the other. If he had a Father, he was made in his likeness. And if he is our Father we are made after his image and likeness. He once possessed a body, as we now do; and our bodies are as much to us, as his body to him. Every iota of this organization is necessary to secure for us an exaltation with the Gods. Our mortal tabernacles decline. The spirit is inseparably connected with the body until death, and it is so designed; but when we get through with our worship in this Tabernacle or building for worship, we dispense with it until we wish to meet again. We are not inseparably connected with it; it may be consumed by the element of fire and pass away for ever. But it is not so with our bodies; if we wilfully loose these, we loose everything that God has provided for the faithful.

This is an item I wished to explain, though we do not know everything. When brother Kimball speaks, I am so well acquainted with his views and style that I easily understand his meaning; but he does not always fully explain his views to the understanding of the people. This is a point of doctrine that is all and in all to us, consequently it is essentially necessary that we should understand it as it is, and not carry away the idea, from what has been said by brother Kimball, that this is a spiritual kingdom and the body is nothing. Brother Kimball understands this doctrine as I do, but he has his method of expressing his ideas and I have mine; and I am extremely anxious to so convey my ideas to the people that they will understand them as I do. Our language is deficient, and I do not possess in this particular the natural endowment that some men enjoy. I am a man of few words, and unlearned in the learning of this generation. The reason why brother Kimball has not language as perfectly and fully as some other men is not in consequence of a lack in his spirit, for he never has preached when I have heard him, that I did not know what he was about, if he knew himself. I know that his ideas are as clear as the sun that is now shining, and I care not what the words are that he uses to express them.

We have foolish Elders, and I have had to contend, time after time, against their foolish doctrines. One of our most intelligent Apostles in one of his discourses left the people entirely in the dark with regard to Jacob and Esau, and he never understood the difference between fore-knowledge and fore-ordination. Fore-knowledge and fore-ordination are two distinct principles. And again, I have had to contend against what is called the "baby resurrection" doctrine, which, as has been taught and indulged by some, is one of the most absurd doctrines that can be thought of. Having had these foolish doctrines to combat, I am not willing that the idea should possess your minds that the body is neither here nor there, and that the work of salvation is entirely spiritual. We have received these bodies for an exaltation, to be crowned with those who have been crowned with crowns of glory and eternal life. Yes, Joseph Smith said, the Lord whispers to the spirit in the tabernacle the same as though it were out of it. That is correct and true.

What you understand with regard to this doctrine and religion, and with regard to the things of God generally, you understand in the Spirit. Take the spirit from the body, and the body is lifeless; but in the resurrection the component parts of our bodies will again be called together, expressly for a glorious resurrection to immortality. Our bodies, which are now subject to death, will return to mother earth for a time, to be refined from that which pertains to the fall of man, which has particularly affected the body but not the spirit. When the spirit enters the body, it is pure and holy from the heavens; and could it reign predominently in the tabernacle, ruling, dictating, and directing its actions without an opposing force, man never would commit a sin; but the tabernacle has to suffer the effects of the fall, of that sin which Satan has introduced into the world and hence the spirit does not bear rule all the time.

When we receive the Gospel, a warfare commences immediately; Paul says, "for I delight in the law of God, after the inward man," but I see another law in my members warring against the law of my mind, and bringing me into captivity to the law of sin which is in my members." We have to fight continually, as it were, sword in hand to make the spirit master of the tabernacle, or the flesh subject to the law of the spirit. If this warfare is not diligently prosecuted, then the law of sin prevails, and in consequence of this some apostatize from the truth when crossing the plains, learn to swear instead of to pray, become high-minded and high tempered instead of learning to be patient and humble, and when they arrive in these vallies they feel so self-sufficient that they consider themselves the only ones that are really right; they are filled with darkness, the authority of the Spirit is not listened to, and the law of sin and death is the ruling power in their tabernacles. They could once testify, by the revelations of Jesus Christ to them that Mormonism, or the Gospel is true; then the Spirit triumphed over the flesh, they walked in the light of God, and great was their joy, and brilliant their hope of immortality and eternal life. The rule of the flesh brings darkness and death, while, on the other hand, the rule of the Spirit brings light and life. When through the Gospel, the Spirit in man has so subdued the flesh that he can live without wilful transgression, the Spirit of God unites with his spirit, they become congenial companions, and the mind and will of the Creator is thus transmitted to the creature. Did their spirits have their choice there is not a son or daughter of Adam and Eve on the earth but what would be obedient to the Gospel of salvation, and redeem their bodies to exaltation and glory. But there is a constant warfare between them, still they must remain together, be saved and exalted together, or neither of them will be saved and exalted with the salvation and the exaltation which the Gospel offers.

Our bodies are all important to us, though they may be old and withered, emaciated with toil, pain, and sickness, and our limbs bent with rheumatism, all uniting to hasten dissolution, for death is sown in our mortal bodies. The food and drink we partake of are contaminated with the seeds of death, yet we partake of them to extend our lives until our allotted work is finished, when our tabernacles in a state of ripeness, are sown in the earth to produce immortal fruit. Yet, if we live our holy religion and let the Spirit reign, it will not become dull and stupid, but as the body approaches dissolution the spirit takes a firmer hold on that enduring substance behind the vail, drawing from the depths of that eternal Fountain of Light sparkling gems of intelligence which surround the frail and sinking tabernacle with a halo of immortal wisdom.

I shall soon be sixty-one years of age, and my spirit is more vigorous and powerful to-day than it has been in any day I ever saw; it is more quick to comprehend, more ready to discern, the understanding is more matured, more correct in judgment, the memory more vivid and enduring and discretion more circumspect, and when I have attained eighty years I shall be better than I am to-day, God being my helper. I am better now than I was twenty years ago. Write it down and read it twenty year hence, and see whether my spirit is not better and brighter than it is today. Need we in spirit bow down to this poor, miserable, decaying body? We will not. Brother Kimball's side has been broken by a fall from a wagon, but he will be mended up, and his life will not be shortened on that account; and we are going to live until we are satisfied.

The Elders of Israel, though the great majority of them are moral men, and as clear of spot and blemish as men well can be, live beneath their privilege; they live continually without enjoying the power of God. I want to see men and women breathe the Holy Ghost in every breath of their lives, living constantly in the light of God's countenance. Brother Kimball says you must keep alive, and give nourishment and vitality to the body, comparing the Church to a tree; that you must help your Prophet and Revelator and keep that portion of the tree alive. God keeps that alive, brethren and sisters. I thank you for your prayers, your integrity, &c., but I feel to-day as I did in Nauvoo, when Sidney Rigdon and others intended to ride the Church into hell. I told them that I would take my hat and the few that would go with me and build up the kingdom of God, asking no odds of them. If you support me, you support yourselves; if you do not choose to do this you will dry up, blow away and be damned.

A tree or plant of any kind that sends its roots into the ground does not gain strength and vitality from the ground alone, but the atmosphere contributes to its support as well as the ground, and it will live longer out of the ground with air than in the ground without it. From the atmosphere and the rays of the sun it gathers elements that we do not see, which operate upon the sap sent up through the roots under the bark into the branches and leaves where it is prepared to make wood and fruit, and give strength and growth to the trunk, roots, and the whole tree.

Then you may cut off all the limbs and roots of some trees, and the atmosphere will make more in great profusion.

I do not expect to preach a lengthy sermon this afternoon, but there is a great deal to be said and done. The Lord Almighty leads this Church, and he will never suffer you to be led astray if you are found doing your duty. You may go home and sleep as sweetly as a babe in its mother's arms, as to any danger of your leaders leading you astray, for if they should try to do so the Lord would quickly sweep them from the earth. Your leaders are trying to live their religion as far as I am capable of doing so? Yes, I do. The power of God is with me continually, and I never mean to live an hour without it.

I am satisfied that we do not realize to the fullest extent our moral and intellectual growth as a people, but let us be straightened up and a fountain of knowledge is opened, a rich mine of intellectual wealth is revealed, and in time we shall find that heaven and earth have come together, for the earth will be celestialized and brought back to the presence of God, who dwells in eternal burnings in the midst of perfection. Then we should be prepared to enjoy the fullness of the blessings and glory God has in store for us. If we live in these bodies as we should we shall be prepared to receive all the glory he has for the faithful. Let us continue the warfare, fight the good fight of faith, sanctify our hearts before the Lord, and day by day perform the labour he has for us to do, and we shall be accounted worthy to receive our exaltation.

May God bless you. Amen.

{15}

"The Kingdom of God,"
A Sermon Delivered on 13 July 1862

(from *Journal of Discourses*, 26 vols.
[Liverpool: Latter-day Saints' Book Depot, 1855-86], 9:286-89)

I will use, for the foundation of my remarks, words found in Rev. 11th chap., 15th verse—"And the seventh angel sounded, and there were great voices in heaven, saying, The kingdoms of this world are become the kingdoms of our Lord, and of his Christ, and he shall reign for ever and ever."

How near to this text I shall preach, I know not; there is enough in it to answer my purpose, and it is one upon which a great deal can be said.

The plan of salvation cannot be told in one discourse, nor in one day, one month, or one year, for it is from everlasting to everlasting, like the Priesthood of the Son of God, without beginning of days or end of life. The Gospel we declare unto you leads to eternal life, and this kingdom is the kingdom of God which he has promised, by the mouths of his Prophets, that he would set up in the last days—a kingdom that must triumph over all the ills that afflict the family of man, and usher in everlasting righteousness.

Man has wandered far from his Maker—far from the path of rectitude his Heavenly Father has marked out for his feet—and is walking in a way strewn with dangers; he has left the true light, and is walking in darkness; rejected the wisdom and intelligence that is from Heaven, and has become benighted in ignorance and unbelief, neither knowing God, nor the object of his own existence upon the earth. This darkness and ignorance must be dispelled by the preaching of the Gospel, and as many as will believe on the Lord Jesus Christ and walk in all the ordinances of God blameless, will be numbered with his Saints and be gathered into his kingdom to be further taught the principles of eternal life.

The kingdom of God in the latter days must triumph upon all the earth, subdue every species of sin, and destroy every source of sorrow to which down-trodden humanity has been subject. The work of making the kingdoms of the world the kingdom of God and his Christ has commenced; and all the inhabitants of the earth, without exception, will yet acknowledge Jesus to be the Christ, to the glory of God the Father. All mankind are individually interested in this Latter-day Work, for all have a future, whether glorious or inglorious.

Man is created for a glorious purpose—for a life that is eternal. A great deal is comprehended in the two words "eternal life;" they entirely exclude death. We have no death to preach, for we should never practice the principles of death, but pursue the path that leads to the continuation of the lives. The world will be revolutionized by the preach[ing] of the Gospel and the power of the Priesthood, and this work we are called to do. In its progress every foolish and unprofitable custom, every unholy passion, every foolish notion in politics and religion, every unjust and oppressive law, and whatever else that is oppressive to man, and that would impede his onward progress to the perfection of the Holy Ones in eternity, will be removed until everlasting righteousness prevails over the whole earth. Such was the design of the preaching of the Gospel in the days of the Apostles.

It is written in the book of the Acts of the Apostles, "And when they found them not, they drew Jason and certain brethren unto the rulers of the city, crying, These that have turned the world upside down, are come hither also." Using the same figure, the Elders of the Church of Jesus Christ of Latter-day Saints are called to right up the world. To turn it over is a gigantic work, but it will be done, for both the righteous on earth, and the sanctified in heaven are working at it, and all power both in heaven and on earth is given to the Saviour by his Father. It is our business to fully comprehend the sayings and doings of the Saviour in his mission on the earth, which is life to all who believe and endure to the end in the pursuit of life eternal.

A life time is too short to tell the extent of the mission of the Saviour to the human family, but I will venture to use one of his sayings, in connection with what I have already quoted from the book of Revelations. When he was arraigned before Pilate to be tried for his life, he said to Pilate, "My kingdom is not of this world: if my kingdom were of this world, then would my servants fight, that I should not be delivered to the Jews: but now is my kingdom not from hence." Connect this saying with "Blessed are the peacemakers, for they shall be called the children of God," and we can understand how the kingdom of Christ is not of this world, because it is established in peace, unlike all worldly kingdoms which are established in war. The motto of his kingdom is "Peace on earth and good will towards men," and hence not after the order of worldly kingdoms.

It was remarked this morning that the Book of Mormon in no case contradicts the Bible. It has many words like those in the Bible, and as a whole is a strong witness to the Bible. Revelations, when they have passed from God to man, and from man into his written and printed language, cannot be said to be entirely perfect, though they may be as perfect as possible under the circumstances; they are perfect enough to answer the purposes of Heaven at this time.

The saying, "My kingdom is not of this world," and the saying, "The kingdoms of this world shall become the kingdoms of God and his Christ," at the first glance would appear palpable contradictions; but when they are read with their proper connections and by a person whose mind is enlightened by the power of the Holy Ghost, instead of contradiction between them there is seen to exist a perfect harmony. Joseph Smith, the Prophet of the last days, had a happy faculty of reducing the things of heaven to the capacity of persons of common understanding, often in a single sentence throwing a flood of light into the gloom of ages. He had power to draw the spirits of the people who listened to him to his standard, where they communed with heavenly objects and heavenly principles, connecting the heavenly and the earthly together— in one blending flood of heavenly intelligence. When the mind is thus lit up with the Spirit of revelation, it is clearly discerned that the heavens and the earth are in close proximity—that time and eternity are one. We can then understand that the things of God are things which pertain to his children, and that the expression, form and sympathies of his earthly children pertain to their Great Father and Creator.

It has been thought by some that the kingdom Jesus established on the earth, when he was here in the flesh, was not the kingdom Daniel saw. Pardon me, if I differ from this view and say that it was the very kingdom that Daniel saw, but it was not then the time to establish it in its fullness, it was not then the time for the kingdom of God to subdue all other kingdoms as it would be in the latter days.

Jesus came to establish his spiritual kingdom, or to introduce a code of morals that would exalt the spirits of the people to godliness and to God, that they might thereby secure to themselves a glorious resurrection and a title to reign on the earth when the kingdoms of this world should become the kingdoms of our God and his Christ. He also came to introduce himself as the Saviour of the world, to shed his blood upon the altar of atonement, and open up the way of life to all believers. When Jesus came to his own they received him not, but said, "This is the heir, let us kill him and seize on his inheritance;" and they caught him and cast him out of the vineyard, and slew him. Had the Jews received him as the heir, and treated him as such, he would have established his kingdom among them at that time, both spiritually and temporally; and they would have gathered the lost tribes that wandered from Jerusalem, would have overcome their enemies, possessed Palestine in peace, and spread to the uttermost parts of the earth and possessed the kingdom under the whole heavens.

Again, at the time the children of Israel left Egypt if they had then received the Gospel Moses had for them, the kingdom would then have been given to them, and it never would have been broken up, and the house of Israel never would have been smitten and scattered to become bondsmen among the nations. If the children of Abraham, Isaac and Jacob, previous to the Egyptian bondage, had been faithful, they would have received the keys and power of the kingdom, and would never have gone into Egypt to suffer four hundred years in bondage, but they by their wickedness rejected the kingdom.

When God speaks to the people, he does it in a manner to suit their circumstances and capacities. He spoke to the children of Jacob through Moses, as a blind, stiff-necked people, and when Jesus and his Apostles came they talked with the Jews as a benighted, wicked, selfish people. They would not receive the Gospel, though presented to them by the Son of God in all its righteousness, beauty and glory. Should the Lord Almighty send an angel to re-write the Bible, it would in many places be very different from what it now is. And I will even venture to say that if the Book of Mormon were now to be re-written, in many instances it would materially differ from the present translation. According as people are willing to receive the things of God, so the heavens send forth their blessings. If the people are stiff-necked, the Lord can tell them but little.

The kingdom that Jesus came to establish is the kingdom Daniel saw, but that stiff-necked, rebellious generation would not receive the Gospel, and he did not fully establish his kingdom at that time. Could the Lord consistently have given them power over their enemies to whom they were subject while in this state of rebellion to God and his laws, they would have become more wicked than the Romans or other heathen nations of the land. Had he given them power over the Egyptians in the days of Moses, they would have become more wicked than the Egyptians, and would have used this saving power to bring upon them a more sure and terrible destruction.

The Lord called upon Moses, and he stood amid the thunders and lightnings of Mount Sinai. Moses was a good and great man, but he had lived with and so often been aggravated by a wicked, murmuring and rebellious people that he could not look upon God in his glory, but he could hear his voice and converse with his Heavenly Father in the pillar of cloud and fire. He was, on one occasion, in company with seventy Elders of Israel, permitted to see the back parts of the Almighty. He received the law of carnal commandments for Israel from the mouth of God. I believe with all my heart that if the children had been ready to receive the Gospel in all its fulness, the yoke of carnal commandments would never have been placed upon their necks. Moses was a High Priest after the order of Melchisedec, and yet he partook of the sins of the children of Israel to such a degree that he could not see the face of God.

The very kingdom that Jesus said was not of this world would in his day have been permanently established in this world, if the people could have received it, but they would not have the man Christ Jesus to rule over them; they turned away from the holy commandments, and preferred fables. When Jesus stated that his kingdom was not of this world, he did not mean to convey the idea that it had no right to be on this earth, but that his kingdom was a righteous, holy kingdom, and not like the wicked kingdoms of the world; and the wickedness of the world was such that he could not then establish his kingdom upon this earth.

When Moses went into the mountain to converse with the God of Israel, the cry was heard in the camp, "where is this Moses?" And they made a moulten calf of the jewellery they had borrowed from the Egyptians, and said, "These be thy gods, O Israel, which brought thee up out of the land of Egypt. And when Aaron saw it, he built an altar before it, and Aaron made a proclamation, and said, to-morrow is a feast of the Lord. And they rose up early on the morrow, and offered burnt offerings, and brought peace offerings, and the people sat down to eat and to drink and rose up to play." There was as much sense in this proceeding as there is in people's worshipping their property and money at the present day.

The earth is the Lord's and the fullness thereof, and he wishes to establish his kingdom upon it. I do not think any person will start a single argument to prove that the Lord does not own this earth and all that is upon it. All Christians acknowledge that the earth is the Lord's and the fulness thereof, and that Jesus is the Christ and heir of all things.

One excellent idea that was advanced this morning, I will venture to carry out a little further. The time was when the test of a Christian was his confession of Christ. In the first Epistle of John it is written, "Beloved, believe not every spirit, but try the spirits whether they are of God: because many false prophets are gone out into the world. Hereby know ye the Spirit of God; every spirit that confesseth that Jesus Christ is come in the flesh, is of God, and every spirit that confesseth not that Jesus Christ is come in the flesh, is not of God. And this is that spirit of antichrist, whereof ye have heard that it should come, and even now already is in the world." This is no test to this generation, for all men of the Christian world confess that Jesus Christ has come in the flesh. This generation, however, is not left without a test. I have taught for thirty years, and still teach, that he that believeth in his heart and confesseth with his mouth that Jesus is the Christ and that Joseph Smith is his Prophet to this generation, is of God; and he that confesseth not that Jesus has come in the flesh and sent Joseph Smith with the fulness of the Gospel to this generation, is not of God, but is antichrist. All who confess that

Joseph Smith is sent of God in the latter days, to lay the foundation of his everlasting kingdom no more to be thrown down, and will continue to keep his commandments, are born of God. All those who believe in their hearts and confess with their mouths that Joseph Smith is a true Prophet, at the same time trying with their might to live the holy principles Joseph the Prophet has revealed, are in possession of the Holy Spirit of God and are entitled to a fullness. When such men go into the world to preach the Gospel though they know not a letter in a book, they will do more real good to erring man than the great and wise can possibly do, though aided by all their learning and worldly influence in the absence of the gift of the Holy Ghost. When the spirit of the preacher is embued with the Spirit and power of God, his words enter the understandings of the honest, who discern the truth and at once embrace it to their eternal advantage.

Every person who seeks to know right, to understand every principle of truth pertaining to the earth and the heavens, and by obedience to the laws of the Gospel to obtain the Spirit of truth from the great Fountain of truth, when he hears a truth, whether moral, religious, scientific, or mechanical, whether it pertains to God, to man, to the heavens, or to the earth, that truth is congenial to his feelings, and it seems to him that he had known it all his life. Notwithstanding the dreadful effects of the fall of man, almost all men delight in truth and righteousness. If men are not righteous themselves, as a general thing they honour and revere a righteous person more than they do the wicked and forward. A few in these latter days have ventured to stem the current of iniquity; defying the finger of scorn they have raised their hands to Heaven saying, "we are for God." They repeat a glorious text, "The kingdom of God or nothing." It is with them, "Heaven or nothing." The Lord must reign and rule.

We did not produce ourselves. We did not make the earth, nor stretch out the starry heavens. We have not sought out the wisdom of him who formed the foundations of the great deep, nor explored the vastness of his skill in the formation of the finny tribes. "Who removeth the mountains and they knew not; who overturneth them in his anger; who shaketh the earth out of her place, and the pillars thereof tremble; who commandeth the sun, and it riseth not; and sealeth up the stars; who alone spreadeth out the heavens, and treadeth upon the waves of the sea; who maketh Arcturus, Orion, and Pleiades and the chambers of the south; who doeth great things past finding out, yea, and wonders without number."

Philosophy has tried to search out God, but it stands aghast amid the great and wondrous works of the great Supreme. It acknowledges a great Designer and Framer of the universe, but how to approach him, it findeth not. This great Being is the God of the Latter-day Saints; to whom we accede the right of reigning over the workmanship of his own hands. It is his right to control the gold and the silver, the wheat and the fine flour, yea, all the elements that have been enumerated by the searching eye of philosophy and science, and those that are past finding out by mortals in their present state. Has an unholy principle, a wicked influence that leads to death, the right to control the ability and power to do good which God has placed in man? No. God alone has the right to control the intelligence that is in the human family, for he is the giver of it.

Religious people talk a great deal about doing wondrous great things for the Lord—about doing this, that and the other for the glory of God. Every good that man performs is, firstly, for his own benefit and eternal welfare, if he continues in well doing, and secondly, for the common good of others, so far as his example and the influence of good done effects others. We may, for comparison's sake, imagine a great king who has many kingdoms to dispose of and many sons to give them to, but one of his sons will not have his kingly father to rule over him, neither will he accept of any of his favours. Now, if any body suffers loss in this case, it is the proud, rebellious son; the father can give the kingdom, that he otherwise would have given to his wayward son, to a more worthy subject. He is all powerful, and bestows ability to whom he will to become powerful like himself. "If I were hungry, I would not tell thee: for the world is mine, and the fulness thereof. Will I eat the flesh of bulls or drink the blood of goats? Offer unto God thanksgiving, and pay the vows unto the Most High."

The generations of men from the beginning have refused to pay homage to their God, and to render unto him that which belongs to him. If men serve God, it is to their advantage; but they suppose that they sacrifice a great deal for God and do him a great service, and are enriching him and impoverishing themselves. Render unto God that which is God's. I care not whether it be gold, silver or copper. When men extract the precious metals from the earth, they breathe the air, drink the water and eat the food that belongs to God.

I could give the reasons why the servants of God, from the beginning, have not been able to establish his kingdom on the earth, but I have not time to do so to-day. In these latter days, the kingdoms of this world will become "the kingdoms of our God and his Christ," and those who have gold and silver and wealth of other descriptions, and refuse to devote it to the Lord, are blind and naked and destitute of that wisdom which comes from above. The breath that is in their nostrils is not really their own. All people live upon the bounty of the Almighty, yet they say that the precious metals are theirs, and they will devote this wealth to their own service, revel in luxury, and do as they please. Those who possess the wealth of this world, possess it by the permission of the Almighty, and then they go heedlessly on in the way to destruction. How long? Until their race is run.

All must have the privilege of proving to God and angels what they will do with the talent and ability God has given them, whether they will waste their blessings in pandering to unholy appetites or use them in the way God has designed they should. This is one great reason why men are permitted to do as they do. It is an orthodox doctrine that God has decreed whatsoever comes to pass. He has decreed many things to come to pass, but not all things. He has not decreed that one man shall blaspheme his name, and that another shall often be found on his knees praying to him; this is left to the free volition of the creature. All the inhabitants of the earth have had the privilege of proving themselves before God in their life time whether they delighted in that which was right or that which was wrong, and according to that, those who have been without law will be judged without law. What better, in the sight of Heaven, are those who place their affections upon earthly wealth, than the children of Israel who worshipped a calf?

Those who wish to join us in this great work, must do as we have done, to obtain that which we have obtained. It is not our business to question the validity of any of the laws and ordinances of God. It is no matter to us how simple the ordinance he requires us to submit to, in order to attain a certain end. He has said, "he that believeth and is baptized shall be saved." If he has instituted baptism in water for the remission of sins, it is not our business to question his right, to do this, by quarrelling with the mode of this ordinance. If he had told us to dig a hole in the ground and bury ourselves for a certain length of time, it is his right to do so, and our advantage to obey. Whenever the Gospel has been preached in any age of the world, the ordinance of baptism has been in force. It had the same validity in the days of Adam, Enoch, and Noah as in the days of Jesus Christ and his Apostles, or as it has now.

An angel of the Lord visited Adam, when Adam was offering up sacrifice. The angel asked him why he was offering up sacrifice. Adam replied, I know not, but this I do know, the Lord has commanded me, therefore I offer up sacrifice. It may be said that Adam was very ignorant. It was designed by the Lord that his previous knowledge should pass from him.

"Jesus answered and said unto him (Nicodemus,) Verily, verily, I say unto thee, except a man be born again, he cannot see the kingdom of God. Nicodemus saith unto him, How can a man be born when he is old? Can he enter the second time into his mother's womb and be born? Jesus answered, Verily, verily, I say unto thee, except a man be born of water, and of the Spirit, he cannot enter into the kingdom of God." A man must be born again before he can see the kingdom of God; and must be born of water and of the Spirit, before he can enter therein.

It may be asked whether any person can be saved, except those who are baptised. Yes, all the inhabitants of the earth will be saved, except those that sin against the Holy Ghost. Will they come into the presence of the Father and the Son? Not unless they are baptized for the remission of sins, and live faithfully in the observance of the words of life, all the rest of their days. "In my Father's house are many mansions." "Enter ye in at the strait gate; for wide is the gate, and broad is the way that leadeth to destruction, and many there be which go in thereat; because straight is the gate and narrow is the way, which leadeth unto life, and few there be that find it." A question was asked Joseph Smith if all would be damned, except the Latter-day Saints. He answered "yes and most of the Latter-day Saints, unless they repent and do better than they have done."

The glory of those who are not permitted to enter into the presence of the Father and the Son will be greater than mortals can imagine, in glory, excellency, exquisite pleasure, and intense bliss. It has not entered into the heart of man to conceive of the greatness of their glory. But the glory of those who enter into the presence of God exceeds all these in glory, as the light of the sun exceeds the light of the moon and stars. All these different glories are ordained to fit the capacities and conditions of men.

Let me say a word in praise of the congregation before me. Here I see people who have gathered from almost every nation of the earth, and they have brought with them their national customs, traditions, education, fashions and language; yet this mixed people dwell together in peace: all nationality gradually subsides, and we see a universal blending into one, possessing the same feeling and spirit of our holy religion, all being determined to promote the kingdom of God on the earth, looking forward to the day of rest. What other community less needs the services of lawyers, magistrates and judges than this community? This is a joy to me.

The Lord designs to set up his kingdom in our day, and the commandments he requires us to obey and the duties he makes obligatory for us are easy. We can perform all he requires of us, without hurting us in the least.

Some contend that there is no virtue in the water, but there is virtue in him who has made the commandment, and he has power to pardon sins. Were I to command you to wash your bodies and you refused to do so, your filthiness would cleave to you, and you alone would suffer the inconvenience.

We break the bread, which represents the Lord's body, as he has commanded, in remembrance of him, and that he will come to earth again when the kingdoms of this world shall become the kingdoms of our God and his Christ. We pour out water or wine in remembrance of his blood which was shed, and in token of the time when he will drink of the fruit of the vine anew with us in his Father's kingdom, when he comes again and the kingdoms of this world becomes the kingdoms of our God and his Christ. The kingdoms of this world must be prepared for his coming by the proclamation of the Gospel, or be wiped out of existence.

The whole would have lost confidence in themselves and in their God. How can it be restored? By beginning to serve God, and then trying to induce every man and woman to join heart and hand in this moral reformation. By associating with those with whom you can trust your wealth, honour, good name, virtue and integrity, and inviting all to join you who are full of integrity and honour, and who will treat you as the angels of God would if they were here. We must restore the integrity and confidence which have been lost to the world. The kings upon their thrones have to pay for their positions, for they cannot trust themselves in the hands of their attendants, without bribery. Only the semblance of honour, integrity and confidence are to be found in the world, and even that brings a high price; however, this general remark has its honourable exceptions. We must find men and women that we can trust with everything that is sacred to us, or the kingdom of God can never be established upon the earth. The Lord will not acknowledge a people who will falsify their word and are unvirtuous; he will not long trust a man of that kind with any of the affairs of his kingdom. He will not trust an unvirtuous people with his Holy Priesthood. He will not trust a people with property—with earthly wealth—who will covet the same and use it to pander to their lusts, and otherwise devote it to the power of the enemy of God and man.

The business of the Latter-day Saints is to bring forth the kingdom of God in the last days, morally, religiously, and politically. Will they do it? I rather think they will, with the help of God. No matter what the enemies of God and his cause do with our name, or with our means; no matter how often they hurl us from our habitations and drive us from city to city, and from county to county, let every one of us be found standing upon the pedestal of truth and virtue, defiling not our persons by sin in any way. Let us esteem all that we are permitted to possess as given to us of the Lord; whether it be gold, silver, goods, houses, lands, or wives and children, they are all the Lord's. These blessings are only lent to us. When we have passed this earthly ordeal and have proven to the heavens that we are worthy to be crowned with crowns of glory, immortality and eternal lives, then the Lord will say these are yours, but until then we own nothing.

Will all believe as we believe? I know not. I would be pleased if all men would believe the truth and practice righteousness. If they have truth in their possession, I wish them to be as generous with it as I am. I freely impart to my fellow-beings all the truth I know of, and all the rules of godliness I am in possession of. My religion teaches me to embrace all truth in the heavens, on the earth, under the earth, and in the bottomless pit, if there is any there. My creed embraces all truth. If you have truth that I have not, let me know it, and it will come to where it belongs; and if I have truth which you have not you are welcome to it. There is no need of debate and contention in regard to truth and error, for debate tends to create a spirit of bitterness.

These is no need for war and bloodshed, for the earth is large enough for all. The elements of which this earth is composed are all around it. Philosophers say the atmosphere is forty miles deep. Be this as it may, there are no bounds to the elements that compose worlds like this. This earthly ball, this little opake substance thrown off into space, is only a speck in the great universe; and when it is celestialized it will go back into the presence of God, where it was first framed. All belongs to God, and those who keep his celestial law will return to him.

Many inquiries are made as to what will become of that portion of the world of mankind who have died without law. When we return to build up the waste places of Zion, then will the Scripture be fulfilled— "Him that overcometh will I make a pillar in the temple of my God, and he shall go no more out: and I will write upon him the name of my God, and the name of the city of my God, which is New Jerusalem, which cometh down out of heaven from my God: and I will write upon him my new name." The servants of God will officiate for the dead in the temples of God which will be built. The Gospel is now preached to the spirits in prison, and when the time comes for the servants of God to officiate for them, the names of those who have received the Gospel in the spirit will be revealed by the angels of God and the spirits of just men made perfect; also the places of their birth, the age in which they lived, and everything regarding them that is necessary to be recorded on earth, and they will then be saved so as to find admittance into the presence of God, with their relatives who have officiated for them. The wicked will be cleansed and purified as by fire; some of them will be saved as by fire. Some will be given over to the buffetting of Satan, that their spirits may be saved in the day of the Lord Jesus. Others will receive their bodies, but cannot be saved in the kingdoms and mansions that are in the presence of God. All the children of man will receive a glory in the mansions of God according to their capacities, and rewards according to their acts in the flesh.

Brethren and friends, do you naturally despise such a doctrine as this, or does it find a response of welcome in your bosoms? My soul says, Hallelujah, every moment I think of the ample provisions God has made for his sons and daughters. They will not welter in hell to an endless eternity, but they will rise higher and higher, and continue to increase in intelligence and love of truth as they advance. There will be an eternal progress in the knowledge of God.

May God bless the people. Amen.

16

"For Many Years I have Sought to Instruct
My Fellow Beings in the Ways of Life and Salvation,"
A Sermon Delivered on 19 July 1863

For many years I have sought to instruct my fellow beings in the ways of life and salvation, and, as far as I had influence, I have endeavored to lead them in the path of right, in their faith, in their morals, and in the government of every passion and impulse of their natures. Whether my daily example has corresponded with my teachings, I will leave all who are acquainted with me to judge. My spiritual walk and conversation have been constantly before the Latter-day Saints, who are my witnesses as to the way in which I have lived my religion.

It is my desire to be saved in the Kingdom of God; and it is my desire that all who can shall be saved in the presence of God and of His Son, Jesus Christ. For this I labor and toil, and with me it is the Kingdom of God or nothing. Nothing can endure, only that which abides in God.

All the triumphs of science are the grand results of revealed truth. All that mankind possesses of true greatness and goodness is the gift of God. All that is not of God and that does not exist to honor Him, will sooner or later return to native element. Consequently, to serve God and to acknowledge Him in His true character and in His works should be the greatest and highest purpose of mankind while they exist here. To deny the existence of God is equal to denying the existence of intelligence. To deny the existence of God is equal to denying the existence of the earth and of all things that live and breathe upon it. Those who worship a God who does not exist, and to worship a bodiless, passionless, partless God, is equal to worshipping something that is non-existent, subscribe to the worship of a fable and walk in total darkness so far as knowledge of the true God is concerned. It must strike [a] sensible person that nothing can be made without a maker, that nothing can be created without a creator, and that no person can be begotten without a father, or brought forth without a mother. These are plain facts which we all naturally know. The earth exists, and it owes its existence to a designer, organizer, and framer. We exist, and owe our existence to a Maker. There is a Supreme Being, and to Him the earth and its fullness, the animate and inanimate, existence owe their being; and this God, Brother Spencer told us this morning, he delighted to acknowledge. In the fashionable world it is quite a remarkable circumstance to find a single person who is willing to openly acknowledge the God of Heaven as the Creator, and upholder of all things. Indeed, it is quite a task for professed Christians even to acknowledge God, hence they are exhorted, "oh, my dear brother, my dear sister, do take up your cross, and be not afraid to acknowledge God," for "he that denieth me before men shall be denied before the angels of God." The man that cannot freely acknowledge God must be devoid of the best portion that intelligence granted to his race, must stand branded as unwise in the midst of created things, and virtually denies before God and angels that he ever possessed true intelligence.

In modern revelation it is said that the Lord is displeased with none save those who do not acknowledge His hand in all things. Who gave the knowledge there is in the world? O, inhabitants of the earth, can you hear it? It was God who gave it. Who gave Robert Fulton knowledge to apply steam and machinery to propel boats? He said that he had dreamed on the subject. Who gave them to him? It was God. Through the achievements of agricultural science, the raw material is produced of which the numerous and varied appliances of civilization are made; and the great attainments in mechanical knowledge have harnessed the elements to powerful and nicely adjusted machinery for making the raw material into articles for clothing and other conveniences. The greatest and wisest of mankind are unable to make a mosquito wing, or a leaf, or a blade of grass, independent of God and His laws.

There are great mysteries connected with the different races of men. Why and how they are made different in their color, intelligence, and physical construction, philosophers and learned men have failed to discover. Why have they thus failed? Because they do not possess the key to their own philosophy. Men may have much knowledge given to them, and yet not possess the key of knowledge.

Brother [Orson] Spencer said that he is thankful that he is located in these sequestered vales, far away from those who have hated, hunted, and persecuted the Latter-day Saints. Why have they so abused this people? Because we hold the key of knowledge that all the world are ignorant of. For this we have been driven to the secluded country. I also am exceedingly thankful that we are here. I used to pray to be delivered from the Christians. I am delivered from them, thank God, and from there [sic] pernicious influences. The nations of Christendom naturally have good common sense, yet it is so perverted that they do not know how to preserve themselves. They know not how to wisely guide their own affairs, nor how to conduct themselves one with another without corrupting each other, and destroying every vestige of honor, virtue, and truth that exists among them. Some of them are willfully blind, and some are ignorantly so. They acknowledge the Bible to be true; they say that it contains the words of God to them; they say that they believe the accounts given by Moses of the creation of man, that God said, "Let us make man in our own image, after our likeness." Yet [in] the most sublime and transcendent stretch of their philosophical and scientific theology, they have not succeeded in finding out the God of Abraham, Isaac, and Jacob, in whom, in their few common sense moments of thought, they believe. The Bible gives Him an image, a likeness, a body, with parts, senses, and passions, which has a location, a family, a home, but we find modern theology has set up an idol to worship which cannot be said to have the likeness of anything that ever did or ever will exist in all the eternities of God, and that does not possess any one of the qualifications possessed by the God of the Saints. It would be much more consistent to altogether set aside the Bible as a revelation of the will of God to man, than to profess to believe in it and then depart from it in practice. It would be more consistent to boldly say that there is no God, consequently no heaven, nor earth, that we are not or that we are anything but what we really are, than to persist in worshipping a phantom of the brain, at the same time persuading ourselves that we are worshipping the true God.

I can tell all the world that we have a Father and a God; that He has a home, a location, a mansion of glory where He dwells, that He is endowed with all the powers of physical and mental constitution possessed by His children, mankind, but that He has those powers developed in a degree infinitely more perfect than they; that He is capable of understanding and supplying the wants of all His creatures, and is touched with the infirmities of His children that live in a sinful world.

Much proof could be produced to demonstrate that good, sober sense is not a prevailing element in the philosophical, political, theological, and scientific knowledge of the world.

When men have surrounded themselves with the comforts of life, when they have accumulated means to live and friends to live with, when they are happy in their peaceful homes removed from the busy bustle and turmoil of life, when they enjoy the society of wives, children, and friends, being charmed and consoled by music made at home, their minds, educated and used and refreshed from the rich stores of their libraries, when in short they have surrounded themselves with every means of home comfort, improvement and enjoyment, what a blessed and happy state of society it would be could such senses of home felicity and contentment and peace be perpetuated and remain forever undisturbed; but no, the husband and father dragged from his peaceful domicile, hurried to the field of sanguinery strife, where he is left bleeding far away from the loved ones at home and the comforts that surround them, which cease to give them happiness in the absence of him around whom they once so often circled in their happy glee.

Petty differences between potentates and rulers of nations have to be arbitrated by shedding rivers of blood, and sending blight and despair into the bosoms of thousands of families whose protectors and friends have fallen in the fields of battle. Intelligence and good sense would devise means to protect every man in the enjoyment of his life, home, country and friends, where they prevail peaceful hours like a river, and war with its dread consequences never comes. Is not the present condition of the world positive and undeniable proof that unperverted sense and wisdom that God gives does not prevail among mankind? Are not the sayings of the prophets literally fulfilled? "Wherefore the Lord said, for as much as this people draw near me with their mouths, and with their lips do honor Me, but removed their hearts far from Me, their fear toward Me is taught by the precepts of men: therefore, behold, I will proceed to do a marvelous work among this people, even a marvelous work and a wonder: for the wisdom of their wise men shall perish, and the understanding of their prudent men shall be hid." Again, speaking of Zion in the last days, "Now also many nations are against Thee, that say, let her be defiled, and let our eye look upon Zion, but they know not the thoughts of the Lord, neither understand they His counsel; for He shall gather them as the sheaves into the floor."

Our nation would have spent many millions of treasure to prevent the Latter-day Saints from coming to these mountains, had they known the counsels of the Lord. They may hunt the Mormons now, but it will do them no good. They have driven us to where the Prophet Joseph said that we should be driven. He said in Nauvoo, "This people will leave here. We have been kicked out of the frying pan into the fire, and the next they do will be to kick us into the middle of the floor, where they do not want us." If we are not now in the middle of the floor, I do not know where the middle of the floor can be.

It is a fashionable practice in fashionable society to profanely swear by the name of God the Father and His Son Jesus Christ, throwing dishonor upon the name of their Maker and upon the name of their Redeemer. God will bring all such into judgment. True ladies or gentlemen, even if they did not believe in the existence of Deity, would not be found using His name profanely; but the true character of a saint is to openly acknowledge God in all things, never taking His name in vain, but using it at all times with reverence and proper solemnity. This also properly becomes every person of intelligence who is in doubt with that wisdom which comes from God. Those who honor and reverence the author of their existence, honor themselves.

While I am speaking of the Christian world, my mind glances at the heathen world; they are as much Christians as those who profess the name of Christ in Christendom. There are no people upon the face of the whole earth but what have once been in possession of the knowledge of the true God, and have, sometime in the past, been in possession of the Holy Priesthood. Why are they so ignorant and benighted in their understanding? And why is the Christian world so lost to every sense of duty to themselves and to their Father and God? It is because they have transgressed the law of God, have changed His ordinances, and broken the everlasting covenant which God made with the fathers. Why is the House of Judah and the half tribe of Benjamin scattered to the four winds of heaven and left to wander to and fro on the earth like lost sheep? It is for the same cause, and because they clamored for the blood of the Savior and wished it to be upon them and upon their children. The other tribes were scattered, smitten and led away for the same cause. If any of them have ever kept the Holy Priesthood among them, they have been led to where no communion could be held with them since they went away.

I declare to the heavens and to the earth, and to all intelligent beings that dwell in them, that we possess the true gospel of the Son of God, that we acknowledge God, our Father, Who lives in heaven, in whose image we are made; that we may dwell with Him, we must be made perfect through suffering as He was. We believe that He is perfect in His power, in His glory and in His exaltation, possessing all things and swaying His sceptre over all things that we know anything about. His power and intelligence are everywhere disseminated. Not a sparrow can fall to the ground without His notice, and the very hairs of our heads are numbered. He goes where He pleases throughout His extended dominions; He is capable of walking through this congregation, or of preaching from this stand, and we would not know Him from one of ourselves. Or He can show Himself in His glory, which could not be endured by persons still in the flesh. We believe in Jesus Christ, the heir of the family, who gave His life for the redemption of the earth, and everything pertaining to it—every flesh that ever lived and walked or crawled on the earth, flew in the air, or swam in the waters, that He may bring forth the Kingdom of God as prepared for Him and present it to His Father spotless; that was the object of His errand in the world. We believe that He was the Son of Mary and of God, precisely as recorded in the New Testament.

I am happy in having the privilege of speaking to my fellow beings who are passing through this territory. I have traveled scores of thousands of miles, often with bleeding feet, and many times without food, to preach the gospel to mankind, and now people are willing to come and hear me. I am thankful for the privilege of speaking to them, and I shall tell them the truth and in whom we believe.

It is stated in the book of Doctrine and Covenants that "Seth was a perfect man and his likeness was the express likeness of his father's, insomuch that he seemed to be like unto his father in all things, and could be distinguished from him only by his age." So it is with Jesus Christ and His Father. They are one and cannot be known apart only as Adam and Seth were known apart. Shall we boldly acknowledge all these things before the world? Yes, and let the world howl as they have—let them howl on. By and by every knee shall bow and every tongue shall confess to the glory of God the Father, that Jesus is the Christ. We had better do this sensibly and willingly. I do not know how other people feel, but I never want to be drive[n] to do anything. I want to willingly do what I do, that I may have credit for what I do. If I am forced to do a thing, then I have no reward. If I wanted to be a soldier in the army, I would willingly go and be one, and fight like a man, but if they undertook to drive me to it, they would have a hard work to perform. What! Go to murder my fellow men? But it is argued that it cannot be murder when men kill each other in a popular war. It is just as much murder as it is for the Indians to kill the passing immigrants.

At the judgment of the quickened dead, popular leaders, who have inaugurated war instead of arbitrating peace, will be held accountable to God for the lives of their subjects which they have caused to be destroyed on the battlefields, and for the thousands of hearts they have broken and for the destitution and suffering they have caused to exist outside the battlefields in trying to maintain what they called the honor and dignity of their nation. Every generous, noble, and God-like impulse that dwells in the breasts of earthly and heavenly beings, cries aloud for war to cease. Is there not room enough in the world for every man to have his farm and his garden? And why cannot the advantages and blessings of commerce be enjoyed by all, without mixing folly, rabidness, and devilism with wise and free institutions?

What say the powers of wickedness? Destroy each other, or make each other as wretched as you possibly can. Heaven says, "Let there be no war among you, my children, and let the bonds of everlasting peace continue to grow stronger and stronger until all are sanctified and I can come and dwell with you, like the children of Israel in the days of the Prophet Samuel, they say make us a king to judge us like all the nations." When this demand was made to Samuel by the Israelites, he prayed unto the Lord, "And the Lord said unto Samuel, hearken unto the voice of the people in all that they say unto thee: for they have not rejected thee, but they have rejected Me, that I should not reign over them." A king was given to Israel with this prophecy for Samuel, after they had seen the great sin in asking (for) a king, "but if ye shall still do wickedly, ye shall be consumed both ye and your king."

The people of the world have chosen kings to rule over them, as Israel did of old, and have refused to acknowledge God to be their king. Hence, desolating wars and their consequent evils have from time to time almost depopulated kingdoms, laying the foundation for burdens and exactions from the survivors to pay the expenses of costly and needless wars and to sustain princes in their luxourious idleness (who) have made slaves of millions who now groan in their chains and cry to God for deliverance. When the wicked rule, the people mourn; while prosperity, peace and plenty flow under the sway of righteous rulers.

It was the overanxious, tyrannical and grasping disposition that rendered it necessary for the American Revolutionary fathers to take up the sword in defense of their liberties. Had the King of England conceded to them, the right of self-government, when they called for it, the effusion of much blood would have been stayed, and that king would have less to answer for before the bar of God.

Laws instituted by nations are to hold in check the turbulent, wicked, and unruly spirits of the people, and to fortify kingly authority and power against insurrection and the vengeance of the oppressed millions. Law is not made for the upright, only to exalt them. The law and order of heaven are given expressly to increase celestial intelligence in the Saints, and to advance them in glory and power eternal. The man who walks uprightly before his God and infringes upon the rights of none, but feeds the hungry and clothes the naked, doing all he can to improve the condition of and happify his fellow-beings, walks above all law, and goes onward and still onward from conquering unto conquering. The laws of God are given to exalt the Saints to a higher state of glory—celestial felicity and power, while the laws of men are too often made and enforced to subject the creature who disobeys them to increased depths of misery and degradation. The law of God enstills into the human soul a hatred of sin by portraying the beauties and advantages of righteousness, elevating it even above the desire to do wrong; the laws of men, consisting chiefly in a code of penalties, against crime, are made more to over-awe the creature than to instruct and elevate the mind above the love of crime. Obedience to the one brings the spirit of God—the Holy Ghost—to enlighten and educate the mind with heavenly wisdom; obedience to the other promises protection of life and property, but in every instance leaves the mind still uninformed and in darkness. "The law of the Lord is perfect, converting the soul." "Great peace have they who love Thy law."

The two ways are before us—the law of life and the law of death; the one gives the sheep a wide range and exalts them to glory, the other unchains the dogs from confinement. The laws of men have a good and salutary influence upon society—keeping the unscrupulous merdurder

[sic] and the desparately [sic] wicked within bounds, encouraging the arts of industry and the progression of political and domestic economy, therefore "let no man break the laws of the land, for he that keepeth the laws of God hath no need to break the laws of the land: wherefore, be subject to the powers that be, until He reigns whose right it is to reign, and subdues all enemies under His feet." "For rulers are not a terror to good works, but to the evil." "Owe no man anything but to love one another, for he that loveth another hath fulfilled the law."

Very often we hear people excuse themselves in their wickedness because of sin which dwells in their mortal bodies, arguing that they were born in sin, and shapen in inequity—born into the world with no good thing in them. This tradition is simply not true, and this favorite argument of theirs will fail them at the bar of God. People are wicked because they list to be wicked. If they were made wicked without their agency, then may it fairly be expected that this same power will make them righteous without any effort of theirs; but seeing that they are wicked of their own free will and accord they are very justly addressed in the language of the prophet, "Let the wicked forsake his ways, and the unrighteous man his thoughts; and let him return unto the Lord and He will have mercy upon him, and to our God, for He will abundantly pardon."

My counsel to all the Saints is to love God and to keep His commandments. And to those who do not wish to be Latter-day Saints, I say live a good, moral, virtuous life, and win the confidence of all your acquaintances, that they may esteem you as a faithful and trustworthy man.

May the Lord bless you, Amen.

17

"Personality of God
—His Attributes—Eternal Life, Etc.,"
A Sermon Delivered on 18 June 1865

(from *Journal of Discourses*, 26 vols.
[Liverpool: Latter-day Saints' Book Depot, 1855-86], 11:119-28)

I wish the strict attention of the congregation, which is so large and widely spread under this low bowery that I fear it will be with difficulty that I can make myself heard by all. To persons who wish to understand and improve upon what they hear, it must be very annoying to only hear the sound of the speaker's voice and not be able to comprehend its signifi-cation.

The gospel of life and salvation has again been committed to the children of men, and we are made the happy partakers of its blessings, and my sincere desire is that all may improve upon the words of life which have been revealed from the heavens in our day. It is written, "And this is life eternal, that they might know Thee the only true God, and Jesus Christ whom Thou hast sent." All nations, tribes and communities of men worship something, it may be a stump, a stock, a tree, a stone, a figure moulded in brass, iron, silver, or gold, or some living creature, or the sun, the moon, the stars, or the god of the wind and other elements, and while worship[p]ing gods which they can see and handle, there dwells within them a crude and undefined impression of a great Supreme and universal Ruler whom they seek to represent and worship in gods made with their own hands; but where he is located, what his shape and dimensions and what his qualifications are they know not. The Apostle Paul found the city of the Athenians wholly given to idolatry; and they called him a "babbler," because he preached unto them Jesus and the resurrection. He disputed in the synagogue with the Jews and with the devout persons, and in the market daily with them who met with him; and standing, in the midst of Mars-hill, he said, "Ye men of Athens, I perceive that in all things ye are too superstitious. For as I passed by and beheld your devotions, I found an altar with this inscription, 'To the Unknown God.' Whom, therefore, ye ignorantly worship, Him declare I unto you."

The Athenians knew not what to worship, and it seems they were willing to worship a god unknown to them, very likely under the impression that he might be the true God, whom they had tried to represent no doubt in various ways.

Wherever the human family dwell upon the face of the earth, whether they are savage or civilized, there is a desire implanted within them to worship a great, Supreme Ruler, and not knowing Him, they suppose that through offering worship and sacrifice to their idols they can conciliate his anger which they think they see manifested in the thunder, in the lightning, in the storm, in the floods, in the reverses of war, in the hand of death, etc., etc.; thus they try to woo his protection and his blessing for victory over their enemies, and at the termination of this life for a place in the heaven their imaginations have created, or tradition has handed down to them. I have much charity for this portion of the human family called heathens or idolators; they have made images to present to their eyes a power which they cannot see, and desire to worship a Supreme Being through the figure which they have made.

There is a Power that has organised all things from the crude matter that floats in the immensity of space. He has given form, motion and life to this material world; has made the great and small lights that bespangle the firmament above; has allotted to them their times and their seasons, and has marked out their spheres. He has caused the air and the waters to teem with life, and covered the hills and plains with creeping things, and has made man to be a ruler over His creations. All these wonders are the works of the Almighty ruler of the universe, in whom we believe and whom we worship. "The earth rolls upon her wings, and the sun giveth his light by day, and the moon giveth her light by night, and the stars also giveth their light, as they roll upon their wings in their glory, in the midst of the power of God." "Behold all these are kingdoms, and any man who hath seen any or the least of these, hath seen God moving in his majesty and power."

All people are conscious of the existence of a Supreme Being: they see Him or His power in the sun, in the moon and in the stars, in the storm, in the thunder and in the lightning, in the mighty cataract, in the bursting volcano, or in the powerful and disgusting reptile, etc. He is also described by some as having no form, attributes, or power, or in other words, "without body, parts or passions," and, consequently, without power or principle; and there are persons who suppose that He consists entirely of attributes universally diffused. Not knowing God they worship His works that manifest His power and His majesty, or His attributes which manifest His goodness, justice, mercy and truth. According to all that the world has ever learned by the researches of philosophers and wise men, according to all the truths now revealed by science, philosophy and religion, qualities and attributes depend entirely upon their connection with organised matter for their development and visible manifestation.

Mr. Abner Kneeland, who was a citizen of Boston, and who was put into prison for his belief, in an essay which he wrote, made this broad assertion: "Instead of believing there is no God, I believe that all is God."

We believe in a Deity who is incorporated—who is a Being of tabernacle, through which the great attributes of His nature are made manifest. It is supposed by a certain celebrated philosopher that the most minute particles of matter which float in space, in the waters, or that exist in the solid earth, particles which defy the most powerful glasses to reveal them to the vision of finite man, possess a portion of divinity, a portion of infinite power, knowledge, goodness and truth, and that these qualities are God, and should be worshipped wherever found. I am an infidel to this doctrine. I know the God in whom I believe, and am willing to acknowledge Him before all men. We have persons in this church who have preached and published doctrines on the subject of the Deity which are not true. Elder Orson Pratt has written extensively on the doctrines of this church, and upon this particular doctrine. When he writes and speaks upon subjects with which he is acquainted and understands, he is a very sound reasoner; but when he has written upon matters of which he knows nothing—his own philosophy, which I call vain philosophy— he is wild, uncertain, and contradictory. In all my public administration as a minister of truth, I have never yet been under the necessity of preaching, believing or practising doctrines that are not fully and clearly set forth in the Old and New Testaments, Book of Doctrine and Covenants, and Book of Mormon.

The Book of Mormon, which we firmly believe to be the word of God to nations that flourished upon this continent many centuries ago, corroborates the testimonies of the writers of the Old and New Testaments, and proves these books to be true. They were given to us in weakness, darkness and ignorance; I will, however, give the translators of King James's version of the Bible the credit of performing their labor according to the best of their ability, and I believe they understood the languages in which the Scriptures were originally found as well as any men who now live. I have in my life-time met with persons who would persist in giving different renderings, and make quotations from the dead languages to show their scholarship, and to confuse and darken still more the minds of the people. To all such I have always felt like saying, there is the Bible, if you are capable of giving us a more correct translation of it than we have, it is your duty to do so. The Old and New Testaments have always answered my purpose as books of reference. Many precious parts have no doubt been taken from them; but the translation which we have, has been translated according to the best knowledge the translators possessed of the languages in which the ancient manuscripts were written, yet as uninspired men they were not qualified to write the things of God.

I believe in one God to us; as it is written, "For though there be that are called gods, whether in heaven or in earth (as there be gods many, and lords many); but to us there is but one God, the Father, of whom are all things, and we in Him; and one Lord Jesus Christ, by whom are all things, and we by Him," and, "They were called Gods unto whom the word of God came." I believe in a God who has power to exalt and glorify all who believe in Him, and are faithful in serving Him to the end of their lives, for this makes them Gods, even the sons of God, and in this sense also there are Gods many, but to us there is but one God, and one Lord Jesus Christ—one Saviour who came in the meridian of time to redeem the earth and the children of men from the original sin that was committed by our first parents, and bring to pass the restoration of all things through His death and sufferings, open wide to all believers the gates of life and salvation and exaltation to the presence of the Father and the Son to dwell with them for ever more. Numerous are the scriptures which I might bring to bear upon the subject of the personality of God. I shall not take time to quote them on this occasion, but will content myself by quoting two passages in the 1st chapter of Genesis, 26th and 27th verses. "And God said, let us make man in our image, after our likeness; and let them have dominion over the fish of the sea, and over the fowl of the air, and over the cattle, and over all the earth, and over every creeping thing that creepeth upon the earth. So God created man in his own image, in the image of God created he him; male and female created he them."

I believe that the declaration made in these two scriptures is literally true. God has made His children like Himself to stand erect, and has endowed them with intelligence and power and dominion over all His works, and given them the same attributes which He Himself possesses. He created man, as we create our children; for there is no other process of creation in heaven, on the earth, in the earth, or under the earth, or in all the eternities, that is, that were, or that ever will be. As the Apostle Paul has expressed it, "For in Him we live, and move, and have our being." "Forasmuch then as we are the offspring of God, we ought not to think that the Godhead is like unto gold, or silver, or stone, graven by art or man's device." There exist fixed laws and regulations by which the elements are fashioned to fulfill their destiny in all the varied kingdoms and orders of creation, and this process of creation is from everlasting to everlasting. Jesus Christ is known in the scriptures as the only begotten of the Father, full of grace and truth, and it is written of Him as being the brightness of the Father's glory and the express image of His person. The word image we understand in the same sense as we do the word in the 3rd verse of the 5th chapter of Genesis, "And Adam lived an hundred and thirty years, and begat a son in his own likeness, after his image." I am quite satisfied to be made aware by the scriptures, and by the Spirit of God, that He is not only the God and Father of Jesus Christ, but is also the Father of our spirits and the Creator of our bodies which bear His image as Seth bore the image of his father Adam. Adam begat many children who bore His image, but Seth is no doubt more particularly mentioned, because he was more like his father than the rest of the family.

We bear the image of our earthly parents in their fallen state, but by obedience to the gospel of salvation, and the renovating influences of the Holy Ghost, and the holy resurrection, we shall put on the image of the heavenly, in beauty, glory, power and goodness. Jesus Christ was so like His Father that on one occasion in answer to a request, "Show us the Father," He said, "He that hath seen me hath seen the Father." The strongest testimony that can be borne to the minds of men is the testimony of the Father concerning the Son, and the testimony of the Son concerning the Father, by the power of the revelations of the Spirit, which every man who is born of woman possesses more or less, and which, if mankind would listen to it, would lead them to the knowledge of God and ultimately, assisted by the ordinances of the gospel, into His presence.

If there is anything that is great and good and wise among men, it cometh from God. If there are men who possess great ability as statesmen, or as philosophers, or who possess remarkable scientific knowledge and skill, the credit thereof belongs to God, for He dispenses it to His children whether they believe in Him or not, or whether they sin against Him or not; it makes no difference; but all will have to account to Him for the way and manner in which they have used the talents committed unto them. If we believe the plain, broad statements of the Bible, we must believe that Jesus Christ is the light that lighteth every man that cometh into the world; none are exempt. This applies to all who possess the least degree of light and intelligence, no matter how small; wherever intelligence can be found, God is the author of it. This light is inherent according to a law of eternity—according to the law of the Gods, according to the law of Him whom we serve as the only wise, true and living God to us. He is the author of this light to us. Yet our knowledge is very limited; who can tell the future, and know it as the past is known to us? It is a small thing, if we were acquainted with the principle. Were we acquainted with this principle, we could just as well read the future as the past.

The Latter-day Saints believe in Jesus Christ, the only begotten Son of the Father, who came in the meridian of time, performed his work, suffered the penalty and paid the debt of man's original sin by offering up Himself, was resurrected from the dead, and ascended to His Father; and as Jesus descended below all things, so He will ascend above all things. We believe that Jesus Christ will come again, as it is written of Him:

"And while they looked steadfastly toward Heaven as He went up, behold, two men stood by them in white apparel; which also said, Ye men of Galilee why stand ye gazing up into heaven? this same Jesus which is taken from you unto heaven, shall so come in like manner as ye have seen Him go unto heaven."

Strange as it may appear to many we believe that Jesus Christ will descend from heaven to earth again even as He ascended into heaven. "Behold, He cometh with clouds, and every eye shall see Him, and they also which pierced Him: and all kindreds of the earth shall wail because of Him." He will come to receive His own, and rule and reign king of nations as He does king of saints; "For He must reign, till He hath put all enemies under His feet. The last enemy that shall be destroyed is death." He will banish sin from the earth and its dreadful consequences, tears shall be wiped from every eye and there shall be nothing to hurt or destroy in all God's holy mountain.

In view of the establishment of the kingdom of God upon the earth by Jesus Christ, John the Baptist proclaimed, that the kingdom of heaven is at hand. "Prepare ye the way of the Lord, make His paths straight;" and, "John did baptize in the wilderness, and preach the baptism of repentance, for the remission of sins." Jesus Christ sent His disciples to preach the gospel to every creature, to the king and the peasant, to the great and the small, to the rich and the poor, to the bond and the free, to the black and the white; they were sent to preach the gospel of repentance and remission of sins to all the world, and "He that believeth and is baptized shall be saved, but he that believeth not shall be damned; and these signs shall follow them that believe: In my name shall they cast out devils; they shall speak with new tongues; they shall take up serpents, and if they drink any deadly thing it shall not hurt them, they shall lay hands on the sick and they shall recover."

The Latter-day Saints, this strange people as they are called, believe and practice this gospel; they believe that the acts of the creatures, in the performance of the ordinances, prove to the heavens, to God, to angels and to the good who are upon the earth—to their brethren and to those who are not their brethren in a church capacity—to those who believe and to those who do not believe, that they are sincere in their belief before God and man. Every doctrine and principle that is laid down in the Old and New Testaments for salvation, this people will persist in believing and practicing; and, for so doing, they have become a byword, and are wondered at by the orthodox Christians of the 19th century, who are truly astonished that anybody, in this enlightened age, should emphatically believe that the Lord and His servants anciently spoke the truth, and intended their words should be believed and practiced by all who desire salvation. It is our privilege, if we so wish, to disbelieve the words of God or a part of them; but we choose rather to believe all the words of God, and are trying to observe all of His precepts, to purify the Lord God in our hearts.

There cannot be found a people upon the face of the whole earth who are more perfect in the belief and practice of the gospel of Jesus Christ than are the Latter-day Saints, and there exists no people who are more easily governed. We have been gathered from many nations, and speak many languages; we have been ruled by different nationalities, and educated in different religions, yet we dwell together in Utah under one government, believe in the same God and worship Him in the same way, and we are all one in Christ Jesus. The world wonder[s] at this, and fear the union that prevails among this, as they are called, singular people. Why is this? It is because the Spirit of the Lord Almighty is in the people, and they follow its dictates, and they hearken to the truth, and live by it; this unites them in one, and causeth them to dwell together in peace; and were it not for pettifogging lawyers and judges who are among us, a law suit would not be heard of in Utah from one year's end to another. When many of these people come to Utah they are poor and houseless, but they go to work and labor away with all their might, without a murmur, under wise and judicious guidance, and in a short time they are able to gather from the soil, the water and the air, the essential and solid comforts of life.

When a lawyer comes into the church, if he happens to have a little common sense left, and will take to ploughing and cultivating the soil, there is a chance for him to make a man of himself; but if he follows his former customs and habits, the chances are against him, he may ruin himself, lose the Spirit of the Lord, if he ever possessed it, and go back into midnight darkness.

It is through the proclamation of the gospel that this great people have been gathered from their homes in distant parts of the earth. It is not in the power of man to accomplish such a work of gathering thousands of men, women, and children from different nations to a distant inland country, and unite them together and make of them a powerful nation. They heard the sound of the gospel, they repented of their sins, and were baptized for the remission of them, and received the Holy Ghost by the laying on of hands; this Spirit caused them to gather themselves together for the truth's sake; they came here because the voice of the Lord called them together from the ends of the earth. They needed not to be persuaded to gather themselves together, for they knew it was the will of God by the power of the Spirit which they had received through the ordinances of the gospel. Here sits brother George D. Watt, our reporter, who was the first man to receive the gospel in a foreign land; there had not been a word spoken to him about gathering to America;

but he prophesied that the land of America was the land of Zion, and that the Lord would gather His people to that land in the last days, and thus he prophesied by the Spirit of prophecy which he had received by embracing the gospel.

Wherever the gospel is preached in all the world, and the people repent, are baptized, and receive the Holy Ghost by the laying on of hands, that Spirit teaches them that America is the land of Zion, and they begin straightway to prepare to gather, and thus the Lord is building up His kingdom in our day. Were it not that I possess the Spirit of truth which reveals to me the purposes of God, it would appear to me a strange work and a wonder; but I can understand that the Lord is feeling after the inhabitants of the earth, and teaching the honest in heart the truth, and diffusing His Spirit among them, and offering to all men life and salvation.

If the message which the Lord is sending among the nations is rejected by them, they will crumble and fall, and cease to exist. The set time has come for the Lord to favor Zion; He is sending His servants to the uttermost parts of the earth to declare the truth to the inhabitants thereof, which they can receive or reject, and be saved or be damned. This is a hard saying—who can bear it? A gentleman asked the Prophet Joseph once if he believed that all other sects and parties would be damned excepting the Mormons. Joseph Smith's reply was, "Yes, sir, and most of the Mormons too, unless they repent." We believe that all will be damned who do not receive the gospel of Jesus Christ; but we do not believe that they will go into a lake which burns with brimstone and fire, and suffer unnamed and unheard of torments, inflicted by cruel and malicious devils to all eternity.

The sectarian doctrine of final rewards and punishments is as strange to me as their bodiless, partless, and passionless God. Every man will receive according to the deeds done in the body, whether they be good or bad. All men, excepting those who sin against the Holy Ghost, who shed innocent blood or who consent thereto, will be saved in some kingdom; for in my father's house, says Jesus, are many mansions. Where is John Wesley's abode in the other world? He is not where the Father and the Son live, but he is gone into what is called hades, or paradise, or the spirit-world. He did not receive the gospel as preached by Jesus Christ and His apostles; it was not then upon the earth. The power of the Holy Priesthood was not then among men; but I suppose that Mr. Wesley lived according to the best light he had, and tried to improve upon it all the days of his life. Where is the departed spirit of that celebrated reformer? It occupies a better place than ever entered his heart to conceive of when he was in the flesh. This is a point of doctrine, however, which I have not time to speak upon at large now, even if I had strength to do so.

The Lord sent His angel and called and ordained Joseph Smith, first to the Aaronic and then to the Melchisedek Priesthood, and Joseph Smith ordained others. He baptized believers and confirmed them and organized the church. The Lord revealed to him that order which is now in our midst with regard to our organization as a people, and there is no better among men. It is the government of the Lord Almighty, and we think it is very good. The Lord is again speaking to the children of men, who have opened their ears to hear, and their hearts to understand; He communicates His will to this people, although they may be ignorant and guilty of a thousand wrongs, and some will apostatize; yet we are the best people upon the earth, the most peaceable, the most industrious, and know the best how to take care of ourselves of any people now living who are not the people of God; and what we do not know God will teach us, and what we cannot do He will help us to perform, if we continue to do His will and keep His commandments; for in doing this we shall live, grow and increase in numbers and in strength, and I pray that we may grow in grace and in the knowledge of the truth, for without this we are nothing. To me it is the kingdom of God or nothing upon the earth. Without it I would not give a farthing for the wealth, glory, prestige and power of all the world combined; for, like the dew upon the grass, it passeth away and is forgotten, and like the flower of the grass it withereth, and is not. Death levels the most powerful monarch with the poorest starving mendicant; and both must stand before the judgment seat of Christ to answer for the deeds done in the body.

To us life is the sweetest of all enjoyments. A man will give all that he has for his life, yet it is compared to a span length, and is swift to its termination like the shuttle that passeth over the weaver's beam. Even when denied the enjoyment of health and of worldly comforts and conveniences, still will men cling to life to the last. The kingdom of God secures unto the faithful eternal life, with wives, children, and friends, in glory immortal, and in eternal felicity and bliss. Life eternal in His presence is the greatest gift that God can bestow upon His children. This life is nothing in point of duration in comparison with the life which is to come to the faithful, and for that reason we say that in this life it is the kingdom of God or nothing to us. With the kingdom of God and the facilities it offers for an everlasting progression in godliness until we know all things as our Father in Heaven knows them, there is no life of greater importance than this life, for there is no life in heaven or on earth to the true followers of Jesus Christ that is not incorporated in His gospel. Those who reject the gospel, when it is proclaimed to them by the authority of heaven, cannot know the Father and the Son, and are cut off from the eternal life which this knowledge alone gives.

We are in the hands of the Almighty as a people, and He is able to take care of us. We entertain no antipathies against any person or community upon this earth; but we would give eternal life to all, if they would receive it at our hands—we would preach the truth to them and administer to them the ordinances of the gospel. But, it is said, you believe in polygamy, and we cannot receive the gospel from your hands. We have been told a great many times that polygamy is not according to Christianity. The Protestant reformers believed the doctrine of polygamy. Philip, Landgrave of Hesse, one of the principal lords and princes of Germany, wrote to the great reformer Martin Luther and his associate reformers, anxiously imploring them to grant unto him the privilege of marrying a second wife, while his first wife, the princess, was yet living. He urged that the practice was in accordance with the Bible, and not prohibited under the Christian dispensation. Upon the reception of this letter, Luther, who had denounced the Romish church for prohibiting the marriage of priests, and who favored polygamy, met in council with the principal Reformers to consult upon the letter which had been received from the Landgrave. They wrote him a lengthy letter in reply, approving of his taking a second wife, saying:—

"There is no need of being much concerned for what men will say, provided all goes right with conscience. So far do we approve it, and in those circumstances only by us specified, for the gospel hath neither recalled nor forbid what was permitted in the law of Moses with respect to the marriage. Jesus Christ has not changed the external economy, but added justice only, and life everlasting for reward. He teaches the true way of obeying God, and endeavours to repair the corruption of nature."

This letter was written at Wittemburg, the Wednesday after the feast of St. Nicholas, 1539, and was signed by Martin Luther, Philip Melancthon, Martin Bucer and five other Reformers, and was written in Melancthon's own handwriting.

The marriage was solemnised on the 4th of March, 1540, by the Rev. Denis Melanther, chaplain to Philip. Philip's first wife was so anxious "that the soul and body of her dearest spouse should run no further risk, and that the glory of God might be increased," that she freely consented to the match.

This letter of the great Reformer's was not a hasty conclusion on their part that polygamy was sanctioned by the gospel, for in the year 1522, seventeen years before they wrote this letter, Martin Luther himself, in a sermon which he delivered at Wittemburg for the reformation of marriage, clearly pronounced in favor of polygamy.

These transactions are published in the work entitled "History of the variations of the Protestant churches."

Ladies and gentlemen, I exhort you to think for yourselves, and read your Bibles for yourselves, get the Holy Spirit for yourselves, and pray

177

for yourselves, that your minds may be divested of false traditions and early impressions that are untrue. Those who are acquainted with the history of the world are not ignorant that polygamy has always been the general rule and monogamy the exception. Since the founding of the Roman empire monogamy has prevailed more extensively than in times previous to that. The founders of that ancient empire were robbers and women stealers, and made laws favoring monogamy in consequence of the scarcity of women among them, and hence this monogamic system which now prevails throughout all Christendom, and which has been so fruitful a source of prostitution and whoredom throughout all the Christian monogamic cities of the Old and New World, until rottenness and decay are at the root of their institutions both national and religious. Polygamy did not have its origin with Joseph Smith, but it existed from the beginning. So far as I am concerned as an individual, I did not ask for it; I never desired it; and if I ever had a trial of my faith in the world, it was when Joseph Smith revealed that doctrine to me; and I had to pray incessantly and exercise faith before the Lord until He revealed to me the truth, and I was satisfied. I say this at the present time for the satisfaction of both saint and sinner. Now, here are the commandments of the Lord, and here are the wishes of wicked men, which shall we obey? It is the Lord and them for it.

I pray that the Spirit of Truth may find its way to each heart, that we may all love the truth more than error, and cling to that which is good that we may all be saved in the kingdom of our God. Amen.

18

"I have a Few Times in My Life Undertaken to Preach to a Traveling Congregation, but My Sermons have been Very Short, and Far Between," A Sermon Delivered on 7 October 1866

(from Brigham Young Addresses, 1865–1869, A Chronological Compilation of Known Addresses of the Prophet Brigham Young, Vol. 5, [Salt Lake City: Elden J. Watson, 1982])

I have a few times in my life undertaken to preach to a traveling congregation, but my sermons have been very short, and far between. If a portion of this congregation have to do walking, I will wait until they get through with their pedestrian exercises, and then I will commence my remarks.

I have a few things to lay before this congregation that I think is worthy of my attention and the attention of the Latter-day Saints everywhere, and that are worthy of the attention of those who do not believe as the Saints do. I shall have a few words for the different classes of people who are assembled here today, if I can elevate my voice so as to be heard. We have had the privilege of meeting together many times in this capacity; the Saints enjoy privileges that no other Christian community enjoy. These blessings and privileges have been enumerated in part before this conference. We have heard the testimony of several of the Apostles this conference, and I hope that we shall have time to hear from the rest of them who are present.

The testimony that has been borne by the Elders in this meeting is verily true. There is no person, who has received the spirit of the Gospel, but what would delight to tell his neighbors, his friends, his relatives, and those with whom he associates, the things of God which he has experienced and witnessed himself. There are but few who have the privilege of coming into this stand to tell the congregations of the Saints their experience; but they can sit down with their friends by their firesides, and talk over their history and experience in this Church and Kingdom.

Most of the civilized nations have had the Gospel preached to them, and many of the barbarous nations. You have heard the brethren testify of what they received when they believed and obeyed the Gospel. It is very true that the Christian world is seeking to know the Lord and to

179

understand His ways; but they do not seek Him in a way to find Him, and to know His will. For revelation from Him they have substituted the wisdom of men, and by this they never can find out God. There are but few individuals who, when they hear the Gospel preached, are willing to humble themselves, and to seek unto the Lord in the name of Jesus for the testimony of the Holy Spirit to bear witness with their spirit in regard to the truth of what they have heard. In this way, and in this way alone, is the Lord to be found. Men can never search out the mysteries of godliness by the wisdom and learning of this world.

We heard a very strong testimony yesterday from Elder Taylor concerning receiving the Gospel. When I first heard the Gospel, I heard it from the most illiterate men that I knew. I cannot say that they were possessed of much more natural or acquired ability than I possessed myself. I heard them in my simplicity with plainness, in the few words which they could use in the English language, the doctrine which they taught to me, and the testimony which they bore concerning the New Testament—the testimony of the Apostles concerning Jesus, and the sayings of the Saviour, and the signs that followed through obedience, I found to be true. I also found that the teachings of the Elders of the Church of Jesus Christ of Latter-day Saints to be a precise pattern of the ancient Gospel taught by Jesus Christ and His Apostles.

There were a great many witnesses in the days of Jesus and the Apostles, and for many years after they had ceased their ministry on earth. We have no history from gentile historians that contradicts the testimony of Jesus and the Apostles. Although we have only the testimonies of eight men left on record that we consider authentic who have testified to the mission of the Saviour. You will find the names of these eight men written in the New Testament. But in the testimony of the Gospel of the Son of God delivered in this our day, not only twelve men have testified, but scores and hundreds and thousands. I think I can safely say, before Elder Taylor heard the Gospel, these were all testifying that they knew by the power of God that Joseph Smith had a divine mission, and that the Gospel and priesthood he had received were true. I was a witness of these things at that time, and shall I pretend to say that I would put up my judgment and sincerity against the decision of the New Testament and the Book of Mormon—and [then] there were Joseph Smith, Oliver Cowdery, David Whitmer, Martin Harris and other witnesses—in the face of all this testimony? I thought it was too much for me to set up myself against it.

I rejoice exceedingly in the effusion of the Spirit of the Lord through our Elders. It is the sweetest music I ever heard. My testimony of the Gospel of the Son of God, as it is revealed in this our day, has gone forth to the world. Brother Woodruff, in his remarks this morning, referred to the first blessings of the endowment in the temple at Kirtland, and took into consideration the importance of the mission of an Elder of Israel. In that endowment brother Joseph, The Prophet, explained one saying in the scripture with regard to the washing of the feet of the Apostles. Jesus washed their feet before His death, and pronounced them clean; Joseph Smith washed the feet of the Elders, or assisted therein; and pronounced them clean if they had done their duty. He told the brethren that the garments of many of them were clean from the blood of this generation.

When I heard the Gospel proclaimed I was diligent to learn whether it was true or false. I had, previous to hearing it, examined every tenet, and every creed of all the Christian denominations I could become acquainted with in my young days; and, in my judgment, pronounced them all to be folly and entirely unlike the system established by Jesus Christ and His Apostles. I was a firm believer in the Old and New Testaments, in Jesus Christ and in the system of salvation which He introduced in His day, and which He told His disciples to go and preach in all the world. When I read the New Testament, and compared the systems held forth in Christiandom I came to the conclusion that there was no such being living upon the earth as a Bible Christian. I was pronounced an infidel by professors of religion; yet the most wicked class I ever saw in my life. I would have been willing, if an highway had been cast up, to have walked on my knees around the world, if, by doing so, I could have found a man who would have told me the things of God. As for the men who stand in the pulpits teaching the people I looked upon them as blind leaders of the blind, knowing nothing of the things of God.

There are a great many smart men living upon the earth, talented theologians, who have taken pains to inform themselves on the subject of Christianity as far as study and learning would aid them. I was acquainted with several learned theologians. One of them had so thoroughly studied the Bible, he said, that if every Bible in the world were destroyed, he could write another one, and not miss or misspell a word, or make a mistake in the pointing of a single sentence. I heard one of those very learned gentlemen preach at a quarterly conference of the Methodist persuasion. He labored over two hours to define the soul of man. This was an item I wanted to learn something about. I could read the Bible with regard to the spirits of men, and the salvation of man, and concerning God and angels, and devils, and good men and bad men; but when the learned preacher took his text to preach upon the soul of man, I was rejoiced, and expected to be informed and edified upon that subject; and when this talented man, this great scriptorian had exhausted two

hours, he wound up the whole with one grand, crowning declaration—
that the soul of man is an immaterial substance. I was disappointed, and
concluded that he was not an ignorant sectarian priest; but a fool. I was
very young at that time, and durst not say a word, for I was only a boy.
This preacher left us more ignorant upon the subject of the soul of man
than when he found us. If there was a fog over it when he commenced,
it was much thicker when he left off than when he began.

Men graduate from institutions of learning to be ministers of the
gospel; they study and pray all their lives; and after all their piety, and
penance, religion and learning, eloquence and noise on the subject of
godliness, they generally come to the conclusion that, "Great is the
mystery of godliness: God was manifest in the flesh." It is certainly a
mystery to them, and as Jesus said to His disciples, "it is given unto you
to know the mysteries of the kingdom of heaven, but to them it is not
given." When I heard the Gospel, it commended itself to my understanding, and I learned this one fact—it is the only true philosophy in
existence. It was so understood by the ancient Apostles and servants of
God; for they took pains to warn the Saints to "Beware lest any man
spoil you through philosophy and vain deceit, after the tradition of men,
after the rudiments of the world, and not after Christ." Man's philosophy
is full of ignorance; it is like the bedstead the prophet Isaiah refers to: it
"is shorter than a man can stretch himself on it; and the covering narrower
than that he can wrap himself in it." We testify to all, both Saints and
sinners, that this Gospel will be preached to all nations, and then the end
will come, which means the end of the reign of the ungodly upon the
earth, and not the end of the earth as some have supposed; but all
unrighteousness will cease, and God and His people will hold the reins
of government upon all the face of this earth, and that is sufficient for us
to know.

This kingdom will not be overthrown. When the wicked lay a
trap for the overthrow of this Church and Kingdom, and spring it,
they always have found themselves taken in their own snares. This has
been the case from the first organization of this Church to this time.
They have succeeded in slaying the Prophet, and his martyrdom brings
his testimony in force, and the inhabitants of the earth are culpable if
they refuse to receive it. The testament is not in force until after the
testator is dead.

We are now partaking of the emblems of the body and blood of
Christ. And we do this to show unto our Father in heaven, to Jesus our
Saviour, to the angels of the earth, that we remember Jesus in His death
and sufferings and the atonement which He has made for the sins of the
world, and that through Him we get salvation after we have submitted
to the requirements of His gospel, and endured in faithfulness to the end

to every word that proceeds out of the mouth of God. It is customary in the world to have sermons preached on the occasion of the sacrament; but I will let these few words on that subject suffice for the present; I will, however, add, that Jesus Christ is the Son of God as I am the son of my father, and was born of the virgin Mary. On this all Christians have stumbled and fallen in ignorance, and they will remain until they are willing to admit the truth. In Jesus Christ we have God manifest in the flesh, He was the only one begotten of the Father (in the flesh) full of grace and truth; was born in humble circumstances, placed in a manger, grew up to manhood, preached the Gospel, established His Church, suffered martyrdom and went back to the Father.

I will now commence my remarks on a few temporal matters which I desire to notice before I take my seat. There is a vast concourse of people here to attend this conference which gives me a fitting opportunity to notice matters which concern us all. Here are those who first made their advent into this valley in 1847, and broke the ground, planted the first potatoes, raised the first corn, sowed the first wheat, set out the first orchards, subdued the country and made it what it is, by means of hard and continued toil. Others have come here who have done nothing to improve the country; but they are here as our visitors and our neighbors, and fellow travelers. My remarks now will be directed more particularly to my brethren and sisters of the same faith with myself. I shall address myself to good, wholesome citizens of this City, and the regions round about. And if any present should happen to be disappointed with regard to the course that I shall pursue in my remarks, try and be as satisfied as you can, and hear what I shall say.

I came into this valley in the year 1847, with others of my brethren and sisters, and we commenced to build a fort, and at the same time we broke a little ground, planted our beans and peas, and potatoes, and cucumbers and squashes, we also planted a little corn, and sowed a little buckwheat. We found a few Indians here, almost, if not quite, in a state of nudity; we also found great numbers of wolves, and hosts of crickets. These were the sole inhabitants of these valleys when the pioneers of 1847 entered them. We commenced to feed the Indians, and as quick as we could, we commenced to give them some clothing. In a few years we commenced to have fruit; we got grape cuttings from California, and I think in '50 the vines began to bear fruit; in '51 I think, we had a few peaches. We kept improving, and pleading with the people to improve the country by engaging in the different branches of agricultural and horticultural pursuits, and by this means to make this country our future home. From 1847 to 1850 we were here almost entirely by ourselves. In 1849 and 1850 the emigration to the Pacific began to start across the country via Salt Lake, in search of gold. In 1850, 1851, and 1852 the great gold excitement and rush across the country occurred. At that time among the thousands who passed through our settlements there were but few but what were kind, and affable, and ready to observe the laws of this Territory or the laws which governed us as settlers here. We had no territorial or state government, but we were actually a republic by ourselves. Sometimes strangers would land among us who had difficulty with each other on the road. They would call upon me as a general thing to do something for them. I would call upon the high council of the Church to adjust their difficulties, and they would always be satisfied with their decisions. We commenced to elect some officers for the City and for precincts. After that, when difficulties were referred to me, I recommended them to those officers, and they came as nigh satisfying both parties as any courts that were ever held on this earth.

At this stage of our history our sisters could travel round and visit the sick with perfect safety by day or by night; and in case of being afraid to pass a house for fear of a dog, a sister would have no hesitation in requesting the protection of the first man who might be passing by, who would kindly see her safely out of danger. This state of things continued for years after our settlement here. Do we see the same safety for females here today? We do not. Can our sisters walk the streets of the City now without being insulted? Seldom, and yet we have not much cause to complain, for there is much more safety here for females than in other cities of the United States. Are men as secure here now as they were then? No. Are our wives and children as secure? No. But there is a class of men here, who have been termed regenerators, who are trying to introduce civilization among us. I am coming to this point in my remarks directly. There are many in our city and country who do not profess to be of our faith, yet who are good and wholesome citizens, and who, by their example and influence, seek to establish and maintain peace and harmony, decorum and every principle of virtue in the community. They call themselves gentiles; we call them so; yet we are all gentiles in a national capacity. Right or wrong, hit or miss, I am going to ask this vast congregation if we shall continue to submit to have gambling halls and drinking saloons in this our city? I wish this vast concourse of people to express themselves upon this matter. If it be the mind of this congregation that we no longer submit to the continuance of such houses, let them raise their hands. (all hands were raised and shouts of "No, we will not submit to it!") We will blot them out, they shall not contaminate our society.

You must learn this one fact, that in republican governments, the people are supreme; where they decree this or that shall be done, that decree is supreme, and legislators, governors, and judges and expounders of the law are mere subordinates all the time and in every case on a republican government. The people are king and the supreme power. (The President now called for a contrary vote, but not a single hand was raised.) When by the authority of the City Council such places are put a stop to, who have the supporters of such establishments got to quarrel with? With the whole people. Let a judge pass a decree that a grog shope, or a gambling saloon shall be established in our City, and we will give him the privilege to get out of the City as quickly as he can. We will observe every wholesome law; but the man who issues an injunction to the authorities of this City to try to compel them to let gambling and drinking halls be kept open, the scarcer he is in this community the better it will be for him. We will observe the law; and uphold and defend the adjudicators of all wholesome laws; but suppose this vast concourse of people here assembled today should pass judgment upon a criminal charged with murder, and should with one voice condemn him to be hanged, who can say a word about it? Not anybody. It is done by the unanimous voice of the people, and who can help it? Not anybody. The voice of the people is supreme, and they will sustain the City Council in breaking up every hell hole there is in this City. I am but one, and I wanted to know what the minds of the people would be on this subject. Enough on this subject.

There is another temporal matter I wish to say a few words upon. I refer to claim-jumping. There has been a few men jumping claims on our parade ground and on the land on the other side of Jordan. Those lands we have fenced two or three times. And then again there are our cow pastures; we want those gentlemen-claim-jumpers to keep off them, and to keep out of our meadows and gardens. Understand me, my friends—(I have a good many friends who do not belong to the Church in this City and throughout the United States, men who are gentlemen of heart and honor; it is not this class of my friends which I am now talking to; but I am talking to a class of men who are searching through the world for chances to get their living out of the labors of others)— Wherever you see a business man who is willing to work his way through this world and do business upon honorable principles to sustain himself and his family, you will see a man who will never do a dishonest action. I am referring to marauders, men who have no conscience, no principle, who are devoid of all honor and respect for other men's rights and property, and they are here, not for the purpose of developing the country, and making themselves industrious and profitable members of society; but they are transient, they care not how quickly they leave here, and they would as lief stay here as anywhere else. It is to this class of men I address myself, and I warn you to keep off our meadows and pasture grounds.

Those lands which I refer to on the other side of Jordan have been fenced at the cost of some $8000.00. The last time the land was enclosed it was fenced with poles. King James Buchanan, who then presided over the United States, sent an army here. They went into that pasture by my permission, and by their delegate, agreed to pay me so much for the use of it. They burnt up the fence, broke through into a neighboring man's meadow, burnt up his fence and used up his meadow. After they had made their encampment at Camp Floyd, they swore that they never was in the pasture. The very men who sent an agent, and who hired the pasture in my office, gave their oath that the pasture referred to was four miles from their encampment. I did not care anything about it; I knew they could not burn up the land, and I also knew that they would have a happy time of it to get the land without obtaining it legally. Let these regenerators who have no father, nor mother, nor possession, nor whereabouts go and take up land that nobody has fenced and laid claim to; go and build a city where you can gamble. Go to Stockton; nobody will hinder you from gambling there, and set up your houses of ill-fame, and grog shops and gambling halls. Take up land there, and make a city and a community to suit yourselves; but if you jump my pasture—well, all I have to say is, get out of it as fast as you can. But, you sware you won't; then I will give you a presumption right that will last you to the last resurrection. I have said enough on this subject.

There are a few men in our government—and I say they are very few, who are determined to destroy us, and break us up. Is there one-third of the inhabitants of the United States who would do this? No. Take away the priests and their influence and you will not find one man to 500 who would want to break us up. The Scribes and Pharasees were the Saviour's greatest enemies. They stirred up the minds of the people. The whole multitude of the Scribes and Chief Priests accused Jesus Christ before Pilate, "saying, we found this fellow perverting the nation." And again: "If we let him thus alone, all men will believe on him: and the Romans shall come and take away both our place and nation." They were afraid that Jesus and His party would become the dominant party in a political point of view. So they say of the Mormons. "If the Mormons are let alone, they will become the dominant party." That will as surely come to pass as the Lord lives; the Saints will ultimately rule and reign upon the earth, and this is as sure as the Lord has spoken it. That party which oppress people, and do wrong, will not continue to be the dominant party. They are now, but they will not be when the power of the wicked is broken by the advancing strides of light and truth. "When the righteous are in authority, the people rejoice; but when the wicked beareth rule, the people mourn." We have a time of mourning in our nation, and the end is not yet, the chastening hand of the Almighty has not yet completed its work.

I think these regenerators, as they are called, are simply bummers. There are two classes of bummers, one of our writers says, one class who have nothing and don't know where they got it; another class who have something, and other folks don't know where they got it. These bummers want our houses and gardens, and wives, and they will not get any of them. Mark it. The Mormons have made all the improvements in this inland country, and have established themselves by their industry and courage, and they now feed their thousands of strangers that stay with them and that are passing through our country. They have made this country a half-way house, as it were, between the Missouri River and the Pacific shore. The strangers who have lived here all agree that this people are the most industrious people upon the earth, and this is the most industrious people in the world, but that they are the most civil community they ever visited; yet there are a few, and but a few, whom we are making rich and who are continually trying to destroy us. I say to such persons—go where there is plenty of land, and open farms and build up cities, and make your grog houses if you wish to, and not seek to introduce institutions among us which are contrary to the genius of our moral, religious and civil organization; we will not have them here, we will spew them out, and cleanse the platter.

You say: "We must do something or go hungry." We have plenty for you to eat, "But have we not got to do something for it?" Yes, go to work at some productive employment, and cease gambling and drunkenness, for it does you no good, but a great deal of harm. We want to hire a few thousand men now, there is plenty of work to be had in the country. We want them on our streets and on our farms; we want them to build our houses and our stores—our private and our public buildings—we want them to build up our cities and our country, and not be continually trying to destroy it. It takes a wise man to build up a city, and any poor drunken, useless, renegade can apply the torch and destroy that which has cost years of toil, and countless treasure to create. That which has taken a life time for a man to accumulate, a child can destroy in a few minutes. Instead of seeking constantly to destroy that which this poor outcast people have accumulated, follow their noble example; build upon the unoccupied lands, and thereby increase the wealth and importance of the American nation and thus prove yourselves gentlemen and loyal citizens as well by works as land swelling professions. In this way you will win the respect of all honorable high-minded, loyal men. I respect you more today than you respect one another, and would do more for you, if you were destitute, than any one of your own class would, for you do not respect yourselves nor one another.

I will now speak upon a subject which I think ought to notice for the benefit of a few who are inclined to be giddy-headed, unstable in their ways, and enthusiastic about something which they do not understand. You are already apprized of the fact that a son of Joseph Smith the Prophet was here in our City not long since. Joseph Smith's first son only lived a few hours; then Joseph Smith, commonly called Young Joseph, was born; then Frederic, and then Alexander; it was Alexander who was in our City lately. The people have not heard me say anything about him one way or the other. I will relate a few facts. The sympathies of the Latter-day Saints are with the family of the martyred prophet. I never saw a day in the world that I would not almost worship that woman, Emma Smith, if she would be a saint instead of being a devil. I feel so today. There is no good thing in a temporal point of view that I would withhold from her; anything that is in my power to do for her, I would willingly do with all my heart, and with an open hand.

There are a few here that knew Joseph Smith, the Prophet, and some of them are apostatizing from the work, which the Lord commanded him to found, to run after Young Joseph Smith, the second son of the Prophet, who has no more authority to set himself up as a president and teacher of a people than any other man has in the sectarian world who possessed nothing of the priesthood of the Most High. Young Joseph Smith does not possess one particle of this priesthood. The Twelve Apostles and the other authorities of this Church would have been exceeding glad if the Prophet's family had come with us when we left Nauvoo for the valleys of these mountains. We would have made cradles for them if they had required them, and would have fed them on milk and honey. Emma is naturally a very smart woman; she is subtle and ingenious, and she has made all her children believe that myself, brother Kimball, and the other members of the Twelve laid the plot which terminated in the death of the Prophet. This charge is especially laid to myself. At the time that Joseph was killed I was in the city of Boston, a number of hundred miles away from the scene of the martyrdom. She has made her children inherit lies. To my certain knowledge Emma Smith is one of the damdest liars I know of on this earth; yet there is no good thing I would refuse to do for her, if she would only be a righteous woman; but she will continue in her wickedness.

Not six months before the death of Joseph, he called his wife Emma into a secret council, and there he told her the truth, and called upon her to deny it if she could. He told her that the judgments of God would come upon her forthwith if she did not repent. He told her of the time she undertook to poison him, and he told her that she was a child of hell, and literally the most wicked woman on this earth, that there was not one more wicked then she. He told her where she got the poison, and how she put it in a cup of coffee; said he, "You got that poison so and so, and I drank it, but you could not kill me." When it entered his stomach he went to the door and threw it off. He spoke to her in that council in a very severe manner, and she never said one word in reply. I have witnesses of this scene all around, who can testify that I am now telling the truth. Twice she undertook to kill him.

From a dream that I had while on my visit to Logan a short time since, I know that spiritualism is the head and front, and the arm and breast and brain, and the eyes and the whole body of Young Joseph's profession and operations. In my dream I saw the Prophet Joseph, and he tried for awhile to sustain the old dwelling, and meditated building around it; but he finally concluded to discard it, and swept the ground clean where it stood to put up an entirely new building. Although this is a matter I have not thought of, yet the dream is true, and expresses the true state of the case.

When Alexander Smith came here, we treated him kindly, and I plead with him to accompany us on our visit north. George A. Smith, his cousin, plead with him to accompany us, but to no purpose. Finally, Joseph F. Smith, who was from home, came back, and saw him, and met him in public in this city. Many of this congregation are acquainted with that circumstance. It was asked him what he thought of the endowment. He replied, "I do not mention it, for I do not wish to hear anything about the endowment." "What do you think of the doctrine of polygamy?" It is his business to preach against polygamy, and his brother Joseph said that his father never introduced it. Several of the sisters testified to him that they were sealed to his father. Well, said he, "if he did have any such revelation, or teach any such doctrine, or practice it, he must have got out of the way," or, in other words he must have been a fallen prophet, if he ever was a true prophet. That is the conclusion they come to when hard pressed with stern facts. Joseph Smith the Prophet taught the gathering; but this new sect deny the gathering.

If there are any Latter-day Saints who wish to be destroyed, run after that family, and I will promise you in the name of the God of Israel that you will be damned. Any person who will follow this man or that man who is wrong, and refuses to submit himself to the ordinances of the house of God and to serve Him and keep His commandments, will perish; all that walk in that path will go to a sure and swift destruction. Young David Smith seems to be the pet of the company, he is heart and hand with his brother Joseph, and with a hundred others who are apostates from the true faith of the Gospel, and who were one with the mob who persecuted and slew the Prophet. When Joseph the Prophet was killed his wife Emma was pregnant. Joseph said, previous to his death, "She shall have a son, and his name shall be called David, and unto him the Lord will look." I am looking for the time when the Lord will speak to David, but let him pursue the course he is now pursuing, and he will never preside over the Church of Jesus Christ of Latter-day Saints in time nor in eternity. He has got to repent of his sins, and turn away from his iniquity, to cease to do evil, and learn to do well, embrace the Gospel of life and salvation, and be an obedient son of God, or he never can walk up to possess his right. It would be his right to preside over this Church, if he would only walk in the true path of duty. I hope and pray that he and the whole family will repent, and be a holy family.

Now, you old Mormons, stop your talking about Young Joseph, and about David going to preside over the Church by and by! I wish he was prepared for it, would repent of his sins, and come in at the door, and be one with us, and walk up to the Twelve and the First Presidency, saying, I am one with you, and am your servant. When Sidney Rigdon swelled up and thought he was the most important man in the Kingdom, I told him where his place was, and that the Twelve Apostles would build up the Kingdom. Joseph more than one score of times told them both in private and in public, that he rolled the Kingdom on to their shoulders, and said I to Sidney, we will build it up, and bear it off, and not follow you one inch. What has he come to? He sits in the midst of the woods East mumbling to himself; but scarcely able to speak an intelligent word; he is almost a lunatic. And where has the rest of the apostates gone? And where has the rest of the apostates gone? And where will they go? Every one of them, bogus Joseph not excepted, will go to destruction, and the Kingdom of God will continue to flourish and spread abroad.

Alexander stated when here, that the Twelve robbed his mother of "the last second shirt to her back." Now, I want to tell this congregation what we did for his mother, and there are sitting round me numbers who can bear witness of the truth of the statement I am about to make. After Joseph's death, when the Twelve arrived home, they selected Newel K. Whitney and George Miller as Trustees-in-Trust for the Church of Jesus Christ of Latter-day Saints. When the Twelve came home, after the death of Joseph, Emma talked poor, poor. In our absence brother Kimball had collected in Willington $1300.00 in gold to pay some debts. He got this money from bro. E. M. Saunders who now lives at St. George. The question arose in council whether Emma should have that money or not. Brother William Clayton knows all about this circumstance, for he was Joseph's clerk, and he knew where the money was to be paid. Brother Kimball said, "I want to pay Emma this money, and let her do as she pleased with it." So he paid it over to her. Whether she paid the debt with it or not I am not prepared to say; but brother William Clayton can tell; but I think we had to pay the debt. This is according to my recollection.

Instead of Emma being robbed by the Twelve, a few days after the death of Joseph she went over to Hyrum's house. Hyrum had a large ring which he wore, and Joseph had one, and Don Carlos had one, these three rings were all alike. She asked Hyrum's wife to let her see that ring. Hyrum's widow brought her the ring, she took it and put it in her pocket. She went over to Don Carlos' widow and wanted to see that ring; she took that also and put it in her pocket, and I think she also took the portrait of Hyrum. Instead of the Twelve robbing her she goes and takes these things from her sisters. She was not satisfied yet. She wanted the Cleveland farm, situated about four miles from Quincy. She thought if she had that farm she could live.

Newel K. Whitney had bought an old Bible; Joseph had run through it and made a good many marks in it for the new translation. This book belonged to Newel K. Whitney. Emma had it in her possession. She wished to exchange this book for the Cleveland farm. She got the deed for the farm; but she was not ready yet to give up the Bible. She complained about her poor, little, fatherless children, and she kept up this whine until she got the farms she wanted, and besides these farms she owned city property worth fifty thousand dollars. We gave her deeds for the farm at Quincy and for the farm on the prairie by the burning ground. We gave her all she asked for. She has made her children inherit lies. Alexander Smith was a little boy when these circumstances transpired, and he believes what his mother has told him. We gave her those farms, and this does not look like robbing her.

I wanted to mention these things, because there are a great many of this people who are ignorant of these circumstances. She got the last acre of land that was in the hands of the Trustee-in-Trust; it all went to Emma for her benefit. When we left Nauvoo my wife carried her crockery to Emma, and I am sure that others did the same. We gave her everything we could not carry away, and let her do as she pleased with them. I recollect very well that I had a nice carriage built in 1845. About the time it was done, Mother Smith said, "How rejoiced I am that that carriage which Joseph promised to me is done." I sent her the carriage, and I do not know but that I would have taken off my shirt and given it to any of the Smith family and run the risk of getting another. Now, you who have got but little sense wait until you get a little more and stop talking and speculating about Young Joseph or anybody else. God is the captain of this company, the general of this army of Saints, and the President of this Church, its ruler and dictator. If I am the instrument which He chooses to use in the prosecution of His great work, it is all right. I am just as willing as any other man to be used.

I told you in the first place that Mormonism is true. There are some other little items that should be mentioned; but I have already spoken at length and I will postpone mentioning them until another time. When we shall adjourn the Conference I am unable to say. We will continue our services until the Spirit of the Lord shall signify to us when to bring our Conference to a close. Let the people feel satisfied and contented to spend a few days to worship the Lord, and let not their earthly affairs give them trouble; for the heavens are full of days and nights and we shall live to enjoy them. May God bless you. Amen.

19

"We Talk a Great Deal about
Our Improvements and Increase in Knowledge,"
A Sermon Delivered on 4 August 1867

(see *Utah Historical Quarterly* 29 [January 1961]: 66–76)

We talk a great deal about our improvements and increase in knowledge. This is a subject for philosophers. There is no question but there is a great deal of knowledge in the world. But how much knowledge have we in proportion to that that does exist in, through and round about the earth, in the starry heavens and in the eternities of the Gods? When we draw this comparison, our knowledge is very limited, and although we hear our Elders talk Sabbath after Sabbath on the principles of the gospel that we have embraced, yet we cannot improve as fast as we would like to. A child of seven or eight years of age when sent to school cannot learn the letters of the alphabet in one day; neither can he learn the English language in one week, month or year, and I will say not in one short lifetime like ours. So it is with regard to learning the principles of the Gospel—the principles of truth and righteousness comprised within the pale of the Gospel.

I want every man and woman here to understand that the Gospel we talk about circumscribes and comprehends the knowledge that is possessed by the Gods, all the holy angels, and I may say the unholy angels; the knowledge, glory, power and excellency, whether it be good or bad, in time and in eternity. We do not talk much like this do we? When strangers come to our meetings they think, probably, that we do not exhibit any knowledge more than they possess. The fact is, we are endeavoring to commence right.

Suppose, for instance, we want to strike a direct line to the North Pole, and in order to do so we take a compass in which the needle is out of order and does not traverse correctly. It may go five degrees to the east or ten degrees to the west; if we start on the line indicated by this needle, do you suppose we will ever reach the North Pole? Never, we will go past it, and by and by we will swing ourselves from the earth, and by going round a few times we would be left in open space, which would be worse than a ship on the ocean without sail, compass or rudder. This is the case with regard to the religions or what I may call the philosophical systems of the day pertaining to the life we now enjoy and that which is to come. If we start right and we continue in the right path—if we do not know everything today, or even as much as we desire and as other people expect us to know—do you not see it will eventually land us right in the fountain of eternal knowledge, so that we will see as we are seen and know as we are known?

The Gospel of the Son of God that we preach is the system of life and of salvation. The inquiry may arise, where did we get this, how came this people called Latter-day Saints into possession of the true principles of eternal life? Are they not disseminated to all the inhabitants of the earth? I will say they have been, but the inhabitants of the earth have rejected them; consequently, they are left in darkness. Nation after nation, people after people have wandered in darkness and ignorance, and have lived and died without the knowledge of the Gospel. (Asked a blessing on the water.)

On some points, that we may call religious peculiarities, we differ from all the rest of the inhabitants of the earth. How? In this, that we profess to have the fullness of the Gospel of the Son of God that is possessed by no other people that we know of. If our life and conduct as individuals and as a people have witnessed to God, to angels and to the inhabitants of the earth that we have something different from all the Christian world, it is time for them to reflect seriously on the matter, and not treat us with jealousy and contumely.

If we, for instance, were to go to that portion of the house of Israel who were left on the land of Palestine when the ten tribes marched to the northern country and learn the tenets of their faith, we should find that they do not possess one iota of truth but what is enjoyed by the Latter-day Saints. Where is the proof? I do not know that I will have time to measure and weigh these points on the present occasion, but the proof is right before us. We may ask them the question, "Do you believe in the God of Abraham, Isaac and of Jacob?" So do the Latter-day Saints. If they believe in the God who told Moses to say to Pharaoh that He was a man of war; so do the Saints. I say, O Israel, ancient Israel do you believe in the God who brought the children of Israel out of Egypt with a high hand and an outstretched arm! "Yes," say they; and so do the Latter-day Saints. Have you faith, that if necessary, He would again shower manna from Heaven and send flocks of quails to allay your hunger and cause water to burst from the rock to quench your thirst as He did when the Children of Israel were passing through the Wilderness? Do you believe that He is the God whom Moses followed and by whom he was dictated? "Yes," says the whole house of Israel. Well, that is the very God that we—the Latter-day Saints—are serving. He is our Father. He is the God and Father of our Lord Jesus Christ—whom the tribe of Judah discard, heaping ridicule upon his name. He is the Father of our Spirits, everyone of us, Jew or Gentile, bond or free, white or black. Is that saying too much? Is there any of us who will reject the idea that He is the Father of the spirits of all living? If there is, it is through ignorance. All the varieties in physiognomy and the different shades of color—the tawney and copper colored, the black and white, are His; and if there be any who are not white and delightsome, it is because their sins and iniquities have brought a curse upon them. But our Father and our God is the Father of the spirits of all living. He is the framer and finisher of our bodies, and He set this machine in motion that has brought forth the whole human family; and He has laid, made and prepared the plan of Salvation for His children that all may be saved who will receive the Gospel.

Here, in our city, are many who profess to be of the tribe of Judah; some are of that tribe and some are of other tribes. Let them go into the houses of this people and they will hear the prayers of the Elders of Israel ascend in behalf of the tribe of Judah; day by day they are borne before the throne of the Almighty for Him to hasten the day when the eyes of the children of Judah shall be opened that they may see, their ears unstopped that they may hear, and that their hearts may be penetrated by the power of God that they may understand the truth as it is in Jesus. These few remarks with regard to the house of Israel will satisfy me.

Now, what have the Christians got that the Latter-day Saints have not got. Has the holy Catholic Church got faith in Jesus that we have not got? Not a particle that is true and pure. But as for the ordinances of the House of God, we say, and we say it boldly, and here is the standard of our faith—the Old and New Testament—that the mother church and all her daughters have transgressed the laws, every one of them; they have changed almost every ordinance of the House of God; and not only so, but like the children of Israel in olden days, they have broken the covenants made with the fathers. We are bold to say this and we will take this book—the Bible—in which Jews and Gentiles believe for our standard and proof.

Has the holy Catholic Church the ordinance of baptism? So they say. What do you say Latter-day Saints? We say they have not. There is but one mode of baptism and that is by being immersed in the water that the subject may come forth out of the water, in comparison like a child at its birth—struggling for breath—emerging into another element. This is the figure that Jesus gave us. Jesus and others were baptized of John, and the disciples of Jesus baptized more; but none of them were baptized by pouring, sprinkling, kneeling, or face foremost, but they were immersed in the water and came forth out of the water.

Have they the Sacrament? Yes, so they say. "Jesus took bread and blessed it and brake it and gave it to the disciples, and said, 'Take, eat, this is my body.' And he took the cup, and gave thanks and gave it to them saying, 'Drink ye all of it.'" Now, I leave it to all whether they carry out this ordinance or not.

Leaving the mother church, we will go to her children—the other churches of Christendom. And here permit me to politely invite my Christian brethren all over the earth, never to speak evil of their mother. "What do you mean?" say they. I mean, do not speak evil of the church from which you have derived your authority and priesthood. You hear the Protestants crying against and depreciating the character of her who bore them. I would say to all that portion of the Christian world not in communion with the Church of Rome, if you must speak evil of your beloved mother, do it very softly; she is your mother and you are her offspring. It is true that the Greek Church does not acknowledge this, and the Protestants more or less deny it, but still if you trace the matter to its source, you will find they derive their authority from the mother church; and she is as good as any of her children.

Yes, I will venture to say that there are just as serious, honest, virtuous and truthful men and women in the holy Catholic Church as there are in any other on the face of the earth, the Church of Jesus Christ of Latter-day Saints not excepted so far as our truth and honesty as individuals are concerned. But go to each and all of the churches of Christendom and can we find the ordinances of the gospel of Jesus Christ practiced amongst them? We may find a few of them.

Mr. Campbell, some years ago, introduced the great principle of being baptized for the remission of sins. This was the reform from the Close Communion Baptists who baptized merely as a test of fellowship. But Mr. Campbell said "Be baptized for the remission of your sins"; they went no further than that. Said I, "I acknowledge that portion of your doctrine to be true but will you please read the scripture following that and see what it teaches?" "We cannot do it; we do not believe in the laying on of hands for the Holy Ghost. No, No, repent and be baptized for the remission of your sins, but we can go no further." How was it anciently. This book—the New Testament—I think says, "Repent and be baptized everyone of you in the name of Jesus Christ for the remission of sins and ye shall receive the Holy Ghost"; and we also read, "And when Paul had laid his hands upon them, the Holy Ghost came on them and they spake in tongues and prophesied." But Mr. Campbell says, "Stop, stop, that needs to be spiritually construed. It does not mean what it says." "Then," I say to Mr. Campbell and his followers, "what proof have you that it is necessary to be baptized for the remission of sins?" If one is the doctrine of Christ, so is the other. Repent ye, therefore, and be baptized for the remission of your sins that you may receive the Holy Ghost. What is the office of the Holy Ghost? It brings things past, present and to come to the minds of all who receive and enjoy it.

Do the Christian world believe in any of the doctrines of the gospel of Christ? They believe in faith in Jesus, and so do we. Many of them believe in strict honesty, so do we. Yet they frequently say, "How dishonest some of your Mormons are!" I acknowledge that some who are called Mormons are dishonest. I am sorry to say so. And then again I should not be sorry for if this gospel gathered none but the good, the words of the Savior would fall to the ground. He said, "The Kingdom of Heaven is like unto a net that was cast into the sea and gathered of every kind." I think we have gathered of all kinds, and this is collateral evidence and security to us that this is the gospel net; and if the world do not acknowledge it now, they will by and by.

We have this gospel, and it behooves us to live according to its precepts. Some are disposed to call us rogues and to say that we are ignorant. I do not care one farthing what the people from one end of the world to the other call me if they will only repent and be baptized for the remission of their sins, receive the Holy Ghost and live according to the dictates of the spirit of Christ. But there are some rogues and some fools, and I would to God that all were foolish enough to believe and obey the gospel and to live it every day of their lives. All who will do this will be saved.

A good deal was said this morning in relation to our organization and possessing a will of our own. Our Father in Heaven has placed within each of our tabernacles the attributes that He, Himself, possesses. He has given to everyone of us—His children—the germ and foundation of all knowledge and wisdom; and we are fashioned, and made and framed for the express purpose of exercising our will that we may become independent and that we may reign, rule and predominate over all things. Brother Heber says that we have not got a will. He meant that we should not let our wills lead us to destruction. We have all a mind, disposition and will, are capable of becoming gods even the sons of God to rule and reign forever and ever. With these wills of ours we will go to the Master—Him whom we have enlisted to obey as our Teacher, Head and Guide, and from Him we will receive our lessons day by day, and we will fashion our wills and passions accordingly. You and I and every individual will do this sooner or later. In doing this, however, we will each follow the promptings of the spirit within us, and there will be the same diversity as we now behold. Here is one man, for instance, says, "I want to go to the gold mines"; another says, "I will go and haul my potatoes"; another, "I will become a merchant"; another will go to making carriages or furniture, and each one uses the volition God has bestowed upon him with that independence that the angels exercise. It is true that we may be so far controlled by circumstances that we cannot do exactly as we please, which is, in part, the theory of the infidel, or what in England are called the Owenites. They pretend to say that every man and woman that lives are wholly controlled by surrounding circumstances; that we have no choice or will of our own, or if we have, the circumstances surrounding us, continually prevent its exercise.

This is true in part. We are capable to some extent of framing the circumstances by which our children will be surrounded. To illustrate, one man says, "I will become a thief"—we have just such characters in our midst—he is raising a family of children who are brought up to steal all they can lay their hands on, and by and by they are found in the penitentiary. Such characters are governed by surrounding circumstances but they are of their own making. If we will deal honestly and justly with one another, we will so control circumstances that the rising generation will become honorable men of the earth—honorable before God and angels. Take a course opposite to this and their names will be cast out as evil, and not for righteousness sake, but for their bad deeds. It is for you and me to live according to the precepts of our holy religion.

There was one question hinted at very plainly this afternoon by Bro. George Q. Cannon, to which I will now refer, that is, whether this people are going to dictate to their leaders, or whether they are going to follow them and obey their counsel. I will tell the Latter-day Saints, one and all, male and female, from beginning to end, that while God keeps me here in this capacity and calling, you will follow me, or we shall separate no more to meet. I can say of a truth, if you will follow me as I follow Christ, we will go into the Celestial Kingdom. The people can do as they please; I do not ask them to follow anything they do not choose to follow. They generally prefer taking their own course, like some of our merchants here, who buy and sell and oppress the people all they can. They are blinded by the spirit of the world; they cannot see things as they are; they act as they please, and by and by, as I told them years ago, if they are not careful, they will get their reward and go to hell.

I had a talk during the past week with one of our merchants, who, I understood, had taken a contract to furnish flour to Camp Douglas at five dollars and twenty-four cents a hundred. While conversing with him, I learned that he had taken but a small contract and that he had the flour and wheat on hand necessary to fill it, and he was disposed to sell, being satisfied that others would have done so if he had not. I could not say much to him on the subject when I heard what he had to say. But what do such prices do for our farmers? They reduce their wages to twenty-five or fifty cents a day. Circumstances are woven around them that this is the inevitable result. To facilitate operations on their farms they have probably got reapers and mowers, thrashing machines, ploughs and other farming utensils on credit from some of these merchants, and being in debt they are obliged to let their wheat go at a dollar a bushel, when it cost them two dollars a bushel, and if their labor were paid for in proportion to that of our mechanics and common laborers, it would be worth from three dollars to five dollars per bushel. If our merchants and producers would be agreed in these matters, the outsiders could not affect the price of wheat or flour one sixpence, and we might have a fair remunerative price for them.

I recollect when Mr. Livingstone was here and the army was at Camp Floyd that he reduced the price of flour and wheat. I told him that it was the most impolitic thing he could do; for if instead of reducing, he kept up the price of wheat to three or four dollars a bushel he would make a thousand dollars where he only made a hundred. I want to inform our merchants, whether in or out of the Church, that these gentlemen here on the hill—I am disposed to call them gentlemen, I am acquainted with some of them, it is not Pat[rick Edward Connor] and his crowd—would rather pay this community ten dollars a hundred for their flour than five. Why? Because they see that this is a laboring community and they ought to have pay for their labor. We ought to be reasonable with one another, and be as willing to give as to receive.

I think I will tell a story in relation to this matter. A few years ago when the people were very anxious to trade off their flour, a company passed through here, the captain of which was a pretty honorable man; he had been through before and was tolerably well-known. When the flour was offered to him for three or four dollars a hundred, said he, "Gentlemen you are a set of damned fools; we do not want this flour short of ten dollars a hundred. Why do you sell it so cheap; you do not get anything for your labor?" I do not say that our quartermasters who purchase here say this, but I guess it comes into their minds sometimes. Some of our friends think they are going to curry favors by selling so cheaply. What is it to them who let out the contracts; it is not they who pay for this flour; neither do those men who are sent to Washington pay for it, but it is paid for out of the millions that are gathered from the taxed hard laboring community of the United States. Do you not think these gentlemen here would as soon let us have a fair price for our flour as to see it gambled away? My solid opinion is that they would; whether it is so or not, it is no matter. I will let this rest.

I want to say to the farmers when you gather your wheat, put it in your bins, and if you owe a merchant, let him wait until the day of judgment unless he will pay you so that you can live. If you owe a man who has it in his power to control your labor and means, and would crush you, tell him to wait. If he were just and generous, he would be willing to let you live, as well as to live himself. It is almost straining my own feelings to say a man should not pay his honest debts, but is it honest for a man who has me in his power to crush out my life? No, it is damnable and will send many an Elder to hell. Equal rights of live and let live is our doctrine.

With regard to this people, I will say, we do not advance as fast as we should. We have characters in our midst who are despicable in the eyes of justice, truth and mercy, but we cannot help it. Let me say to you, Latter-day Saints, that the man who refuses or rejects counsel pertaining to his temporal affairs will sooner or later go out of this Church and will go down to misery. Is this a hard saying? Yes, very hard. The feeling of a great many is that they should actually have the privilege of dictating their temporal affairs without being molested or meddled with. But stop! stop! Let me ask a question—I will say of the whole Christian world—when you get to heaven, do you not expect whether you are farmers, merchants, tradesmen, or whatever your calling may be to be subject in all things to the voice of Him who has the right to rule and dictate? Yes, everyone of you, and I want to say that if this order of things is not carried out on earth by the Latter-day Saints, God will choose another people who will carry out this principle to the very letter. Some will say, "I do not agree with Brother Brigham in temporal affairs." Who cares whether you do or not? You can do just as you please, but you who despise counsel in anything whatever, will, unless you repent, soon lose the spirit of this gospel and will be filled with the spirit of apostasy; that is to say the spirit of Christ will no longer dictate, prompt, and comfort you, but will give place to the spirit of darkness, mourning and discontent, and by and by you will go and join the bogus Josephites, for the Latter-day Saints will be so wicked that you will want to get away from them. It is true we are wicked. Jesus came to save sinners and if we were not sinners, we should be as independent of Him as Amasa Lyman. But I need the blood of Christ and I also need the revelations of the Lord Jesus Christ to lead, guide and direct the affairs of this Kingdom. Do you need the same? Yes. Let a woman rise up in rebellion against her husband that lives his religion, and I will promise her sorrow and woe. Do I desire this? No, ladies I do not, but I would that all would live so as to receive the spirit of peace and comfort and enjoy an increase of it as long as they live on the earth. Children who rise in rebellion against their parents will receive the spirit of discontent and uneasiness; it will grow upon them; they will be dissatisfied everywhere, and the spirit of apostasy will grow upon them and they will go down to destruction. Every man that refuses counsel, or sets himself up as a guide to this Church or people had better go where his company is, for he has got one somewhere; but we will not follow him one inch.

I have said a good deal about the faith we have embraced and about the course this people ought to pursue; if we had time to go into the philosophy of this life and show what it is worth, it would be interesting. This life is one of the most precious lives ever given to any creature in heaven, earth, or hell; and this earth is one of the most beautiful planets if we were disposed to make it so. The wretchedness, misery and woe on the earth are through the wickedness of the children of men. The children of God have rebelled—they have transgressed the laws, changed the ordinances, broken the laws, and every man has turned his own way, and the spirit of the Lord is not with them without it is to convict them.

I recollect when I first joined the Church a certain Elder making this assertion—that all had gone out of the way; the question was asked him, "Do you suppose that John Wesley is damned and in hell?" "Yes," said he, "he is weltering with the damned in hell." It was one of the most unwise expressions that could be made, and the man who made it was as ignorant as Henry Ward Beecher who has said that "to be born was the greatest misfortune that could befall man."

John Wesley is just as happy as he can be, or as he ever anticipated; but he is not with the Father and the Son, nor ever will be unless the ordinances are administered for him, and they will be by and by.

Do you recollect what Brother Macdonald said this morning about redeeming the dead? By and by when the world is subject to the law of Christ and we can build temples to the Lord, the responsibility of redeeming the dead will rest upon us. Then, if you and I do not, our children will enter the temples of the Lord and go through all the ordinances for every good man and woman that ever lived on the earth who have died without the privilege of hearing the gospel.

I have detained you long enough, and have talked long enough. May God bless you.

20

"The Source of Intelligence, Etc.,"
A Sermon Delivered on 29 May 1870

(from *Journal of Discourses*, 26 vols. [Liverpool:
Latter-day Saints' Book Depot, 1855-86], 13:170-78)

If I can have your attention I will talk to you a few minutes. Speaking as much as I have in public makes me feel most forcibly that I have both stomach and lungs, hence I would like to have stillness in the house. I see some sisters withdrawing in consequence of their children not being quiet; I am very much obliged to them, and trust that others will do likewise if they cannot keep their children still.

I am not in the habit of making many apologies nor very many preliminaries when I speak to a congregation. Sometimes I feel to say a few words that might be called apologetic in rising to address a congregation, having that timidity which most men feel on such occasions. I have seen few public speakers in my life who were capable of rising and speaking directly upon a subject, unless it had been studied or perhaps written beforehand. To speak extempore, on the impulse of the moment, without reflection, requires considerable steadiness of the nerve. This is a matter that I have reflected upon a good deal, for in my experience I have learned that there is a modest timidity in the feeling of almost all persons I ever saw when called upon to speak to their fellow-beings. This is frequently the case in private circles as well as before the public. I think I understand the reason of it; it is a matter which I have studied. I find myself here on this earth, in the midst of intelligence. I ask myself and Wisdom, where has this intelligence come from? Who has produced and brought into existence, I will say, this intelligent congregation assembled here this afternoon? We are here, but whence have we come? Where did we belong before coming here? Have we dropped accidentally from some of the planets on to this earth without order, law or rule? Perhaps some, in their reflections, have come to this conclusion, and think that is all that is known in relation to this matter. I inquire where is this intelligence from which I see, more or less, in every being, and before which I shrink when attempting to address a congregation? I ask the question of my friends, my brethren and of every man that lives: Suppose that you, through duty, are called to speak to a private family, to a small congregation, or even to children in a Sunday school, do you not feel this same timidity? Where is the man who can rise to address children without feeling this same modesty? I have seen a very few in my life who could rise before a congregation, in a prayer meeting, or go on the stage of a theatre, or anywhere else, and speak with perfect ease and confidence. I think they have great reason to be thankful for their self-confidence; but where they obtained it or whether it is inherent whether they are destitute of real refinement or have a surplus of it, it is not for me to say. I know that I do not possess this faculty. When I speak to a congregation I know that I am speaking to the intelligence that is from above. This intelligence which is within you and me is from heaven. In gazing upon the intelligence reflected in the countenances of my fellow-beings, I gaze upon the image of Him whom I worship—the God I serve. I see His image and a certain amount of His intelligence there. I feel it within myself. My nature shrinks at the divinity we see in others. This is the cause of that timidity to which I have referred, which I experience when rising to address a congregation.

I rise with pleasure this afternoon to speak to my friends, brethren and sisters, and to the strangers who are here; and I will take the liberty of looking at my people—my brethren and sisters, as they are, and we will look at each other as we are. I look at others as they are, and we will look at each other as we are. We will chat a little together, and I will give both Saints and strangers a few of my views. First to the Saints, I will say that you and I have professed to believe in God who reigns in the heavens, who formed the earth and the planets. No matter whether He rules the celestial, terrestrial or telestial, you and I have professed to believe in that Supreme Being who has set this machine in motion. He governs by law. He has reduced His offspring, His legitimate offspring, to all the sin, darkness, death and misery that we find on this earth; He has also provided means and, in connection with the attributes He has implanted within us, has instituted ordinances which, if we will receive and improve upon, will enable us to return back into His presence. I say to the Latter-day Saints, live your religion! Live so that the Spirit of the Lord will dwell within you, that you may know for a surety and certainty that God lives. For me to tell you that there is a God in heaven, that Jesus Christ is the Savior of the world; for me to tell you that Jesus will give his holy Spirit to them that believe on him and obey his Gospel, would be fruitless to you unless you obey his requirements. I know that the Latter-day Saints are looked upon by the world as dupes—as a low, degraded, imbecile race, and that we are so unwise and short-sighted, so vain and foolish, that through the great amount of enthusiasm within us, we have embraced an error, and have been duped by Joseph Smith. You who have obeyed the principles he preached know whether you are deceived or not. I know for myself and you know for yourselves.

Now let me ask you, if you trust to my faith, to my word and teachings, counsel and advise, and do not seek after the Lord to have His Spirit to guide and direct you, can I not deceive you, can I not lead you into error? Look at this and see to what mischief it would lead, and what an amount of evil could be done to a people if they did not live so that the Spirit of the Lord would dwell with them that they might know these things for themselves. It is my request, my prayer, exhortation, faith, wish and earnest desire that the Latter-day Saints will live their religion, and that they will teach their children all things pertaining to God and godliness, that they may grow up into Christ, their living head.

I would ask of my friends or foes, no matter which—I mean those who do not believe as I do—those who look upon us as a set of fanatics, I would ask a few questions of the world of mankind, of the greatest philosophers, of the greatest geniuses, and of the men of the most profound knowledge on the face of the earth, Can you tell me where you get your knowledge? Say some, "The schoolmaster taught me thus and so; my mother taught me thus and so; or I have learned it from books." Can you tell me the origin of this knowledge? Can you direct me where I can go and get the same knowledge? Was this inherent in you? Was it developed without any nourishment, or instruction—without the life and intelligence which came from the vision of the mind? Ask the mechanic—Who influenced you to bring forth this and that improvement in mechanism? Who influenced Professor Morse to believe that he could stretch a wire round this building or any other, and then, by applying a battery at one end of the wire, that he could receive an answer at the other? Who taught Robert Fulton that he could apply steam so as to propel a vessel? Did his mother, his schoolmaster or his preacher tell him this? No, he would have spurned the idea.

Now, all this is in my remembrance. I lived near by those who assisted Mr. Fulton in building his steamboat. He could not be dissuaded, by any means, to desist from his operations. I ask what was it that influenced the mind of Fulton in this direction? It was that invisible influence or intelligence that comes from our Creator, day by day, and night by night, in dreams and visions of the mind. "I see it, I know it," said he. I recollect him telling some of our neighbors who assisted him in building the first steam vessel that ever was built, "I know that I can apply steam so as to propel this vessel from here to New York. I know it just as well as I live." I recollect a Mr. Curtis, a carriage maker, who lived in the State of New York; said he, "I have a little property, and I will spend all I have to assist Mr. Fulton to put his project into successful operation, for I have faith in it."

This is a question which I would like the scientific and philosophic world to answer, Where do you get your knowledge from? I can answer the question; they get it from that Supreme Being, a portion of whose intelligence is in each and every one. They have it not independently; it was not there until put there. They have the foundation, and they can improve and add knowledge to knowledge, wisdom to wisdom, light to light, and intelligence to intelligence. This power to increase in wisdom and intelligence so that we can know things for ourselves is within every one of us.

Now, I ask the wise, where did you get your wisdom? Was it taught you? Yes, I say it was taught you. By your professors in college? No, it was taught you by the influence of the spirit that is in man, and the inspiration of the Spirit of God giveth it understanding; and every creature can thus add intelligence to intelligence. We all know that if we learn one page of a book to-day, we can learn another to-morrow, and yet retain that which we learned previously; and so we can go on step by step, from day to day, improving the faculties with which God has endowed us, until we are filled with the knowledge of God.

The "Mormons" believe all this. I ask strangers and the philosophers of the world, Is there any harm in it? Is it any harm for you and me to exercise faith in God? We have faith, we live by faith; we came to these mountains by faith. We came here, I often say, though to the ears of some the expressions may sound rather rude, naked and barefoot, and comparatively this is true. Is that a fact? It is. Shall I explain this? I will in part, and I will commence by satisfying the curiosity of almost everybody that comes here, or with whom our Elders converse when away. A great many men and women have an irrepressible curiosity to know how many wives Brigham Young has. I am now going to gratify that curiosity by saying, ladies and gentlemen, I have sixteen wives. If I have any more hereafter it will be my good luck and the blessing of God. "How many children have you, President Young?" I have forty-nine living children, and I hope to have a great many more. Now put that down. I impart this information to gratify the curiosity of the curious.

"President Young, did you come here naked and barefoot?" I will say, very nearly so. "How many of your wives had shoes to their feet, after leaving every thing you had in the State of Illinois?" I do not think that more than one or two of my wives had shoes to their feet when we came here. We bought buckskins of the Indians and made moccasins of them. How many of these Elders had whole pantaloons when they reached here? I do not believe a dozen of them had. They had worked in the dead of winter ferrying the people across the river until they had nothing, and they came here naked and barefoot, that is, comparatively.

We had to have faith to come here. When we met Mr. Bridger on the Big Sandy River, said he, "Mr. Young, I would give a thousand dollars if I knew an ear of corn could be ripened in the Great Basin." Said I, "Wait eighteen months and I will show you many of them." Did

I say this from knowledge? No, it was my faith; but we had not the least encouragement—from natural reasoning and all that we could learn of this country—of its sterility, its cold and frost, to believe that we could ever raise anything. But we travelled on, breaking the road through the mountains and building bridges until we arrived here, and then we did everything we could to sustain ourselves. We had faith that we could raise grain; was there any harm in this? Not at all. If we had not had faith, what would have become of us? We would have gone down in unbelief, have closed up every resource for our sustenance and should never have raised anything. I ask the whole world, is there any harm in having faith in God? Have you faith? Ask Mr. Pullman if he had faith that he could build a car more convenient than any the travelling community enjoyed before, and he will say that he had faith that he could build cars in which ladies and gentlemen might travel through the country with all the ease and comfort they could desire; and he showed his faith by his works, as we read of the ancient worthies doing. You know James says, "Show me your faith without works, and I will show you my faith by my works." Mr. Pullman and others can show their faith by their works. We show our faith by our works. Is there any harm in this? I ask the whole Christian world, is there any harm in believing in God, in a supreme power and influence?

The Christian world believe in God, but they say He has no body. Christianity does not teach any such thing. "God has no parts and He is without passions," say the Christian world. I do not read the Scriptures aright if this is the fact. I read that God loves, that God hates. I read that His eyes are over the works of His hands; that His arm is stretched out to save His people; that His footsteps are seen among the nations of the earth. If He has no feet, He certainly can make no impression; if He has no hands or arms he cannot reach down to save His people. I read that the Lord's ears are open to the petitions of His people; but if He have no ears how can He hear. This is the way that I read the Bible, and I ask, is there any harm in reading and understanding it thus? There are a great many infidels now, who were formerly among our Christian friends and brethren, who are ignoring the Bible in their public schools. I do not. Is there anything in the Bible that should not be read by the scholars in schools? If there be, leave out such parts, or rather replace the language there used, with phraseology more in accordance with modern usage, so that the principles contained in the Bible may be taught in your catechisms or other books. I know that there is some plain talk in the Bible, plainer than I heard this morning; but that plain talk was the custom of the ancients. The mere phraseology there used is not of much consequence, it is the true principle which that book teaches which renders it so valuable. If any of you, ladies and gentlemen, were to step on a steamboat and cross over to Liverpool, you would hear language and see customs that you never heard or saw in Yankee land. It is the same with regard to the Bible, the phraseology is that which was customary centuries ago; but no matter what the language is, that is merely custom. But I will say that the doctrines taught in the Old and New Testaments concerning the will of God towards His children here on the earth; the history of what He has done for their salvation; the ordinances which He has instituted for their redemption; the gift of His Son and his atonement—all these are true, and we, the Latter-day Saints, believe in them.

Some, in their curiosity, will say, "But you Mormons have another Bible! Do you believe in the Old and New Testaments?" I answer we do believe in the Old and New Testaments, and we have also another book, called the Book of Mormon. What are the doctrines of the Book of Mormon? The same as those of the Bible. "What is the utility of this book—the Book of Mormon? Has it been of any use whatever to the people anywhere?" O, yes. "Where and when?" I will refer to one of the sayings of Jesus recorded in the New Testament. Just before his crucifixion he said to his disciples, "Other sheep I have which are not of this fold; them also I must bring, and they shall hear my voice; and there shall be one fold and one shepherd." After his crucifixion he came to this continent, chose Twelve Apostles from among the people and sent them forth to preach his Gospel. He also did many mighty miracles. He was seen to come from heaven down into the midst of the people. He organized his Church amongst them, healed the sick, and left his Church and Gospel in their midst. I am sorry to say that we see the descendants of this very people now in a very low and degraded state. I refer to the aborigines or native Indians of this continent. But this is in consequence of their apostasy and turning from God. The aborigines of this country are the descendants of this very people whom Jesus visited, to whom he delivered his Gospel, and among whom he organized his Church. They were obedient for over three hundred years, and served God with an undivided heart, after which they began to apostatize. For three hundred years the people on the continent of North and South America were benefitted by the work of the Savior in organizing his Church and revealing every principle and ordinance calculated to assist them back into the presence of God. Is not that good?

"What good does it do you, Latter-day Saints?" It proves that the Bible is true. What do the infidel world say about the Bible? They say that the Bible is nothing better than last year's almanack; it is nothing but a fable and priestcraft, and it is good for nothing. The Book of Mormon, however, declares that the Bible is true, and it proves it; and the two prove each other true. The Old and New Testaments are the stick of

Judah. You recollect that the tribe of Judah tarried in Jerusalem and the Lord blessed Judah, and the result was the writings of the Old and New Testaments. But where is the stick of Joseph? Can you tell where it is? Yes. It was the children of Joseph who came across the waters to this continent, and this land was filled with people, and the Book of Mormon or the stick of Joseph contains their writings, and they are in the hands of Ephraim. Where are the Emphraimites? They are mixed through all the nations of the earth. God is calling upon them to gather out, and He is uniting them, and they are giving the Gospel to the whole world. Is there any harm or any false doctrine in that? A great many say there is. If there is, it is all in the Bible.

When I first commenced to preach to the people, nearly forty years ago, to believe the Bible was the great requisite. I have heard some make the broad assertion that every word within the lids of the Bible was the word of God. I have said to them, "You have never read the Bible, have you?" "O, yes, and I believe every word in it is the word of God." Well, I believe that the Bible contains the word of God, and the words of good men and the words of bad men; the words of good angels and the words of bad angels and words of the devil; and also the words uttered by the ass when he rebuked the prophet in his madness. I believe the words of the Bible are just what they are; but aside from that I believe the doctrines concerning salvation contained in that book are true, and that their observance will elevate any people, nation or family that dwells on the face of the earth. The doctrines contained in the Bible will lift to a superior condition all who observe them; they will impart to them knowledge, wisdom, charity, fill them with compassion and cause them to feel after the wants of those who are in distress, or in painful or degraded circumstances. They who observe the precepts contained in the Scriptures will be just and true, and virtuous and peaceable at home and abroad. Follow out the doctrines of the Bible and men will make splendid husbands, women excellent wives, and children will be obedient; they will make families happy and the nations wealthy and happy and lifted up above the things of this life. Can any see any harm in all this? "Oh, but you Mormons are such a strange people. It is true that we have found things in Utah different from what we expected, but still you people are so strange!" Why, what did you expect? Did you expect to see men and women with fins like fishes? We are right from your country—from England, France, Germany, Massachusetts, Maine, New Hampshire, Vermont, New York, from the South, from every State in the Union; what did you expect to see? We lived with you, went to school and to meeting with you; but still the saying is, "Oh, the Mormons are a strange people." It is true that we are; but in what does our peculiarity consist? We do not believe in litigation, quarreling, or in having contention with each other. We take the low and degraded and lift them up. If it would be any satisfaction to any man in the world to know what advantages President Young has had, I will say that I used to have the privilege of cutting down the hemlock, beech and maple trees with my father and my brothers: and then rolling them together, burning the logs, splitting the rails, and fencing the little fields. I wonder if any of you ever did this? You who came from England, or from the rich prairies of Illinois or Missouri never did. Well, this was my education. "Did you not go to school?" Yes; I went eleven days, that was the extent of my schooling.

Now, if we can take the low and degraded and elevate them in their feelings, language and manners; if we can impart to them the sciences that are in the world, teach them all that books contain, and in addition to all this, teach them principles that are eternal, and calculated to make them a beautiful community, lovely in their appearance, intelligent in every sense of the word, would you not say that our system is praiseworthy and possesses great merit? Well, this is all in that book called the Bible, and the faithful observance of the principles taught in that book will do this for any family or nation on the earth.

We are not anxious to obtain gold; if we can obtain it by raising potatoes and wheat, all right. "Can't you make yourselves rich by speculating?" We do not wish to. "Can't you make yourselves rich by going to the gold mines?" We are right in the midst of them. "Why don't you dig the gold from the earth?" Because it demoralizes any community or nation on the earth to give them gold and silver to their hearts' content; it will ruin any nation. But give them iron and coal, good hard work, plenty to eat, good schools and good doctrine, and it will make them a healthy, wealthy and happy people.

This is the great mystery with regard to the Latter-day Saints. We have got a code of laws that the Lord Almighty has left on record in the book called the Old and New Testaments. This same code is contained in the Book of Mormon, also in another book we have, called the Book of Doctrine and Covenants. These doctrines are taught in all these books, and taught alike.

Now then, does the voice of the Lord, as heard from the heavens, ever teach men and women to do wrong? Never. You see a man or woman, in any community, no matter where they are or who they are, that is inclined to do a wrong act to themselves or anybody else, and they profess to do that under a religious influence, and you may know that their ideas of religion are false. Ladies and gentlemen write that down. His religion is false who does not have love to God and to his fellow-creatures; who does not cherish holiness of heart, purity of life, and sanctification, that he may be prepared to enter again into the presence of the Father and the Son.

The question was asked a great many times of Joseph Smith, by gentlemen who came to see him and his people, "How is it that you can control your people so easily? It appears that they do nothing but what you say; how is it that you can govern them so easily?" Said he, "I do not govern them at all. The Lord has revealed certain principles from the heavens by which we are to live in these latter days. The time is drawing near when the Lord is going to gather out His people from the wicked, and He is going to cut short His work in righteousness, and the principles which He has revealed I have taught to the people and they are trying to live according to them, and they control themselves."

Gentlemen, this is the great secret now in controlling this people. It is thought that I control them, but it is not so. It is as much as I can do to control myself and to keep myself straight and teach the people the principles by which they should live. Do all do it? No, and the consequence is we see wickedness in the land. Men do very wrong. Who is guilty? The Lord? No. The religion we have embraced? No. The counsel we have given? No. I have had the question asked me, in the days of Joseph, "Mr. Young, I suppose that you would obey Joseph Smith, let him tell you to do what he might?" "Well, I think I would." "Suppose that he should tell you to kill your neighbor or to steal, or to do this, that or the other, that is wrong, would you do it?" I would reply, "Wait till I am told. I have never yet been told from heaven, by Joseph Smith, the Old or New Testament, the Book of Mormon or the Book of Doctrine and Covenants, to do a wrong thing; and I will wait until I am, before I say what I would do; that is time enough."

"Well, have you not committed wrong?" I may have committed a great many wrongs for want of judgment or wisdom—a little here and a little there. "But have you not done great wrongs?" I have not. I know what is in the hearts of almost every person who comes to this city. It is hurled throughout the length and breadth of our country like lightning that Brigham Young and the "Mormons" are guilty of doing this, that and the other, I need not reiterate; and it is often asked, "Have not you Mormons been guilty of this or that crime or evil?" I answer, no, ladies and gentlemen, we have not. It is the wicked who do these crimes; it is men who will go to hell; and then they try to palm them off on the just and righteous. You can imagine what you please of the stories you have read about the people of Utah from the pens of every lying scribbler who has been here. Imagine what you please, but write this down, publish it in your little paper (the *Trans-Continental*), that a Saint will never do wrong if he knows it. If a man will do a wrong thing wilfully, he is not a Saint. When you hear of Brigham Young, and of his brethren who are in the faith of the holy Gospel, doing this wrong and that wrong, wait until you find out the truth before you publish it to the world.

We have been asked a good many times, "Why do you not publish the truth in regard to these lies which are circulated about you?" We might do this if we owned all the papers published in Christendom. Who will publish a letter from me or my brethren? Who will publish the truth from us? If it gets into one paper, it is slipped under the counter or somewhere else; but it never gets into a second. They will send forth lies concerning us very readily. The old adage is that a lie will creep through the keyhole and go a thousand miles while truth is getting out of doors; and our experience has proved this. We have not the influence and power necessary to refute the falsehoods circulated about us. We depend on God, who sits in the heavens. Our trust is in Him who created the heavens, who formed the earth, and who has brought forth His children on the earth, and who has given the intelligence which they possess. He has given them the privilege of choosing for themselves, whether it be good or evil; but the result of our choice is still in His hand. All His children have the right of making a path for themselves, of walking to the right or to the left, of telling the truth or that which is not true. This right God has given to all people who dwell on the earth, and they can legislate and act as they please; but God holds them in His hands, and He will bring forth the results to His glory, and for the benefit of those who love and serve Him, and He will make the wrath of men to praise Him. All of us are in the hands of that God. We are all His children. We are His sons and daughters naturally, and by the principles of eternal life. We are brethren and sisters. What is it that makes the distinctions we see in the classes of the children of men? We see the low and the degraded, like the aborigines of our country; what is the cause of their being in their present condition? It is because of the rejection by their fathers of the Gospel of the Son of God. The Gospel brings intelligence, happiness, and glory to all who obey it and live according to its precepts. It will give them intelligence that comes from God. Their minds will be open so as to understand things as they are; they will rejoice in being blessed themselves and in blessing their fellow beings, and in being prepared to re-enter the presence of the Father and the Son. This will be their delight. Is this so? It is.

I was very much gratified a day or two ago with a little circumstance that transpired while a company of ladies and gentlemen were visiting me. We were talking over some circumstances relating to our coming to the valleys, and our hardships after we got here. I said it was faith in the Lord Jesus Christ that enabled us to endure. A lady present said, "That is right, I believe in exercising faith in him. Have faith in God, for God will bless all who have faith in Him, no matter who they are nor by whom called; if you have faith in God, and live according to the light you have, God will lead you to glory."

I delight to hear a person give an intimation of their having faith in God; to hear it said, "I believe in Jesus Christ. I believe in his crucifixion and atonement, and in his ordinances." These ordinances we are trying to live, that we may glorify God, and prepare ourselves to build up His Zion on the earth, that the world may be filled with peace, knowledge and joy.

God help us to do so!

21

"I Hope the Brethren and
Sisters will Remember What has been Said,"
A Sermon Delivered on 30 June 1873

(from *Deseret News*, 23 July 1873)

I hope the brethren and sisters will remember what has been said by Brother George A. Smith. In the first place he spoke concerning the patriarchs of the Church. If you will remember what has been told you, you can gather a little more from time to time, and you will understand the nature of this priesthood, and this office. I have it in my mind to give this congregation a short history of the introduction of the office of a patriarch in the midst of this people. Most of the Latter-day Saints have a historical knowledge of the brethren being driven from Jackson county, Missouri, in 1833; also of the gathering of the strength of the Lord's house together by Joseph, and going up to Missouri in 1834. My brother, Joseph Young, and myself were in this camp. When we were on our return home my brother Joseph spoke very frequently with regard to patriarchs and patriarchal blessings, and finally said he, "When we get to Kirtland I am going to ask Brother Joseph Smith if we can have the privilege of calling our father's family together and receiving a patriarchal blessing under the hands of our father." Brother Joseph Young saw the Prophet Joseph Smith, and said he, "I do not see any inconsistency in this at all, and I think it would be a good thing." A day was appointed for the family to gather together, and Brother Joseph Smith was asked to attend this meeting. He came, and while we sat chatting together on the things of the kingdom, the Prophet said, "I believe it will be necessary for Father Young to receive his patriarchal blessing and be ordained a patriarch, so that heaven bless his family;" and after our little meeting was opened Brother Joseph Smith laid his hands upon Father Young and blessed him and gave him an ordination to bless his family—his own posterity. When this was done Father Young laid his hands upon the children that were there, commencing at the eldest and continuing until he had blessed all that were in the house. We were not all there, some of the brothers and sisters were absent. After that, Brother Joseph Smith said, "I think I will get my father's family together and we will have a patriarchal blessing from Father Smith." He did so. In a few days he called his father's house together and gave him the authority to bless his children, and Father Smith blessed his children. In the course of a few weeks, I think, Brother

Joseph Smith received a revelation to ordain patriarchs, and he called his father's family together again, and gave his father the full ordination of patriarch for the church; and in this revelation the Lord instructed him to have a record kept, in which should be written all the blessings of the patriarch of the church, and from these circumstances were ordained a few, but only a very few, patriarchs.

We have passed along now for many years with but few patriarchs in the church. At our last conference I felt very much impressed to introduce the subject of ordaining patriarchs. We talked the matter over, and we concluded we would set apart a number that were worthy—those of considerable age—and give them the blessing of a patriarch. Since that time we have ordained quite a number. We are ordaining some here, and this will be continued, probably, until there is a patriarch in all the branches of the church, especially in every large branch. This is a little history of the coming forth of this office in the midst of this people. Now I will tell you the reason why I mention it.

From the time that Joseph obtained a knowledge of the plates in the hill Cumorah he received little by little, a little at a time. "When he first obtained a knowledge of these plates, I apprehend that he knew nothing, in comparison, of their contents and the design of the Lord in bringing them forth. But he was instructed little by little until he received the Aaronic priesthood, then the privilege of baptism for the remission of sins, then the Melchizedek Priesthood, then organizing a church, &c., and this is the travel of this prophet Joseph first and we, following up, and we receive a little here and a little there, and so we increase, and if we live according to the revelations that are given to us we will continue to increase in understanding. The Lord never reveals all to a person at once. A man may have a vision and the heavens be opened to his mind so that he may see a great deal, but he will retain only a little.

Now I want to say a few words to the brethren and sisters, with regard to cities of Enoch, and to portray what might be enjoyed by a portion or all of this people if they were living in the capacity of a city of Enoch. To do this fully would be exceedingly difficult, but it can be seen in part by the vision of the Spirit. I wish to bring this one particular thing before the minds of the people. We have a great deal to say with regard to property—the share that so entraps the affections of the Latter-day Saints. It is my humble opinion that if the time had come for us to commence and organize these branches in this place, and in the next settlement, and throughout the valleys of the mountains, I would rather undertake to control the purses of those who have means than to control the doings of the poor. For instance, I will relate a little circumstance. I think it was in 1850, we built a very nice house, in a very nice location, in which to place some widows. We wanted to make them happy and comfortable. When we had prepared the house and everything for their reception we could not get one of them to go into it. They must live where they chose to live; they must dictate where they would go, decide what house they should live in, and the very room or chamber which they would use, and we have had more difficulty with those whom we have fed and clothed than with those who are wealthy. I will relate a little circumstance that transpired in Independence, Jackson Co. A poor man with his wife and seven or eight children came up there. I do not think that the children had ever had a shoe to their feet or a second dress to wrap around them, and hardly a first one, and it was as much as ever the man could do to keep anything on his feet. His shoes were so bad that he had to "withe" them up. I do not suppose you ever saw such a thing as that; I do not expect you have in the mountains, but the Yankees have. When a shoe was about three-quarters worn out they would tie the tops to the bottoms with leather strings, and finally when they got so bad that they could not hold them on they would put a "withe" around so that they could wear them. I expect that if this man had any shoes, they had to be "withed" on his feet. Well, he came there and offered his services to the church. Said he, "I will give all my services to the church and ask nothing in return, if my family can be well clothed, well fed, and have a good house to live in." He was informed that he had better go to work and do something for his family before he could do anything for the church. I believe that he and the church dissolved partnership. This, which I have been relating to you, is just about the spirit of the people. You take the poor man who has not a penny in the world, and do you think you are going to have the privilege of dictating his time? No sir, but we can dictate the purse without difficulty. We have rich men; some of them are wealthy. I would rather undertake to control the purse of a millionaire in this church than some men not worth a dime in the world, and who never will be unless somebody gives it to them. There is more need to labor and contend against the disposition and the will of the poor, miserable, ignorant, poverty-stricken brethren than those who are wealthy and have got a little learning and a little idea of a human being. This is my experience. Ask the brethren who are poor, What do you say? Become equal? "Yes," say they, "we will hold up both hands for that." What do they mean? They mean for those who have wealth to give it to them, and let them spend as much as and where they please, and as ill as they choose. But you take them, and if they want to go a fishing, "Yes sir," say they, "I guess my time is my own, and I guess I have a right to go a hunting, or a fishing. I have a right to go over to this place or that place, when I please, and I shall not ask any man when I may go or when I may come." This is the disposition of the people, and the more ignorant they are, the more argument and reasoning, and the longer it will take to bring them to an understanding of what is right and what is wrong.

As for the real advantages of living as a family, why those who contemplate can see at once, that, if we were in a family, governed and controlled by the priesthood, all this needless riding, running, hallooing, &c., would cease. Another thing, I will say to the young ladies especially, that if I should live to have the dictation of a stake of Zion that would live according to the Order of Enoch, this nonsensical reading would cease. This "yellow covered" literature would not come into the houses of the Saints. We should dispense with this, and cast it from us; if it were here, we would cast it out and sell it to the paper makers, and let them make it up into paper to use for a better purpose, to make our own books. In such a state of society we would have every person study that which would be useful. Here are our young women—now I am not going from home to get this experience. I hope that my children know as much about the Bible, Book of Mormon or the Doctrine and Covenants as they do about yellow covered books. But you ask many of our young people about these stories: "What a beautiful story there is in" such and such a paper! Or "what a beautiful story there" is in this paper or in that. They know all about it. The proprietors of these papers get men and women to write stories with no other foundation than the imaginations of their own hearts and brains, and our young women and boys read these lies until they get perfectly restless in their feelings, and they become desperate, and many of our girls—I am not accusing any one here, I think they pay attention to their business a little better, they have got cows to milk instead of novels to read—but in our part of the land many of our young women just hope and pray, if they ever thought of prayer, "I do wish some villain would come along and break open my room and steal me and carry me off; I want to be stolen, I want to be carried away, I want to be lost with the Indians, I want to be shipwrecked and to go through some terrible scene, so that I can experience what this beloved lady has experienced whom I have been reading about." Oh, how affecting! and they read with the tears running down their cheeks, until their books become perfectly wet, and they do so wish that somebody or other would come and steal and carry them off. If I had the dictation of a society, all this would stop, you would have none of it. I would have every person learning something useful. We would come together for two hours after the labors of the day and we would read the Bible, Book of Mormon, Doctrine and Covenants, Voice of Warning, history, geography; perhaps we would get up a class for the study of law, for we have to meet the world as it is. We would study physic, anatomy, surgery; the history of our own nation and of other nations; we would have classes in which our German brethren might teach the young people, and the old ones too, the German language, and when that was through with we would have the best of the instruction imparted in the English language or in other languages, or in something that would be profitable and useful to pupils in their future life. We would teach them good manners, how human beings, should conduct themselves in their social intercourse. I do not profess to understand pure, true etiquette as it should be displayed among an intelligent people, like the Americans, but I can tell you what I meet. I have a great many visitors at my office. Occasionally a gentleman comes, and occasionally a lady. But on the countenance of many of those I see, some of them professing to be the elite of the nation, ignorance and impudence are unmistakably portrayed. Occasionally a man comes along who is connected with a railroad, newspaper, book, or some public business, and he is full of boasting and vanity. "I have been a judge," "I have been a sheriff," "I have been a constable or magistrate," or "I have been a general," or something or other. "Would it be convenient for you to pass me over your railroad." What should such persons be called? Shall we use the vulgar phrase, and say they are public bummers, ignorant of the first rules of etiquette. Perhaps they think the ignorance is me; and if they do it is very well. I frequently meet people of this class. "Why bless your heart, I guess I am ready for anything. I have got money." Yes it is money, money, and some people think that makes a gentleman or a lady, and that money is all the accomplishments they need. I wish they understood true etiquette—the true principles of manhood.

I beg your pardon, I have now occupied twice the time allotted me. I want to say a little more with regard to the Order of Zion, but I will stop.

{22}

The Resurrection.
A Discourse by Brigham Young, President
of the Church of Jesus Christ of Latter-day Saints,
Delivered in the New Tabernacle. Salt Lake City
at the General Conference, Oct. 8, 1875

**(Salt Lake City: Deseret News
Steam Printing Establishment [1875])**

I wish to present to the Latter-day Saints the doctrine of the resurrection in its true light. To satisfy the philosophy of my own mind in regard to this doctrine, I shall be under the necessity of commencing with the words of God as we find them in the beginning, or rather the beginning of the history we have of the earth. We admit the history that Moses gives of the creation or organization of this earth, as stated in his writing, to be correct. The philosophy of my mind, with all the experience I have gained by observation and knowledge of facts, tells me that there is nothing made, formed or fashioned without a Being to make, form or fashion the same. Then my own reasoning teaches me that myself as a mechanic, with all others upon this earth, and those also who dwell in the heavens. When we commence any work of mechanism, have an object in the same. God had an object in view when He framed this earth and placed vegetation and all creatures upon it, and man was brought here for the high object of an increase of wisdom, knowledge, understanding, glory and honor—each and every person, creature or thing in its own order and time, that all may harmonize together and receive this glory and honor. The particles that compose the earth were brought together for a certain purpose by its great Author. This purpose was, and still is, to bring this earth and all things upon it into a higher state of glory and intelligence. In the beginning there were laws given by which all nature was to be governed or controlled. It is true that man transgresses these laws and would change them if he had the power to do so. But there are laws which he cannot disturb, and which operate regardless of man's actions. Among these is the law which pertains to the resurrection of the body of man, and also to the resurrection of the earth; for this earth has to undergo a great change, or, in other words, has to be resurrected.

Abel, the martyr, was the first man of whose death we have any account. He brought his offering to the Lord and was accepted. This proves that he was a righteous man, and by his righteousness he so far

218

sanctified the particles of this earth that comprised the component parts of his body that they became entitled to a glorious resurrection, which he undoubtedly obtained when Jesus arose. If Abel had been eaten by dogs or lions, the component parts of his body never could have gone to compose the component parts of any other bodies. Why? Because the laws which govern the elements would not permit this to be done.

The question may be asked. Do not the particles that compose man's body, when returned to mother earth, go to make or compose other bodies? No, they do not. Some philosophers have asserted that the human body changes every seven or ten years. This is not correct, for it never changes; that is, the substance of which it is composed do not pass off and other particles of matter come and take their place. Neither can the particles which have comprised the bodies of men become parts of the bodies of other men, or of beasts, fowls, fish, insects or vegetables. They are governed by a divine law, and though they may pass from the knowledge of the scientific world, that divine law still holds and governs and controls them. Man's body may be buried in the ocean, it may be eaten by wild beasts, or it may be burned to ashes, and they be scattered to the four winds, yet the particles of which it is composed will not be incorporated into any form of vegetable or animal life, to become a component part of their structure. Are they gross, tangible, and in their organized capacity, subject to decay and change? Yes, and if buried in the earth, they undergo decomposition and return to mother earth; but it is no matter how minute the particles are, they are watched over and will be preserved until the resurrection, and at the sound of the trumpet of God every particle of our physical structures necessary to make our tabernacles perfect will be assembled, to be rejoined with the spirit, every man in his order. Not one particle will be lost.

I have a few questions to ask the philosophical world especially those who are well skilled in chemistry: Is this earth, the air and the water composed of life, or do they, or any portion of them, consist of inanimate matter, or of that that has no life in itself? Another question: If the earth, air and water, are composed of life, is there any intelligence in this life? The philosopher may take his own time to answer these questions, and when he has satisfied himself he may ask himself again: Are those particles of matter life; if so, are they possessed of intelligence according to the grade of their organization? As far as we are concerned, we suggest the idea that there is an eternity of life, an eternity of organization, and an eternity of intelligence from the highest to the lowest grade, every creature in its order, from the Gods to the animalculae. Bear in mind, you who are believers in the resurrection or in the works of God, that man has sought out many inventions and has striven hard to learn the mysteries of God and godliness by his worldly wisdom, yet there are many things which science, with all its tests, cannot find out. Matter may be divided into an infinitude of atoms, until they pass beyond the power of the microscope to discover them, and the most skillful chemist who dwells on the earth knows not whither they go. My position is, and which I declare to the Latter-day Saints, it is beyond the power of man, without revelation from God, with all his science to know whether these particles that compose our bodies go into other creatures to form the component parts of their bodies, or whether they merely pass into the already organized body to resuscitate it and contribute to its sustenance. I declare to the Latter-day Saints, and to all living upon the earth who have intelligence to understand, that the particles that comprise the component parts of our bodies will never enter into other bodies to form the elements of their bodies; but these very identical particles that now compose our bodies will be resurrected and come together by the power of the trump of God and will be re-united to form the body—excepting the blood, which will not be necessary to our existence in an immortal state—and then be prepared to receive the spirit, preparatory to their exaltation. Query: Would not the particles that compose the body of our Savior, according to their intelligence, oppose the idea of becoming part of any other body but His? Again: Would not the Saints, who are faithful in magnifying the Priesthood of the Son of God, object to the particles which now compose their bodies, and which they have sanctified through obedience to that Priesthood, entering into and forming parts of other bodies than their own—bodies which their spirits had not possessed and of which they knew nothing in this life?

Although some may think that the substances of which our bodies are composed are borrowed for our use during this mortal existence, it is not so, neither will they be thrown off at death, never to be restored; and though in the resurrection the bodies of the righteous will be raised immortal and free from all corruption, they will be none the less tangible or perceptible to the touch of those who are permitted to handle them. The question may be asked: Will the bodies of those who do not observe the laws of God, and which are not sanctified by obedience to them, come forth in the resurrection? Undoubtedly they will; but not at the same time nor to the same glory that they do who observe the laws of God.

The earth, also, abideth the law and filleth the measure of its creation, and though it shall die, it shall be resurrected in glory, a sanctified creation, suitable for the residence of celestial beings. The elements will be burned and purified, and be renewed, but not one atom of earth's organism will be lost; for that which is governed by law shall be preserved by law. And for everything which our God has created He has prescribed laws. There is nothing so minute as to escape His notice, there is no creation so immense as to transcend the bounds of His power; all are alike subject to the operation of His decrees. He called matter from chaos and created the earth, and the heavens are studded with planets, the glorious workmanship of His hands. He has hung those mighty orbs in space, and their courses are fixed. And by the exercise of His power the original elements which have formed the bodies of men will be brought forth in the resurrection—bone to bone, sinew to sinew, flesh to flesh, not one hair shall be lost—and all this in obedience to law, that the substances which have formed the tabernacles of men, or of beasts, or of fowls, or of fish, shall not be intermingled or lost; but shall be all restored to their own places, though they may have been swallowed up in the depths of the sea, or have been scattered to the four winds of heaven

To illustrate these facts connected with the resurrection of the body, we will quote from the revelations which the Lord has given to His children: . . .

[Publisher's note: Throughout the remainder of this sermon Brigham Young quotes from the following scriptures and other works *verbatim* without additional explanation or commentary: Ezekiel 37:1-14; Job 19:25-27; Daniel 12:2; Luke 20:37; 24:36-43; John 20:24-27; 5:25, 28, 29; Revelation 20:6, 13; Matthew 27:52, 53; Philippians 3:20, 21; Romans 8:11; 6:4, 5; 1 Corinthians 15:16-22, 35-39, 42-44; 1 Thessalonians 4:14-16; Mosiah 16:7-10; 2 Nephi 9:6-8, 11-13; Alma 11:41-44; 40:21-23; Helaman 14:15, 16; 3 Nephi 23:7-13; Mormon 9:13; Doctrine and Covenants 88:14-20, 25-28, 95-98; 29:13, 23-26; 43:18; 45:45, 46; 63:49-52; Pearl of Great Price, pp. 10, 21; *History of Joseph Smith*, March 20, 1842, February 9, 1843 (Doctrine and Covenants 129), April 2, 1943 (Doctrine and Covenants 130:18-23), April 7, 1843, May 17, 1843 (Doctrine and Covenants 131:7, 8), and June 11, 1843.]

"Philosophy of Man upon the Earth—
The Great and Grand Secret of Salvation—
Are We One—Nature of Stewardship—
Increase of Temples—Hear Ye, Mothers,"
A Sermon Delivered on 8 October 1876

(from *Journal of Discourses*, 26 vols. [Liverpool:
Latter-day Saints' Book Depot, 1855-86], 18:257-64)

I hope to be able to make myself heard by this large congregation. This moving of feet, whispering to each other, the crying of children, and the noise made by those who are walking, are like the murmuring of many waters. When there is perfect quietness, I am satisfied that my voice can be heard all over this house, and no one who is blessed with good ears for hearing need miss a word. I should feel more satisfied if I could prevail on our brethren, when speaking from this stand, to speak directly in front, so that they could be heard as far as possible. Many of our experienced Elders, in their conversation to the people, turn first to the right and then to the left, and every time they turn either way, a portion of the congregation is unable to distinctly understand that which is spoken; whereas, if they were to speak directly to the front, the voice would divide and go equally to each part of the house, and all would hear. Whether I shall be able to continue my remarks to any length I do not know; I shall try, however, to use judgment in speaking, so as not to injure myself.

I will give a short text, to both Saint and sinner, and I think if we were to include ourselves among the latter and say we are all sinners, we would come nearer the fact than to class ourselves among the former, although we hope to be Saints, are trying to be Saints, and probably a great many of those who are called Latter-day Saints will yet become Saints indeed.

First, the philosophy of man upon this earth. This cannot be learned by studying the sciences of mankind, it is only understood by the revelations of God to ourselves. I will give you a part of my own visions upon this matter. Mankind is composed of two distinct elements; the first is a spiritual organization in eternity, the second is a natural organization on this earth, formed out of the material of which this earth is composed. Man is first spiritual, then temporal. As it is written in the revelations of God to man, all things were first created spiritual, and secondly temporal.

That is, spirits were begotten, born and educated in the celestial world, and were brought forth by celestial bodies. By tracing this subject a little we might understand how this is brought about. The spirits before inhabiting bodies are as pure and holy as the angels or as the gods, they know no evil. This, their first estate, is the commencement of their experience.

These spirits I shall leave for the present, and refer to our first parents, Adam and Eve, who were found in the Garden of Eden, tempted and overcome by the power of evil, and consequently subject to evil and sin, which was the penalty of their transgression. They were now prepared, as we are, to form bodies or tabernacles for the reception of pure and holy spirits. When the body is prepared, at the proper time, the spirit enters the tabernacle, and all the world of mankind in their reflections and researches must come to this conclusion, for the fact is they can come to no other—that when the mother feels life there is an evidence that the spirit from heaven has entered the tabernacle. So far, this is the philosophy of our being. As has been said, in consequence of sin, the body is subject to sin, and it requires all the efforts and power that man can exert in order to resist temptation that this pure and holy spirit may bring into subjection the body, so that it may be sanctified by the Gospel or the law of Christ. The inquiring mind will ask, Why is this so? Simply that we may know good from evil; all the facts which you and I understand are by contrast, and all glory, all enjoyment, every happiness and every bliss are known by its opposite. This is the decree, this is the way the heavens are, the way they were, and the way they will continue to be, forever, and forever. Never was there a time when evil was not in existence, but the time will come when this evil will pass away and be no more, so far as this world is concerned, and nothing will be able to endure only that which is pure and holy, and Christ will destroy death and him that hath the power of death. This applies to this earth, and the ordeals which it passes through with those that are upon it until the winding up scene.

But to return to this organization. We find a pure spirit inhabiting the tabernacle of the creature which is always prompting the individual to good, to virtue, to truth and holiness; all of which emanate from that source of purity from which this spirit came. And here the evil that came through transgression that is in this tabernacle, is warring with this pure spirit, it seeks to overcome it, and is striving with all its power to bring this spirit into subjection, into bondage to the law of sin. This is the warfare which Paul refers to when speaking of the "thorn in the flesh," which is no more or less than the spirit contending against the flesh, and the flesh against the spirit. This pure spirit will remain in a condition to receive the operations of the spirit of God, which has gone forth into the world, and which lightens every man that comes into the world, regardless of his condition, birth or education; the spirit of Christ lightens them all, and instructs their pure spirits, which are organizations in the germ and in their growth, to become independent beings, even sons and daughters of the Almighty; and it will continue to thus operate until this body, this sinful tabernacle, has warred against the spirit and overcome it to such a degree as to entirely subject it to the man of sin. And when the flesh attains this victory over the spirit, then is the time spoken of when man has sinned to that degree that, says the Apostle, "ye shall not pray for them, for they have sinned a sin unto death." Then the spirit of the Lord ceases to strive with them, they no longer receive light, having passed the day of grace. Until then every man and every woman is on saving ground, and they can be redeemed from sin.

How is it that the Latter-day Saints feel and understand alike, are of one heart and one mind, no matter where they may be when they receive the Gospel, whether in the north or the south, the east or the west, even to the uttermost parts of the earth? They receive that which was promised by the Savior when he was about to leave the earth, namely, the Comforter, that holy unction from on high which recognizes one God, one faith and one baptism, whose mind is the will of God the Father, in whom there dwelleth unity of faith and action, and in whom there cannot be division or confusion; when they received thus further light, it matters not whether they have seen each other or not, they at once become brothers and sisters, having been adopted into the family of Christ through the bonds of the everlasting covenant, and all can then exclaim, in the beautiful language of Ruth, "Thy people shall be my people, and thy God my God!" And the fact that we receive this Comforter, the Holy Ghost, is proof that the spirit in warring with the flesh has overcome, and by continuing in this state of victory over our sinful bodies we become the sons and daughters of God, Christ having made us free, and whoever the Son makes free is free indeed. Having fought the good fight we then shall be prepared to lay our bodies down to rest to await the morning of the resurrection when they will come forth and be reunited with the spirits, the faithful, as it is said, receiving crowns, glory, immortality and eternal lives, even a fullness with the Father, when Jesus shall present his work to the Father, saying, "Father, here is the work thou gavest me to do." Then will they become gods, even the sons of God; then will they become eternal fathers, eternal mothers, eternal sons and eternal daughters; being eternal in their organization, they go from glory to glory, from power to power; they will never cease to increase and to multiply world's without end. When they receive their crowns, their dominions, they then will be prepared to frame earth's like unto ours and to people them in the same manner as we have been brought forth by our parents, by our Father and God.

I have often remarked that if the Latter-day Saints and all the world understood the philosophy of their own being, they would bow in humble reverence to him who is the Author of our being and the author of all wisdom and all knowledge known among the children of men. It is very little comparatively that we do know, and but very little we can really comprehend. It is believed that our scientists and philosophers are very far advanced, and that wonderful progress has been made in the nineteenth century; but notwithstanding all the knowledge and power of philosophy which so distinguishes our age, who among our most learned can create as simple a thing as a spear of grass or the leaf of a tree? No one; this can only be done through the natural process; no one can organize the simplest particle of element independent of the laws of nature. When the philosopher of the age reaches that perfection that one can waft himself to the moon or to the north star, or to any other of the fixed planets, and be there in an instant, in the same manner that Jesus did when he ascended to the Father in heaven and returned to the earth again, then we may begin to think we know a little. When we shall possess the power and knowledge to cause heavenly planets to take their position, giving them their laws and boundaries which they must obey, and which they cannot pass, then we may begin to feel that we possess a little wisdom and power.

The great and grand secret of salvation, which we should continually seek to understand through our faithfulness, is the continuation of the lives. Those of the Latter-day Saints who will continue to follow after the revelations and commandments of God to do them, who are found to be obedient in all things, continually advancing little by little towards perfection and the knowledge of God, they, when they enter the spirit world and receive their bodies, will be able to advance faster in the things pertaining to the knowledge of the Gods, and will continue onward and upward until they become Gods, even the sons of God. This I say is the great secret of the hereafter to continue in the lives forever and forever, which is the greatest of all gifts God has ever bestowed upon his children. We all have it within our reach, we can all attain to this perfected and exalted state if we will embrace its principles and practice them in our every-day life. How accommodating, how glorious and divine are the dealings of God with his fallen children! We have been called from darkness to light, from the power of Satan to the living God. By obeying the whispering of this Holy Spirit, which we have received by virtue of obedience to the Gospel, which prompts us to purge from within us all sinful desire, we can say we are no more in the world, but we are in Christ, our living head. The philosophy of our coming out from the world is the putting off the old man sin, and the putting on of the new

225

man Jesus Christ. How is this to be done? After we believed the Gospel we were baptized for the remission of our sins—and by the laying on of hands we received the Holy Spirit of Promise and felt that "we shall be one." I felt that I should no longer have need to keep a day-book and ledger in which to keep my accounts, for we were about to consolidate and become one; that every man and every woman would assist by actually laboring with their hands in planting, building up and beautifying this earth to make it like the Garden of Eden. I should therefore have no farther occasion to keep accounts, I should certainly accumulate and earn more than I needed, and had not a single doubt but what my wants would be supplied. This was my experience, and this is the feeling of every one who receives the Gospel in an honest heart and contrite spirit.

But how are we now? What is our present condition?

Are we one temporally? Just about as much as Babylon is. One says, "I am for the mines, I am engaged on my farm or my factory, I am so engaged in my mercantile business that it absorbs all my time, therefore do not trouble me, do not infringe on me." And who are they? Generally they are men who, like myself, came here not only poor, but in debt. I was driven from my homes and possessions, five times stripped of my earthly possessions. When we arrived in this valley, we were in a destitute condition. Others came here as destitute as we were, but are now comparatively wealthy—how do they feel? They wish to do just as they please. Ask them if they believe that the law of God requires us to enter into a general copartnership in all our business relations, living and working together as one family? They will tell you, "No, I don't believe any such thing." Those of this class who are merchants will say, "I want to get rich, I will buy where I please, and will set at a hundred per cent., five hundred per cent., or a thousand per cent., if I can." You may do so if you will, but your end will be lamentable. You count the men who have broken up their homes and gone in search of gold, and then count those who have carried out my advice, and you will readily acknowledge that the latter class is by far the better off, not only financially, but morally and spiritually. You, my brethren and sisters, who were poor when you came here, but who now, through the blessing of God, ride in your carriages and live in fine houses, enjoying all the comforts of life, as well as good health, and the society of friends, how do you feel? As for myself, I have not the slightest feeling in my heart that I own a single thing. What I am in possession of, the Lord has merely made me a steward over, to see what I will do with it. Now, my brethren and sisters, do you feel the same? If you do you will each enquire what is my duty? One duty is to go to work and build this and other Temples, and the other ones can be built long before we can finish this one. Shall we do so? I say we will. If we had reached that perfect state of unity which we should have long before this, and still hope that we yet shall, do you suppose we would ask a man to pay Tithing on ten bushels of wheat, or a hundred or a thousand? No, all that would be necessary under such circumstances would be to say, brother so-and-so, from you we want so much, and from another so much. "Yes," they would say, "Take it. I have nothing. It is all the Lord's, let it be used to do him service in the building up of his kingdom." "What would you do, brother Brigham, if you were required to give up all your substance? Just what I have always been willing to do. I would continue to do my duty and trust in God for the results; that is what I have done all my life. This, doubtless, seems foolishness in the eyes of the world, they cannot understand it, neither have they any means of understanding it, for "the things of God knoweth no man but the Spirit of God." Before I embraced this Gospel I had studied the creeds of the Christian world. When I inquired of them with regard to heavenly things, why we came here, and the nature of the relationship we sustained to God and to heavenly beings, could I get any information? No, not the least idea. I once heard one of the leading Elders in the Episcopal Methodist Church undertake to explain to his congregation one of the simplest of things, namely, "What is the soul of man?" After he had labored for two long hours, having exhausted his language, for knowledge he had none, he straightened back in the pulpit and said, "My brethren and sisters, I must come to the conclusion that the soul of man is an immaterial substance." What a pretty thing to look at! Excuse me. As far as the spirit and feeling of many of these people are concerned with regard to morality, and their endeavors to send the Gospel to the heathen nations, it is excellent. And there are, doubtless, millions of just as honest people among the several religious denominations as are amongst the professedly Latter-day Saints. But they have not the Gospel, they are in darkness with regard to the plan of salvation, and their teachers are blind guides, totally unable to give the people the living word, the way of life. If they live up to the best light and knowledge they have and can get, they are safe, and in a saved condition. What is the sin of the ministry and people of the present Christian denominations? It is that light has come to them and they reject it. The condemnation of the Jewish nation was that light had come into the world, but they chose darkness rather than light, because their deeds were evil; so says the Savior. The same Gospel that Jesus taught to those who rejected him, is entrusted to us to preach to the whole world with the same consequences which must reach them at some time, in some condition.

We have been hunted and driven from place to place, and the wicked have sought our destruction, simply because we offer to them the light, the truth, the everlasting Gospel. Although we have been robbed of our homes and possessions, they have not succeeded in destroying us yet.

Will they succeed? I think not. The Lord has said he would gather his people for the last time, which he is doing; he will not suffer that they shall be overcome, and the kingdom wrested from them as heretofore. Neither will he be mocked and derided when he comes this time—not because the wicked would not repeat the same treatment if they were permitted—but because he will come in judgment, taking vengeance on the wicked and on the ungodly, and with the besom [sic] of destruction the refuge of lies and all those who love and make lies will be swept from the earth, and few men will be left. If the Latter-day Saints do not desist from running after the things of this world, and begin to reform and do the work the Father has given them to do, they will be found wanting, and they, too, will be swept away and counted as unprofitable servants.

Latter-day Saints, go and take up a labor with yourselves, urge yourselves to the belief that the Lord is God, that his eyes are upon the works of his hands, that even the sparrow does not go unfed, nor a hair of our heads fall to the ground unnoticed. Labor with yourselves until you have confidence in God and in his revelations to us; become one in temporal things as well as spiritual things as fast as you can. Enter into the compact, the association we call the United Order, that we may commence to do the work we have undertaken to do.

Now, I will make a proposition, and you may have five years to do the work I am about to assign you. To the people of the Sevier Valley, Millard County, Iron County, Piute County, Beaver County, with Juab, Kane, Washington, and Sanpete Counties, I will say, Go to work and build a Temple in Sanpete. As soon as you are ready to commence, I will provide the plan. The ground is already selected. We do not ask whether you are able to do this; but ask yourselves if you have faith sufficient to do it, for we know that you are perfectly able to do it if you are willing, and do it inside of three years from next April. Then to the people of Box Elder County, the Malad Valley, Cache Valley, Soda Springs, and Bear Lake Valley, Rich County, and the people on Bear River, I say, unite your labor and commence as soon as you can to build a Temple in Cache Valley. Again, to the people of Weber County, Davis County, Morgan and Summit Counties, Salt Lake County, Tooele and Utah Counties, with the people east and west, I will say, Go to work and finish the Temple in this city forthwith. Can you accomplish the work, you Latter-day Saints of these several counties? Yes, that is a question I can answer readily, you are perfectly able to do it, the question is, Have you the necessary faith? Have you sufficient of the Spirit of God in your hearts to enable you to say, Yes, by the help of God our Father, we will erect these buildings to his name. There will be little money comparatively needed, it is nearly all labor, such as you can perform. If the people had paid their Tithing, and paid the hands employed on the Temple in proportion as I have done, that building would have been finished before now. But I am not obliged to build Temples for the people; this is our common duty, in order that all may have the privilege to officiate for themselves and their dead. How long, Latter-day Saints, before you will believe the Gospel as it is? The Lord has declared it to be his will that his people enter into covenant, even as Enoch and his people did, which of necessity must be before we shall have the privilege of building the Centre Stake of Zion, for the power and glory of God will be there, and none but the pure in heart will be able to live and enjoy it. Go to now, with your might and with your means, and finish this Temple. Why, for what reason? The reasons are very obvious, and you understand them.

A few words to the sisters—you mothers who are trifling with the ordinances of the house of God, and the blessings that are proffered to you, I will say that the time will come, if you persist in doing so, when you will mourn, and will be willing to give worlds, if you possessed them, for the privilege of living your lives over again. Some of you are treating with contempt the oracles of the kingdom of God upon the earth, and in the commission of this sin you trifle with your own salvation, as well as the salvation of your children. Repent, and turn unto God, and teach your children the importance of doing the same, and of the sacredness of the ordinances and the laws of God. It is the mother's influence that is most effective in moulding the mind of the child for good or for evil. If she treat lightly the things of God, it is more than likely her children will be inclined to do the same, and the Lord will not hold her guiltless when he comes to make up his jewels; he will disown all such when he comes to claim his own, and will say, Go hence, I never knew you.

The question may be asked, Are you going to discontinue to give endowments here? I think it is very probable that you will have to go where there is a Temple, or go without. In consequence of our having been driven from our homes, and because of our destitute circumstances, the Lord has permitted us to do what we have done, namely, to use this Endowment House for Temple purposes. But since, through the mercies and blessings of God, we are able to build Temples, it is the will and commandment of God that we do so.

I thank you for your attention. We will adjourn this Conference until the 6th day of April next, to meet at ten o'clock a.m., in the Temple at St. George. We intend to dedicate it then. We shall dedicate some parts this fall, and commence to work in it.

I feel to bless the people, and say, May Heaven be kind to you. Amen.

{24}

"When I have asked My Counsellors or Any of the Brethren of the Twelve" A Sermon Delivered on 21 May 1877

(from *Deseret News*, 6 June 1877)

When I have asked my counsellors or any of the brethren of the Twelve with regard to the selection of the presidency of this Stake of Zion [at Logan, Cache County], the reply has been, "Make your own choice, Brother Brigham, and we will vote for them." This is correct and the proper method of nominating such officers. We will give you the liberty of voting as you please, but as for the appointment that is with us to say. This is ordered, it is so revealed and so written, and we must abide by it. The Lord in founding this work did not ask the opinion of the world as to what they thought of this, that, or the other. Suppose the prophet Joseph had sought the opinion of the orthodox world with regard to his right to receive revelations from God, how long do you think he would have waited before they sanctioned his appointment, or acknowledged that the Lord had the right and that it was his privilege to appoint whomsoever he would? The appointment of Joseph was from God, and it was in the authority of the priesthood of the Son of God that Joseph was called, ordained and set apart as an apostle, prophet and elder in Israel, and if it had been referred to the Christian world for their approval and sanction, I think the Lord would have waited until this time. They would have got up here, there and everywhere, saying, "I oppose it."

I shall nominate, as President of this Stake of Zion, Moses Thatcher. [Carried unanimously.] It is Brother Thatcher's privilege to choose his counsellors if he wishes so to do, and it is our right and privilege to give them to him. I shall, therefore, nominate William B. Preston as his first counsellor. [Unanimously carried.] And Milton D. Hammond, who is now Bishop at Providence, as his second counsellor. I am not intimately acquainted with Brother Hammond; but I understand he is a man of good, sound judgment, a man who lives his religion and who is capable of giving counsel in almost all matters pertaining to the building up of the kingdom of God upon the earth. This is what I learn respecting him. What do you think, brethren and sisters, of this nomination? [It was seconded and carried unanimously.]

We will now present the names of the High Council for this Stake of Zion. [The names were read and they were voted for by the

Conference.] When we organize a Stake of Zion we set apart a High Priest to preside over the High Priests in that Stake. He either selects his two counsellors, or we give them to him. There is but one quorum of High Priests in any Stake of Zion. For the Elders we also appoint a President and two counsellors to preside over them. When they number ninety-six, there will be a full quorum; but it is not so with the High Priests. It matters not whether they number fifty, five hundred or five thousand or more, in a Stake of Zion, there can only be one quorum and one president; they thus differ from the Elders. Then if there should be a sufficient number of Elders to make two quorums, we would select two presidents with their counsellors, but if there were more than enough to form one quorum, and not sufficient to make two, they could meet with the first quorum until there should be enough to form a second quorum.

Forty-eight Priests form a quorum. We will have a president set apart for the Priests' quorum, who will also have two counsellors. And when there are forty-eight Priests more it will then be time to organize another quorum. The teachers and deacons will be organized too. Twenty-four form a quorum of teachers, and twelve a quorum of deacons. The Seventies are scattered all through our settlements; we do not organize them; they are already organized in their several quorums. As for mass quorums, I do not acknowledge such organizations. In consequence of operations carried on under that name I have felt disposed to change it and instead of calling them mass quorums, name them "muss" quorums. At almost every place where they have met together, there has been quarrelling between the Seventies and the Bishop. This was first brought to my notice, by learning that when bishops gave out notice for the people to come together at a certain time, it was not an infrequent thing for the presidents of the mass quorums of the same wards to give out their appointments for the Seventies to meet at the same hour. This would be done for the purpose of showing what great authority they had and to get up a quarrel. A president acting in this manner ought to be cut off from the Church. The Seventies are Apostles; and they stand next in authority to the Twelve. The First Presidency organize and regulate the affairs of the Church wherever they can go, or they instruct others to do it. When the First Presidency are not here, and the Twelve are here, they then attend to these matters, and their authority, by a unanimous feeling and faith in the gospel, is the same as that of the First Presidency. Next in order to them stand the Seventies. If through the providences of God the First Presidency and the Twelve were taken away, then it would be the duty of the Seventies to preach the gospel, build up the Church, and ordain every officer requisite in order to establish the Church; to ordain high priests, bishops, high counsellors, patriarchs, and set in order the whole church in all the world. This is according to the revelations given to us. This dissension has come between the seventies and the High Priests in consequence of some poor, miserable, beggarly whiners who craved after power, and who did not know what to do with the authority they already possessed. Some of these high priests would go to Joseph saying: "Brother Joseph, do you think the Twelve have any more power than we have?" "Brother Joseph the Seventies, are they ordained to as high authority and power as the High Priests? Are the Seventies equal to the High Priests? Brother Joseph, it cannot be so, it must not be; the High Priests must be the greater, and they are first." Now, even to this day, there is contention, and I do not know but even among the first elders of Israel there may be argument as to which should come next—if anything were to happen to the First Presidency and the Twelve—the High Priests or the Seventies. Is the apostleship an outgrowth of the high priesthood, or is the high priesthood an outgrowth of the apostleship? Or, in other words, which is the highest office in the church? The office of an apostle. The apostleship is the highest authority that can be imposed upon man upon the earth. I recollect when Brother Don Carlos Smith was ordained president of the high priests' quorum, he got up a genealogical tree, and written along the trunk of this tree were the words, "The High Priests." A little distance up the trunk a limb shot out away off, which represented the ["]Twelve Apostles." This is not according to the revelations which have been given to us. When a man is ordained an apostle, he is ordained to every calling pertaining to the holy priesthood, a man on the earth can hold; but when he is ordained a high priest, he is ordained a priest after the order of Melchisedek; it is then his right to officiate in all the offices below him. I suppose I ordained hundreds of Seventies in early days. Brother Joseph Smith has come to us many times, saying, "Brethren, you are going to ordain Seventies. Do not forget to confer the high priesthood upon them. Ordain each of them to the high priesthood, and to be one of the seventy apostles." That was my language in the ordination of the Seventies, and that is the way I ordain them now. Whether in doing so I mention the high priesthood or not, that is included. In consequence of this a little inquiry arose among the high priests respecting the high priesthood and the apostleship. The Twelve Apostles had been ordained, and every one of them happened to be high priests excepting Brother Heber C. Kimball and myself; we were elders. The fact that we were not high priests and had never been ordained to the high priesthood was taken to Brother Joseph. These cavilers wanted him to take some action about it. They wanted to know if we should not be ordained high priests. Such a suggestion made Joseph righteously angry. Said he, "My brethren, with as much as I have taught you, and as many revelations as have been given on the subject of the priesthood, that you should ask such a question! It would be an insult to the priesthood of the Son of God to ordain a man a high priest after he had been ordained an apostle; for the apostleship holds all the keys of the priesthood upon the face of the earth, to build up the kingdom of heaven, to sanctify the people and prepare them to enter into the presence of God the Father. Now, to say that such a man, holding this priesthood, should be ordained a high priest is an insult, and I want to hear no more about it." But this agitation about the high priesthood has ever since been a matter of speculation with a few.

I say that a man that craves for office and authority does not know enough to magnify the office of a deacon; for, if he did, he would not say a word about authority, he would ask for wisdom that he might know how to magnify the priesthood placed upon him. With regard to the authority of the Church and Kingdom of God upon the earth in its organization, read the Book of Doctrine and Covenants for yourselves. We have a new edition, you can read it. Acquaint yourselves with the power and authority of the priesthood and learn how the Church is organized. I have spoken of these things before, and yet some will say, "I want to know if the Seventies have so much authority as the High Priests." I say unto you, Latter-day Saints, that the Seventies follow the Twelve Apostles, and the Twelve Apostles follow in the wake of the First Presidency, and the First Presidency follow in the wake of Peter, James, and John. But for the Seventies and the Twelve to have equal authority in their decisions with the First Presidency they must be unanimous, as is written in the Book of Doctrine and Covenants. The priesthood which Peter, James and John held while in the flesh was the highest ever bestowed upon the children of men, and it was conferred upon Joseph and Oliver, and without it they never could have built up the Kingdom. Then after this came along the high priesthood. I have been told since I came here that Sidney Rigdon ordained Joseph a high priest. I would ask, who ordained Sidney Rigdon? What priesthood he had he got from Joseph, and then he turned around and ordained Joseph to an office, the authority to hold which he had received from Joseph! It would be unwise. If Sidney had done this, I think I would have heard of it. You can read how Joseph and Oliver got this apostleship. Then after the Conference in Kirtland, in 1831, Joseph received a revelation to ordain high priests, which he did. As far as his being ordained a high priest, it would be as proper to call for a priest, teacher or deacon to ordain me a high priest. The Lord sent his messengers, Peter, James and John, to ordain him to the highest authority that could be given. I trust that these remarks will put a stop to such foolish and absurd questions. Read the revelations and understand them.

[At this point Elder Geo. L. Farrell was elected President of the High

Priests' Quorum and Elders Charles O. Card and Thomas C. Ricks were elected as his counselors.]

The presidency of the Stake can complete this organization. They can select presidents for the Elders' Quorum, Priests', Teachers' and Deacons' Quorums and organize everything properly in the entire Stake, and then it is done. I have been showing you how to organize a Stake of Zion. There is no need of delay or of adjourning over from one meeting till another. If you want to make presidents of quorums, select your men and organize them. But, you may say, "We may get some one who is not worth anything." Then he has a chance to prove himself, and if he is not suitable you can put another in his place at the next quarterly conference.

With regard to the authority in a Stake of Zion, all the members are amenable to the High Council with their president at their head. Suppose one of the Twelve were living here who should be guilty of lying, swearing, drinking, or purloining his neighbor's goods. He would be amenable to this High Council, and he should be dealt with. Now a question arises—can you try him and deal with him as with a lay member? No; you can try him, prove his guilt, place it upon record, and then by the united voice of the people of this Stake of Zion, you could withdraw your fellowship from him; but you could not cut him off from the Church. In one of my discourses it is stated that one of the Twelve could be cut off from the church by the local authorities of the branch or ward where he might be residing when dealt with; but it should have been stated that this action on the case would be only so far as that branch or ward was concerned. But, on the other hand, let the members of this High Council, or the presidency of this Stake get out of the way, begin to drink, swear, lie or steal, the apostles could cut any one of them off from the church, send them adrift and appoint others in their places. That is the difference between the authority of the Twelve Apostles and the authority of the High Priesthood. There is authority and there are degrees of authority, and there is a difference in degrees, callings and the authority of the priesthood. If there should be one apostle left on the earth, he can regulate and set in order the whole of the church and kingdom of God. If there is one seventy left he could do so. This order is not my getting up, it is the Lord's doings; high priests may mourn over it, the Lord has said it, and I have no right to say it is not so; it is so. I know some of you might say, "Did not Brother Joseph take high priests out of the quorum of seventies and place them in the high priests' quorum and put others in their places? Yes; but what did he do this for? I can tell you—it was to satisfy the continual teasing of ignorant men who did not know what to do with authority when they got it, and I think most of those high priests who were so anxious upon this subject afterwards apostatized. You have my word for it, I believe there were none of the whisperings of the spirit suggesting that movement, and I will give you my reasons for thinking so. They set their watch for Joseph whenever he preached on the subject. They invited him to preach at their quorum meetings on the difference between a high priest and a seventy. There had been caviling and bickering in relation to this subject; he condescended to try to do something for them. He preached upon this subject, and I say he stooped to the level of those whiners to try to do something for them. When he got through with his sermon, I thought I never heard less brought forth. I could not discern that he brought forth any light, and it was the only time in my life that I ever heard Brother Joseph speak without bringing forth light and knowledge, but I could not discern anything in this. If we enquire of the Lord, if there is one man upon the face of the earth that can get to the ears of the Lord and can get him to hearken to him, he would know how it is; for there is nothing in the Doctrine and Covenants upon which an idea can be based that the High Priests have precedence over the seventies.

In the first calling of the Seventies the Prophet Joseph ordered that every one of them be set apart to the high priesthood, which is the highest priesthood except the apostleship, and to ordain each as one of the seventy apostles. If there are those present who had my hands laid upon their heads in the Kirtland Temple, they can testify that I am telling it just as it was. Some will treasure up these things in their heart, and will remember them just as I have done. From the first time I saw the Prophet Joseph I never lost a word that came from him concerning the kingdom. And this is the key of knowledge that I have today, that I did hearken to the words of Joseph, and treasured them up in my heart, laid them away, asking my Father in the name of his Son Jesus to bring them to my mind when needed. I treasured up the things of God, and this is the key that I hold today. I was anxious to learn from Joseph and the spirit of God. The spirit of revelation that was given to me has revealed to me many things which have been done. If you, my brethren, are quick to comprehend, and if you love the truth, you will treasure up these things and ponder upon them in your hearts, and when you are asked with regard to them they will be revealed to you. In my doctrinal teachings I have taught many things not written in any book, ancient or modern, and yet, notwithstanding the many things I have told the people. I have never looked into the Bible, the Book of Mormon, or the Doctrine and Covenants, or any of our church works to see whether they agreed with them or not. When I have spoken by the power of God and the Holy Ghost, it is truth, it is scripture, and I have no fears but that it will agree with all that has been revealed in every particular.

I will say to these three brethren, selected for the presidency of this Stake of Zion, that it will be their duty, just as quick as they can attend to it, to go to every ward and see that it is regularly organized, and ordain those who are to be bishops to the high priesthood and then set them apart to the bishopric, each bishop with two counsel[l]ors, and then see that the several quorums of elders, priests, teachers and deacons are organized, and also to see that every person is brought within the jurisdiction of a ward; not a family or an individual to be left out; no matter if they live ten miles off, they must be enrolled in the ward, and the proper persons must know what they are doing, as well as to know what the Seventies, the High Priests and Elders and all are doing. They must see whether all these are doing their duty, living their holy religion, or whether they are breaking the Sabbath by hunting their stock or chopping wood in the canyon, fishing or hunting, or whether they indulge in drinking intoxicating drinks, or whether they steal, lie, speak evil of their neighbor, or do anything which violates the principles of our religion.

There are many persons who, if they were asked, Do you know that Joseph Smith was a prophet of God? Do you believe in the doctrines he taught? they would testify that they do, using the strongest language at their command. Will they run horses or in any way break the Sabbath? Yes, but they swear they know "Mormonism" is true. Such men must be brought into line, or we will sever them from our fellowship. It is the duty of these presidents to see that every ward in this Stake is thoroughly organized. And the Seventies, let them be diligent, help to build this temple and do all they can to strengthen and support their brethren who preside, acting as any other members of this Stake of Zion should, in being obedient to the bishops. If they were scattered over the whole world, they could be notified to come together when it is necessary to do business in the capacity of their calling.

When temples are built you will not see seats provided for the Twelve, not in this temple at any rate. The upper seat on the stand in the east end of the building will be for the First Presidency; the next seat below will be for the presidency of the Stake of Zion; the next seat below will be for the presidency of the High Priests' Quorum. The upper stand at the west end of the temple will be for those holding the Bishopric; the next will be for the presidents of the Quorum of Priests after the order of Aaron, the next below for the presidents of the Quorum of Teachers; and the next for the presidents of the Quorum of Deacons. What, says one, no seats provided for the Twelve, is not this their home? No, their homes are all over the earth, preaching the Gospel, building up the kingdom, regulating the affairs of the kingdom of God upon the earth; and we take them in as visitors. Are there places to be provided for the

Seventies? No, the temples have seats provided for the First Presidency and the local authorities and not for the travelling ministry. The Twelve and the Seventies are travelling quorums to all the inhabitants of the earth. In the Stakes of Zion the Seventies should be willing to labor as directed by the bishops and the presidency of the Stake. They may meet with the high priests or with the elders as they may choose and they will always be welcome if the high priests and elders feel as they should do.

We desire Elder Thatcher and his counselors—Elders William B. Preston and Milton D. Hammond—to give expression to their feelings before the congregation respecting the appointments they have received.

[Brother Thatcher said, in substance, he would do the best he could under the direction of his brethren, the Lord helping him, to magnify the office and calling which had been given him; and Brothers Preston and Hammond expressed themselves similarly.]

[President Young resumed.]

We will now ordain and set these brethren apart to preside over this Stake of Zion.

[Elder Thatcher was then ordained a high priest and set apart to preside, and Elders Preston and Hammond being already ordained high priests, were set apart as his counsel[l]ors.]

You have heard the ceremony that I have used in ordaining and setting these brethren apart to preside over this Stake of Zion; but the most of our Elders in laying their hands upon the heads of persons to confirm them members of the church, after they have been baptized, will seal all the blessings upon them that a patriarch would in giving them their patriarchal blessing, and wander on to subjects that have no relevancy to the ordinance they are attending to. When we commenced work in the Temple at St. George, I had this stopped. I took the ceremony that belongs to baptising and the ceremony that belongs to confirming, and had them written out for the brethren to commit and use when officiating in those ordinances. If you notice I did not use any superfluous language in ordaining and setting apart these brethren. This is the proper way to do.

Some elders, who appear to think they do not preach enough at other times, when asked to open a meeting with prayer, will not forget to preach a pretty good sermon before they stop praying. They will pray for everything on and above the earth as though they offered their secret prayers in public.

Brother Joseph once asked Brother George A. Smith to close a meeting. Brother George A. said, "My prayers are too short." Said Joseph, "That is the reason I ask you." Let your prayers and sermons always be short, right to the point.

It is now time to close our meeting. We leave Brother Thatcher and his counsel[l]ors to complete the organization of this Stake of Zion. In doing this they may confer with the brethren of the Twelve if they choose.

I would be pleased, if time would permit to hear the sentiments of my brethren, the Twelve, on these topics on which I have touched; but I think they will all agree with me. As I remarked yesterday, we differ in our words more than we differ in our sentiments. There are not two men who can preach the same sermon, with the same words. We are all alike respecting our faith in the Gospel and the building up of the kingdom.

With regard to this Temple ground, I will pass my judgment upon the soil on which we intend to build the Temple, and say to all, that unless it is disturbed by some unseen hand, it is just as good a foundation as I could wish for, unless we had solid rock. I do not think we could have it better. We want the brethren to take hold. The presidency of the Stake will call for a certain number of men from the various wards. I trust they will be on hand, ready to be organized for this work. When men get accustomed to the work, I would suggest that they be kept on in preferance [sic] to changing them for raw hands. Let the people sustain these hands and their families, so that they can be kept steadily at work at the Temple. We have called Bro. Charles O. Card to superintend the work on the Temple for the present, and told him what to do and how it should be done. The first thing to be done is to get the lime ready, pile up the sand, get away the dirt before you haul any rock; then have your roads prepared for the drawing of the rock. Let from twenty to fifty masons be kept constantly at work until the building shall be completed. I pray our Father in Heaven, in the name of Jesus Christ, to bless you all. Amen.

"The Wilderness was Kinder to Us than Man"
(from *Talking with a Prophet.*
What Brigham Young Himself Said About His Successor.
A Fool or a Child Could Lead the Mormons—
His Views of the Spirit and
Forces of Mormonism, Its Organization and
Its Government—Humility the Great Virtue.

[*New York Herald*, ca. September 1877]

The wilderness was kinder to us than man, and even when at the worst we had no desire to turn back. [Some have guessed that if Joseph Smith had not been very fortunate in a successor, his revelations would have died with him. Such men] know nothing at all about the revelation of the Church of Jesus Christ of Latter Day Saints. It didn't depend on Brigham Young or any other man to lead the new Israel or to bring them across the plains. A child or a fool could have done it. Do you think God sets so much store by the little difference between a man of sense, or even of genius, and a fool, as to let his work miscarry on that account? His law works forever; He would not have sent us a cloud by day or fire by night, as He did to His people old; that would not try our faith and teach us His ways. He would have given a cow to lead us, and we would have looked into that cow's face and followed it wheresoever it might lead; or He would have caused new herbage to spring up in the trackless waste, and we would have known that the angel of the Lord, though invisible, was pressing the arid sands with sacred feet, and would not fail until He led us into the promised land.

There are three things that pain me. One is to hear saints dwell on Joseph's little shortcomings, as if it made any sort of difference what the idiosyncracies of a prophet or any other man might be, if he is all right on the main lines. That is all we have any business with. There are some people that even grace can't haul up out of the slough of detail into the largeness of the spirit. I have no doubt that there were Israelites who refused to follow Moses because he did or did not part his hair in the middle, and some of that breed are handed down to the present time and are here with us now, and follow Brigham Young and shout, "Our servant Brigham is the lion of the Lord," and remember it against Joseph that he went with one suspender and forgot to put on the regulation Mormon underclothes. They think that if he had had his garments with the holes cut in the breasts and knees and elbows, he would not have got bullet holes in his body.

Another thing I don't like is to see so many saints think I am going to live forever, and, among those who don't go so far, that no one else will ever make as good a ruler for the Mormon people. What I just said about leadership in crossing the plains, I say about leadership here in the Valley. We were not divinely led into the Valley to be left to our own devices. The Mormon people have principles to guide them, and the Spirit. When the gold fever broke out in California, and the whole land was drunk with the lust of wealth, and the plains became a highway to the Pacific, filled with men whom greed made inhuman and monstrous, great was the passion of the saints to follow them. But they overcame it. Many of them dug in the river to drive away their desire, and worked at the public works till they fell under the strain and slept—but even then dreamt of gold, and woke up with the desire to risk all for gold. But they were heroes as well as saints, and went again to work on the public works—feeling safer there than if working at their own private business and farms. For this was what they came out to the desert to do: "To build Zion, to make the wilderness rejoice and blossom as the rose." The worn-out and hungry gold diggers were only too glad to exchange their gold for our corn, and beef, and tanned hides, and home-made cloth, our butter, and cheese, and horses. And so we got gold, gold, gold. But we never gave up our principle for it, our principle that the earth belongs to the Lord, and that his saints must take it as an inheritance and make it blossom. No matter who is head of the church in the wilderness—that child there would make as good a head as any, perhaps better than any. For the greatest man that could be called to it must become as simple as that little child before God would breathe his spirit into him. He must be always asking, "Lord, what wouldst thou have me to do?" If an angel should come from heaven, he could not tell the people other than what we have always known—to live our own lives worthily, to bear with each other in all charity, to cultivate the earth, and to hold ourselves in readiness to go out and preach to every creature.

The other thing I don't like is to have people watch me, or what they call my way of doing things, as if I had a fixed way, and imitate it, and even try to make me stand by it years after, when the circumstances are changed. I have had more anger on account of this than on accout of any other thing, and with my best people, too, and those old enough to know better, if age counts for anything in the matter of wisdom, which is doubtful. Sometimes I think that the worst thing that can happen to a man is to grow old. His experience becomes like a solid wall around him, and he grows blind trying to look through that, and he takes his own memories for the facts of the new changing world around him; and then if the spirit comes to reveal the truth of life to him, he tries to reconcile it with his own opinions, and that is living death; it tells in their faces, their manners, and their voices. Nothing keeps a man young and up to his times like being open to the inspirations of the Spirit.

[Some men have asked if Joseph Smith selected me for leader of the saints because of my humility.] Joseph's words were, "For humilty and obedience, I have found none like unto our brother Brigham." These words have become for me a kind of test of men. When I see a saint full of himself, his own opinion and his own way, I find myself looking at him with the sad eyes of Joseph. It seems to me that humility and obedience are something very profound, and too deep for me. But Joseph Smith was a poet, and poets are not like other men; their gaze is deeper, and reaches the roots of the soul; it is like that of the searching eyes of angels; they catch the swift thought of God and reveal it to us, even at the risk of forgetting their underclothes and their suspenders.

I have half a dozen children by different mothers that seem nearer alike and more attached to each other than almost any full brothers and sisters I could mention. I say seem, for a great deal of the difference between people is only seeming; the real character often lies below all the seeming—and when we get at that we find many people very much alike. Take my John W. and Brigham, Jr. Could any two children of the most different parents seem more unlike, yet in all the essentials of character, truthfulness, courage, love of God, and good will to men, there is not the choice of two peas between them; and there are hundreds of the Valley boys just the same. I think on the judgment day men will be called to account for only very few simple fundamental qualities, and all the pecularities that catch the eye and engage the attention now will be swallowed up in death. But that is no reason why we shouldn't notice them in life, and rejoice in them, for it is only through them that we can tell t'other[?] from which.

Of all the qualities that will perish in the grave, I think humor is the best. Indeed, I'm not sure that it will not survive death, for it often hangs on to the last. I have known saints, the best of saints, too, whose last word was a joke, perhaps about not liking the prospect of their souls going *naked* into the other world, and before the joke was ended they were dead. Perhaps they ended it on the other side. Who knows? It is all mystery. I used to run to humor in my sermons, and next day be sorry for it; but I found years after, when I had forgotten the sorrow and the sermons, that people remembered the humor. I sometimes think God must enjoy humor, and that he won't be strict in reckoning with a humorist. Sometimes one and another of my wives complain of a child; but when I take it in hand I find it had only been chuck full of humor. I have learned some things since my son Brigham was a boy. He was full of practical jokes and fun, and if I should skin him to the bone that's what I'd find. He wore moccasins and stepped like a cat and moused through the whole settlement. God forgive me for being so hard on that boy, but I acted according to my lights. I'm not saying that I know much better what to do now, but I know better what not to do. Anyway I'm but a young beginner. A man needs many wives and children before he learns how to treat one properly.

The next scourge will be the scourge of Reason, when men will go mad over trying to put the whole law and all the prophets into their little heads, like matches in a box; all cut and dry, and ready to go off by friction.

Index

A

Aaron, 1, 2, 152

Aaronic priesthood, Joseph Smith learns of, 214

Abel, 4, 7; resurrected at time of Jesus, 218-19

Abraham, 2, 5, 10, 109, 132; administered to by Melchisedek, 54; cannot build a temple, 23; foreordination, 2, 4, 131-32; promise to, 5

Adam, 5, 19, 47, 49, 56, 102, 132, 223; as creator, God the Father, 93-101; brought from another planet, 95, 126; every world has one, 93; fruit of garden change resurrected bodies, 98; gospel and ordinances in his day, 89, 156; his sacrifice, 156; pass gospel to Methuselah, 54; plural wives, 96; relation to Jesus Christ, 97, 106; resurrected being, 96, 97

adultery, punishment to have blood shed, 108

aging, 141-42

agriculture, first in valley, 183

air, full of life and nourishment, 124-25

Alma, 4

America, visit of Jesus Christ, 207

Ananias, 22, 96

anatomy, study of, 216

Ancient of All Days, 100

animal kingdom, law of, 141

animal magnetism, a true principle taught by Jesus Christ, 83-85

anointings, 20

apostasy, of Christianity, 48, 105, 137; of Saints, 145, 190, 200; shedding of blood for those who leave church, 110

apostles, 48; relation to high priests, nature of calling, 232-34; seventies as, 231-32; whether can be cut off by local leader, 234; why no seats in the temple, travelling quorums, 236-37

astronomy, 49

Atonement, 19

B

Babel, tower of, 45

baptism, 139, 156, 195; and Mr. Campbell, 196; for sick in Nauvoo temple, 24; Jesus Christ and, 139; Joseph Smith and, 214; of earth, 71, 100, 141; preached by Adam, Enoch, Noah, and Jesus Christ, 155

baptism for dead, 18-25; written down, 237

Baptists, 124, 196

Barak, 4

Beecher, Henry Ward, 201

Belial, 110

Benjamin, tribe of, 47

Bible, Brigham Young not read in years, 89; Kings James Version, 170; need not agree with new scripture, 235; proved true by Book of Mormon, 149, 207; scholarship, 151, 170, 181-82; stick of Judah, 207-208; teaches God has body, 162, 206-207

bishops, and seventies, 231-32; planning for Utah War, 117; seats in the temple, 236

blacks, 30, 195; curse because of Cain, no priesthood until all descendants of Adam receive, 132-33

blood atonement. See shedding of blood

bodies, 125, 144, 145

Book of Mormon, 113, 209; antiquities prove, 141-42; first response to, 50-51; no need agree with new scripture, 235; proves Bible is true, 149, 170, 207; stick of Joseph, 208; translation of, 151

Box Elder County, 117

Bridger, Jim, on Great Basin, 205-207

Bristol (England), 50

Bucer, Martin, 177

Buchanan, James, 185; politics of his election, 117-18

business, 165, 185, 199-200

C

Cain, God's foreknowledge, 3, 7; his curse, 132-33

Caleb, 4, 109

California, 54-55; and gold, 63-64, 71, 240

calling and election sure, 19

Calvinism, 52

243

patriarchal blessing, 213-14, 237

patriarchs, 214; and Smith family, 13, 17; can be ordained by seventies, 231-32

Paul, 3, 96, 168-69

peculiar people, 5-6, 208-209

persecution, of church, 112, 113-14, 161-62, 163, 211, 227-28

Peter, 22, 233

Pharaoh of Egypt, 71, 131

Philip, Landgrave of Hesse, and polygamy, 177

Phillip of France, and spirit writing, 78

philosophy, 75, 78, 125, 162, 169, 172, 182, 193, 204, 225

pilgrims, 105-106

Pioneer Company, 26-30, 183

Pittsburgh (Pennsylvania), 15

plan of salvation, 19, 43-44, 225-26

planets, given position and laws by gods, 225

polygamy, 76, 101, 177, 241; Alexander Smith and, 189; Brigham Young's family and, 94-95, 205; history of, 178; Martin Luther and, 177

poverty, 59, 215

Pratt, Orson, 48, 72-73, 170

prayer, which turns into a speech, 237

pre-existence, 1, 4-5

predestination, 3

pregnancy, out of marriage, 101-102

Presbyterians, 51, 124

Preston, William B., 230, 237

priesthood, 1-2, 4-5, 12, 14, 41, 74, 130, 157, 164, 231, 232-35; and blacks, 132-33

priests, 231, 234, 236

property, becoming, 214-16, 226, 227

prophesy, 48

prophet, only God choose, 12; whether can lead astray, 35, 121. See also leaders

prostitution, 102, 178. See also monogamy

Protestantism, 45, 196

Provo (Utah), 120

Prussia, 114

Pullman, Mr., 206

Q

Quakers, 51, 124

Queen Victoria, 46

Quincy (Illinois), Joseph Smith's farm, 191

Quorum of the Twelve, 17, 34, 111, 113, 238; apostasy in, 34-35; Joseph Smith's apostles to assist in resurrection, 99; power in relation to other quorums, 231-32; seventies next in authority, 231-32; why should lead church, 11-17

R

races, 161

Rahab, 4

reading, recommended, 216-17

Rebecca, 6

Reorganized Church of Jesus Christ of Latter Day Saints, 187-88, 200

reprobation, 1, 123, 131

Republicans, 117-18

resurrection, 55, 56, 67, 68, 144-45, 218-21, 224; baby, 144; first, 41, 73, 129, 140, 142; Joseph Smith as President of the Resurrection, 99; last, chance for some if blood shed, 110; of earth, 70-71, 218, 220; of Jesus Christ, 96; of just, 39, 41; of particles composing the body, 128; requires resurrected being with keys, 96, 141; second, 129; last, 42

revelation, 2, 35, 86, 149-50, 214

Revolutionary War, 166

Ricks, Thomas C., 234

Richards, Willard, 1

Rigdon, Sidney, 12, 13, 14, 15, 17, 37-42, 146, 190, 233

Rome, 45

S

Sabbath. See Sunday, working on

sacrament, 49, 51, 156-57, 182-83, 195-96

Salt Lake City (Utah), 116-17, 183-84, 185

Salt Lake temple, 141, 226

salvation, 34, 37, 49-50, 57, 74, 89, 158; none for sinning against the Holy Ghost, 156, 175; for those buffeted by Satan, 158; universal, 129

Sampson, 4

Samuel, 4

Satan, 13, 15, 40, 54, 55, 56, 80, 84-85, 158

Saunders, E. M., 190

Savior, a position, 38, 57, 94, 95

science, 160, 162, 172, 204, 225

Scotland, 16, 46

scripture, 3, 90, 235; cited

—1 Corinthians 15:22, 5